FROM GRIFFIN TO AXOLOTL

MCGILL-QUEEN'S IBERIAN AND LATIN AMERICAN CULTURES SERIES

Series editor: Nicolás Fernández-Medina

The McGill-Queen's Iberian and Latin American Cultures Series is committed to publishing original scholarship that explores and re-evaluates Iberian and Latin American cultures, connections, and identities. Offering diverse perspectives on a range of regional and global histories from the early modern period to twenty-first-century contexts, the series cuts across disciplinary boundaries to consider how questions of authority, nation, revolution, gender, sexuality, science, epistemology, avant-gardism, aesthetics, travel, colonization, race relations, religious belief, and media technologies, among others, have shaped the rich and complex trajectories of modernity in the Iberian Peninsula and Latin America.

The McGill-Queen's Iberian and Latin American Cultures Series promotes rigorous scholarship and welcomes proposals for innovative and theoretically compelling monographs and edited collections.

FROM GRIFFIN TO AXOLOTL

Reimagining the Bestiary in Contemporary Hispanic Literature

AILÉN CRUZ

McGill-Queen's University Press
Montreal & Kingston • London • Chicago

ISBN 978-0-2280-2631-0 (paper)
ISBN 978-0-2280-2632-7 (ePDF)
ISBN 978-0-2280-2633-4 (ePUB)

Legal deposit fourth quarter 2025
Bibliothèque et Archives nationales du Québec

Printed in Canada on acid-free paper that is 100% ancient-forest-free, containing 100% sustainable, recycled fibre, and processed chlorine-free.

This book has been published with the help of a grant from the Federation for the Humanities and Social Sciences, through the Awards to Scholarly Publications Program, using funds provided by the Social Sciences and Humanities Research Council of Canada.

Funded by the Government of Canada | Financé par le gouvernement du Canada | Canada

Canada Council for the Arts | Conseil des arts du Canada

We acknowledge the support of the Canada Council for the Arts.
Nous remercions le Conseil des arts du Canada de son soutien.

McGill-Queen's University Press in Montreal is on land which long served as a site of meeting and exchange amongst Indigenous Peoples, including the Haudenosaunee and Anishinabeg nations. In Kingston it is situated on the territory of the Haudenosaunee and Anishinaabek. We acknowledge and thank the diverse Indigenous Peoples whose footsteps have marked these territories on which peoples of the world now gather.

Library and Archives Canada Cataloguing in Publication

Title: From griffin to axolotl : reimagining the bestiary in contemporary Hispanic literature / Ailén Cruz.
Names: Cruz, Ailén, author.
Series: McGill-Queen's Iberian and Latin American cultures series ; 10.
Description: Series statement: McGill-Queen's Iberian and Latin American cultures series ; 10 | Includes bibliographical references and index.
Identifiers: Canadiana (print) 20250227274 | Canadiana (ebook) 20250227363 | ISBN 9780228026310 (softcover) | ISBN 9780228026327 (PDF) | ISBN 9780228026334 (ePUB)
Subjects: LCSH: Bestiaries—Latin America—History and criticism. | LCSH: Latin American literature—20th century—History and criticism. | LCSH: Spanish literature—20th century—History and criticism.
Classification: LCC PQ7081.C78 2025 | DDC 860.9/3620904—dc23

This book was designed and typeset by Sayre Street Books in Baskerville Pro.
Copyediting by Correy Baldwin.

McGill-Queen's University Press
Suite 1720, 1010 Sherbrooke St West, Montreal, QC, H3A 2R7

Authorized safety representative in the EU: Mare Nostrum Group BV, Mauritskade 21D, 1091 GC Amsterdam, the Netherlands, gpsr@mare-nostrum.co.uk

This book is dedicated to bibliophiles everywhere.

CONTENTS

FIGURES

FROM GRIFFIN TO AXOLOTL

INTRODUCTION

I was in my early twenties when I first flipped through the pages of a bestiary. I had the curious feeling that, rather than encountering something new, I was dusting off animal tales tucked away in the attic of my mind. The facsimile, lush with illuminated letters and boasting animals of strange proportions atop golden landscapes, presented me with truths I thought I had acquired elsewhere: the fox is cunning, the lion is brave, bees are hard-working. These ideas, learned as a child and carried into adulthood, cause me to smile when I encounter a fox scurrying as the sun sets in my neighbourhood, or watch a bee extract pollen. As it turns out, adapted and sometimes diluted versions of the bestiary exist as threads in the fabric of general culture. The realization, combined with my native Spanish and lifelong fascination with literature, gave way to an investigation spanning several years and countries that culminates in the present work. This is a book about the bestiary, a literary genre that is part of the roots of our collective imaginary, the adaptability that allowed it to survive centuries, and its resurfacing in Latin America and Spain.

The bestiary – traditionally defined as short, animal-centred texts, often illustrated, used for Christian moralizing within medieval society – derived its form from the anonymous text the *Physiologus*, which dates back to somewhere between 200 CE and 400 CE. Translated into dozens of languages and having enjoyed prolific dissemination until the twelfth century, the book borrowed from Indian, Hebrew, Egyptian, Greek, and Roman myths and folklore to create vivid allegories. These works imparted morals by decoding lessons incarnate in animals and nature. As is the case with foxes, lions, and bees, the impact of the bestiary was so widespread that to this day we attribute specific qualities to specific creatures. As the medieval period gave way to the Renaissance, however, and humanist preferences shifted toward scientific methodologies, the allegorical beast became nearly extinct. The change in philosophical and cultural currents caused the bestiary to remain dormant for several centuries.

During the nineteenth century and the beginning of the twentieth, the drive to dehumanize political adversaries and a renewed interest in nature and human/animal dynamics foreshadowed the eventual reappearance of the bestiary genre in South America. Works including Esteban Echeverría's "El matadero" (1871), Horacio Quiroga's *Cuentos de la selva* (1918), and Leopoldo Lugones's *Fuerzas extrañas* (1906), and later works like Julio Cortázar's *Bestiario* (1951), Clarice Lispector's *A Paixão Segundo G.H.* (1964), Manuel Puig's *El beso de la mujer araña* (1976), and Copi's *La ciudad de las ratas* (1979), reinvigorated questions about humanity, animality, and the precarious line in between.

The second half of the twentieth century also saw an impulse to question Cartesian rationalism, the Kantian man, and the very anthropocentrism underlying Western society. Michel Foucault's concept of monstrosity and biopower, summarized in the maxim "to make live and let die," Donna Haraway's explorations of post-human possibilities and interspecies dynamics, Giorgio Agamben's reduction of Western politics to biopolitics, and Emmanuel Levinas's ontological distinction between the "I" and the Other are but a few examples of this critical impulse. The field of animal studies also gained momentum during this time.

While not the subject of this book, animal studies at its very heart encourages the examination of the representation of animals in history and culture, and, most pertinent to the present work, literature. Stemming from utilitarian philosopher Jeremy Bentham's suggestion that it is animals' capacity to feel pain, rather than their power of reason, that entitles them to moral consideration, the field holds that there are several ways of relating to the animal. Under the category of "likeness" we find anthropomorphism and zoomorphism, the former prescribing human attributes onto animals and the latter attributing animal characteristics to humans. Branching from Otherness we find concepts such as Descartes's mechanomorphism, that is, his encouragement to view animals as unfeeling machines (Garrard 2023, 131).

Under Otherness we also find the alternative suggested by Greg Garrard, *allomorphism*, in which *allo* (other) is the "acknowledgment of the wondrous strangeness of animals, which often involves an overtly sacred language" (143). Many of the bestiaries analyzed in this work, and in the broader corpus in general, dedicate entries to the likeness and difference experienced when standing before an animal. The various authors and artists featured in the chapters that follow explore the similarities and differences between humans and animals, beasts, and imaginary beings. These growing preoccupations, combined with the experimental nature of the Latin American avant-garde and Boom periods that saw the fashionable reclaiming of medieval forms like exempla, fables, and allegories, led to the first significant cluster in the Hispanic bestiary's trajectory.

Jorge Luis Borges (1899–1986), the Argentine writer most famous for his works *Ficciones* (1944) and *El Aleph* (1949), contributed to the acclaim of Latin American literature with short stories and essays centred around themes of infinity, dreams, mirrors, and mythology. He was the first to play with the traditional form of the bestiary, publishing *Manual de zoología fantástica* in 1957. In 1967, Borges published *El libro de los seres imaginarios*, an expanded version of *Manual*, illustrated by prolific Argentine artist Silvio Baldessari (1916–1987), an elusive yet ubiquitous presence, best known for iconic paperback covers. True to his encyclopaedic proclivities, Borges invited creatures from all corners of the world to inhabit his pages, ranging from American beasts like the hidebehind and the gillygaloo to the Chinese dragon, and included fictional creatures like Kafka's famed Odradek. The Mexican writer Juan José Arreola (1918–2001), acclaimed for his short stories and his exploration of absurdist and existentialist ideas, followed shortly after, with the exquisite poetic prose of *Punta de plata* (1958). The entries in *Punta de plata* were inspired by Héctor Xavier's (1921–1994) silverpoint drawings of animals from Mexico City's Chapultepec Zoo. Xavier was among the most influential Mexican sketch artists of the twentieth century as well as a key member of the Generación de la Ruptura (the Breakaway Generation), responsible for breaking the stronghold that muralists including Diego Rivera and David Alfaro Siqueiros had in Mexico. Unlike Borges, Arreola's bestiary features only animals found in zoos, and plays with different creatures' perceived qualities, like the seal's lust or the rhinoceros's likeness to robust military machinery.

During his exile in Mexico, Central American author Augusto Monterroso (1921–2003), celebrated for his humour and originality in both his short stories and microtextos (flash fiction), published *La oveja negra y demás fábulas* in 1969, infusing the genre with his characteristic wit and incisiveness. Some entries are a single sentence long, and a few objects, including a neurotic hand mirror, managed to slip into his work. In 1965, Chilean poet and diplomat Pablo Neruda (1904–1973), best known for having won the Nobel Prize in Literature and for his ever-varying literary style, published *Bestiary/Bestiario*, a bilingual verse bestiary accompanied by Uruguayan American artist Antonio Frasconi's (1919–2013) striking woodcuts. While prose bestiaries were undoubtedly more common during the genre's peak in the twelfth century, verse bestiaries nonetheless existed, most notably Philippe de Thaon's *Bestiaire* and Guillaume le Clerc's *Bestiaire*, both from the early thirteenth century. Nicolás Guillén (1902–1989), hailed as Cuba's national poet and known for drawing from his Spanish and African heritage, was next to experiment with a verse bestiary. In 1967 he published *El gran zoo*, its entries accompanied by the paper doll–like illustrations of Fayad Jamís (1930–1988), a fellow poet and member of the modernist Cuban painters' group "Las Once." Guillén was the first writer to extensively feature human beings in a space that had been for centuries reserved for animals. Last to this group of influential twentieth-century authors was Mexican short-story writer, essayist, and winner of the Cervantes Prize, José Emilio Pacheco, who published *Álbum de zoología* in 1985. Like Guillén and Neruda, Pacheco's bestiary was published in verse form. In 1993 *An Ark for the Next Millennium*, a bilingual edition of Pacheco's original bestiary, was published, illustrated by Francisco Toledo, the widely acclaimed and prolific Mexican painter and sculptor. These works' temporal proximity to one another, combined with their decades-long circulation in the Hispanic literary world, marks this cluster as a significant moment in the trajectory of the bestiary from a medieval artifact to a contemporary literary form. Due to their authors' prominence and their influence on subsequent bestiaries, these texts are treated here as canonical.

Despite their indisputable influence and significance in the evolution of the genre, seven bestiaries do not constitute the resurgence of a genre. Through travels to the publishing hubs of the Spanish-speaking world – that is, Buenos Aires, Mexico City, Barcelona, and Madrid – and through much trial and error, I curated a corpus of eighty Hispanic bestiaries published in the twenty-first century. Fifteen of these bestiaries are featured here as representative of the most novel and innovative interpretations of the genre, while the full corpus can be found in the appendix. Although the authors deemed canonical are South American, the corpus studied in this book hails from both sides of the Atlantic. This cross-Atlantic analysis is based on the shared language between Spain and the Latin American countries from which the authors and illustrators originate. Beyond a common language, Spain and Latin America share a history stemming from colonialism and its present-day consequences. The two regions have also seen significant cultural exchange over the decades, with many prominent authors and artists moving back and forth between Spain and Latin America. Borges, for instance, lived in Spain for several years, as have numerous acclaimed writers including Isabel Allende and Gabriel García Márquez. The relevance of this cross-Atlantic approach is further cemented by various elements of daily life, including Catholicism, constant cultural exchange through media, and devastating dictatorships and censorships. The various stops in the evolution of the bestiary make it so that many possible segmentations could be justified, and this book offers one possible grouping.

Although the chapters that follow this introduction focus on the Hispanic branch of contemporary bestiaries, a wider resurgence transcending canons has been gaining momentum. This inter-canon proliferation, much like the one belonging to the Hispanic canon, presents a wide array of interpretations of the genre. Some authors use the bestiary to encode a historical and political perspective, such as Antoinette Burton and Renisa Mawani's *Animalia: An Anti-Imperial Bestiary for Our Times* (2020), which explores the role of animals in British imperial history, or Leigh Claire La Berge's *Marx for Cats: A Radical Bestiary* (2023), a work that explores the animality present in Marxist thought. Some bestiaries are tied to a specific writer's imagination, such as J.K. Rowling's *Fantastic Beasts and Where to Find Them* (2001). A similar phenomenon can be observed with the creatures dreamed up by Kafka, Rudyard Kipling, and J.R.R. Tolkien, among many others. Mark Podwal's *A Jewish Bestiary: Fabulous Creatures from Hebraic Legend and Lore* (2021) celebrates the creatures intrinsic to a culture, and the whimsical yet instructive *The Amazing Dr. Ransom's Bestiary of Adorable*

Fallacies, written by Douglas Wilson in 2015, teaches the reader logic. Joanna Bagniewska's *The Modern Bestiary: A Curated Collection of Wondrous Wildlife* (2022) recounts tales too wild to seem true, including that of zebra finches who announce hot weather to their eggs by singing, and immortal jellyfish who reverse the aging process when stressed. Caspar Henderson's *The Book of Barely Imagined Beings: A 21st Century Bestiary* (2012) takes inspiration from Borges and expertly blends disciplines including zoology, natural history, and literature to produce a witty, thought-provoking work. The renewed interest in the bestiary, reflected in both its proliferation and the academic attention it has received, demonstrates that there is an indisputable place reserved for the bestiary in our contemporary literary landscape.[1]

This book is the first in any tradition to employ ancient and medieval bestiaries as a foundation through which to contextualize and appreciate canonical and contemporary ones, in turn scaffolding the potential for further investigation within other canons. By examining the various aspects of medieval works, including beasts[2] featured, illustrations, and the interaction between reader and text, I established the medieval basis that underpins the investigation. This medieval base demonstrated that, unlike with medieval bestiaries, the content of the canonical works and subsequent twenty-first-century bestiaries is not predictable. Elements like didactic, moral teachings, or a particular roster of beasts can no longer be expected. Each bestiary represents a break away from tradition, concerned with twentieth- and twenty-first-century literature or longings, instead of Christian medieval teachings and allegory. As the bestiary evolved and its objectives changed, so did the relationship between text and image. Initially used as mnemonic devices suited for illiterate medieval audiences, the images that accompany bestiary entries quickly took centre stage, at times obscuring the text. Frasconi's woodcuts in Neruda's *Bestiario*, for instance, stomp on the work's verses, sometimes in the form of a horse, other times in the form of a cat. In works like *200 años de monstruos y maravillas argentinas* (2015), Christian Montenegro's illustrations mock their textual counterparts, and in *Animalia exstinta*, Hugo Horita's mixture of the biological and technological serve to sustain a large-scale ruse.

The enormous geographical and temporal distance between these instances of the genre, as well as the radical change in their textual and visual content, raises the question of how we might be able to tell if we are dealing with a bestiary at all. After establishing the genre's parameters through its medieval origins, the book operates under the premise that the bestiary is invariably recognizable through its form. The illustrated entries, titled and accompanied by a brief literary or poetic description of the creature in question, are what differentiates the bestiary from a book of fables, a codex, or an encyclopedia. It is in the bestiary's content that innovation takes place. An example of this content shift exists in *200 años de monstruos y maravillas argentinas*, since it discards animals altogether, capitalizing on the notion that a beast is inherent in all humans, and humans' tendency to view and treat the Other as animal. Due to this phenomenon, I redefined the term "bestiary" as "a collection of titled, independent short texts, often accompanied by an image, about real, mythical, or implied beasts." This definition encompasses the trajectory of the bestiary, spanning from medieval works to contemporary interpretations. As a result, this project observes the evolution of a literary genre and traces how much it can be pushed and distorted before becoming something else.

The purpose of *From Griffin to Axolotl* is to highlight the bestiary as a prominent phenomenon in contemporary Hispanic literature, and to contextualize this latest iteration of the genre within the wider history of the bestiary. Rather than a series of unrelated coincidences and flukes, the proliferation of the contemporary Hispanic bestiary is the result of literary currents and a response to the changes in the social imaginary. In order to place these works into a larger constellation, the book explores how the bestiary's main components – text and image – lend the genre its plasticity, its kaleidoscopic ability to resonate with audiences miles and centuries away from its original context. Depending on the angle through which we approach the works' entries, they reveal different colours, offering new facets and ideas. In this book I offer one possible way of categorizing and studying contemporary Hispanic bestiaries. While this was my preferred configuration, these works could be endlessly reshuffled and rearranged. I hope, through the next six chapters, to encourage readers to dream up their own taxonomies and categories. Most of all, I hope to accompany readers through these as they discover and remember spectacular creatures belonging to a magnificent literary tradition.

1

ORIGINS OF THE BESTIARY GENRE

But ask now the beasts, and they shall teach thee; and the fowls of the air, and they shall tell thee.

Job 12:7 (King James Version)

The genre of the bestiary originated with the anonymous text *Physiologus* around 200 CE.[1] The tales and stories in the *Physiologus* were rooted in Indian, Hebrew, and Egyptian legends and were later combined with Greek and Roman folklore. The fusion was absorbed into Alexandrian books of paradoxology and medical-magical discourse (Curley 1979, ix). Alexandria, the genre's city of origin, fostered an environment in which pagan and Christian allegory freely mixed (Barber 1993, 9). Around the first century, scientific writers such as Pliny the Elder and Aelian introduced legends and myths to the early Christian world (Benton 1992, 69). It was not until the unknown author of the *Physiologus* collected these various concepts and added Christian dogma that the prototype for the medieval bestiary was formed. Scholars speculate that the work was translated from Greek to Latin around the fourth century (George and Yapp 1991, 2; Dines 2012, 30), causing its contents to grow from forty to over one hundred entries (Curley 1979, xxx). This Latin, expanded version of the *Physiologus* thus became the base for what would become a bestiary a few centuries later.

The etymology of the word *physiologus*, or "the naturalist," sheds light on the range of interpretations and disciplines associated with the work of the *Physiologus*, which carried over into the bestiary. Aristotle first used the term to describe pre-Socratic philosophers such as Anaxagoras, Empedocles, and Democritus, whose theories on the processes and occurrences of reality were based on observation of the natural world, particularly animal life. The term was later used by Diodorus Siculus and Cicero to describe the Etruscans, who interpreted omens from Zeus in lightning patterns. By the early Christian era, the different etymologies caused the word to range in meanings related to zoology, science, religious practices, and theology (Curley 1979, xi). The breadth of possible meanings attributed to the word perfectly encapsulates the various functions that bestiary entries would go on to have.

Honouring the two aspects attributed to its name, naturalist and theologian, the *Physiologus* offered the reader a catalogue of short texts on various animals, trees, and even rocks. Different meanings were projected onto each animal in the belief that truth could be distilled from the dynamics and peculiarities of nature. Animals acted as instruments of understanding, void of reason, exemplified by the words of Saint Isidore of Seville (d. 636 CE), whose *Etymologies* were absorbed and featured in bestiaries: "It is a great sin to believe that God would entrust his counsel to cows" (2006, 267). Laden with allegory, each animal was seen as part of a hermeneutics that offered a glimpse into the kingdom of heaven, which was invisible but for the flashes revealed through the cunning of a fox or the zeal of the bee. Most versions included an explanation of the allegory bestowed onto an animal.

An explanation on allegory is necessary, as its precarious status has always been dependent on philosophical and literary vogues. In *The Vitality of Allegory*, scholar Gary Johnson claims that allegory belongs to the same family as metaphors, simile, synecdoche, and metonymy (2012, 4). Allegory develops along simultaneous compositional (author) and hermeneutic (reader) tracks (27). Johnson proposes a four-part structure that characterizes all allegorical narratives as containing "an object or phenomenon to be represented and transformed, a literal narrative that enacts the transformation, a secondary narrative that emerges from the figural interpretation of the literal narrative, and the author's intention" (11). The following entry from *The Aberdeen Bestiary* (ca. 1200)[2] exemplifies the structure: "There is an animal called the beaver, which is extremely gentle; its testicles are highly suitable for medicine. Physiologus says of it that, when it knows that a hunter is pursuing it, it bites off its testicles and throws them in the hunter's face and, taking flight, escapes."[3] Short clarifications follow the allegory, facilitating the reader's understanding of the moral lesson in the entry: "But if, once again, another hunter is in pursuit, the beaver rears up and displays its sexual organs. When the hunter sees that it lacks testicles, he leaves it alone. Thus every man who heeds God's commandment and wishes to live chastely should cut off all his vices and shameless acts, and cast them from him into the face of the devil."[4] The phenomenon represented and transformed here is the danger of not completely rejecting vices. The literal narrative is the beaver's vivid self-castration – emphasized through its Latin and Romance names – and forfeiture of its genitals to the hunter, while the secondary narrative implied is the pious person who gives up all vices so that the devil will leave them be. The author's intention is to communicate that one cannot be too careful or overzealous when avoiding vice and temptation. This entry also negates the common misconception that allegory is merely an extended metaphor. No specific qualities or behaviours of the beaver betray the quietness or inoffensiveness of a pious person. The reader only obtains equivalence after they have formulated a notion of the text, and after the metaphoric formula of $x = y$ has failed them. This therefore leads to Johnson's proposition of a definition for the allegory, one that, despite centuries of fluctuation in popularity and meaning, does not stray far from Quintilian's or Isidore's concept,[5] as "that class of works that fulfills its rhetorical purpose ... by means of the transformation of some phenomenon into a figural narrative" (2012, 8). Because of this, a bestiary entry cannot be retold as "a beaver self-castrates" or "a bird self-immolates," for an entry's literal narrative is insufficient for its comprehension.

The bestiary's nature, intrinsically allegorical, could shift its content depending on context, as exemplified by the phoenix entry in the *Physiologus*. The description of the phoenix begins with an excerpt from the Bible: "The Savior said in the Gospel, 'I have the power to lay down my life, and I have the power to take it again' [John 10:18]. And the Jews were angered by his words" (Curley 1979, 13). Abruptly, the subject changes to an Indian bird called the phoenix, which every five hundred years enters the forests of Lebanon, bathes his two wings in fragrance, and signals to a priest of Heliopolis, a key city of worship in Ancient Egypt, who then heaps the altar with brushwood. Once covered in sacred oils, the bird enters Heliopolis and self-immolates. The next day, the priest examines the ashes leftover to discover a worm that, by the third day, will be a full-sized bird again, greet the priest, and fly back to its home. *Physiologus* warns that if the phoenix can end its life and then resuscitate, only fools could be angry at God for doing the same. The phoenix is revealed to represent the Saviour: "descending from the heavens, he left his two wings full of good odors (that is, his best words) so that we, holding forth the labors of our hand, might return the pleasant spiritual odor to him in good works" (14). The allegory of the phoenix demonstrates that, like his terrestrial counterpart, Christ can die and be reborn.

Physiologus's pagan elements (the bird's Indian origins, its habitat in the forests of Lebanon, the priest from Heliopolis, a Greek word meaning "city of the sun") reflect their context, and mirror societal changes. The role of the presumably pagan priest is significant; he is tasked with catalyzing the sacred process of rebirth. The rebirth not only takes place every five hundred years, but it also specifically happens during the Coptic month of Phamenoth, thereby emphasizing the formidable mix of religions and cultures represented in each bestiary entry. The strong yet balanced fusion between pagan and Christian religions is an important element present in the Bodleian bestiary's interpretation of the phoenix and will be revisited shortly.

Though pinpointing when the *Physiologus* became a bestiary has proven difficult, it is generally accepted to be when a significant number of new chapters emerged, as well as when the material was combined with other sources. As mentioned in the introduction, a bestiary is a collection of short descriptions about real and imaginary animals, followed by a moral explanation based in the teachings of Christian faith. Typically, bestiaries began with the book of Genesis, describing the creation of waters and firmament, and then moved on to birds, fishes, animals, and finally, man. These entries were followed by Adam's naming of the animals, thereby introducing the stewardship inherent in man's responsibility over all of God's beasts. As bestiaries expanded to fit more and more creatures still, animals were grouped according to their kind, "just as they were created, birds on the fifth day and beasts on the sixth" (Grout, n.d.). As we will see throughout this book, the descriptions of animals found in bestiaries were not derived from observation, but rather from *auctores* (authorities), including the previously mentioned Pliny the Elder, Aelian, and, of course, the *Physiologus*. This means that for contemporary readers used to a scientific understanding of animals, the qualities attributed to the creatures populating European bestiaries might seem charmingly inaccurate, if not comical. Here it is worth contextualizing that medieval life was vastly different than contemporary life. Most people never left their home village and information was expensive and difficult to find – renderings of animals even more so. Lions and whales, then, cohabited in bestiaries alongside bonnacons, basilisks, and unicorns, as fantastic and unreachable as their imaginary counterparts.[6] As the analyses in the following pages move back and forth between medieval, twentieth-century, and contemporary works, it is important to heed art historian Janetta Rebold Benton's warning: "When admiring the inventiveness of the medieval artists we must be careful to avoid augmenting it with our own" (1992, 18).

Luxurious and costly to produce, most medieval bestiaries belonged to ecclesiastical libraries and varied depending on their sources. Different manuscripts' versions of the *Physiologus* lead to different bestiaries, depending on which version of the *Physiologus* was combined with which other sources. M.R. James was the first to divide the bestiaries into four distinct families, which Florence McCulloch and Brundson Yapp further subdivided. The B-I version of the bestiary provides an example of the alphanumeric system used to categorize the works. The "B" refers to the version of the *Physiologus* that contains thirty-six specific entries, while the "I" indicates that, save for seven entries, each entry is influenced by Isidore of Seville's *Etymologies*. The conversion of the *Physiologus* into a bestiary is better described as an evolution than a metamorphosis, since, additions aside, much of the *Physiologus* is featured intact in the later medieval form. The two works most often combined with the *Physiologus* were Saint Ambrose's *Hexameron* (ca. 370 CE) and Isidore of Seville's *Etymologies* (ca. 700 CE) (Barber 1993, 3). Though all bestiaries can be traced back to the three texts, the most immediate source for a bestiary was the authority of a previously written one, and the process was dependent on compilers, editors, and scribes. Latin bestiaries peaked in popularity during the twelfth and thirteenth centuries, and once translated into the vernacular they continued to enjoy near-biblical status well into the fifteenth century (4–5).

Bestiaries, unlike the *Physiologus*, were often decorated or had space for illustrations, particularly the vernacular versions (McCulloch 1962, 70). There are several reasons behind this phenomenon. It was initially believed to be because of the overall increase in manuscript illustration seen in the twelfth century. New monasticism and learning were also simultaneously adding to a demand for and creation of more illustrated texts, since, up until the twelfth century, manuscripts were exclusively illustrated by the monastic scriptoria for liturgical purposes (Mezzalira, Cavallo, and Mainardi 2001, 23). The illustrations also served as mnemotechnic devices with which to aid the retention of Christian dogma by the laity, particularly illiterate women and children (Rowland 1989, 14). An accompanying image of a lion, for example, could help a story better instil the fear of God in a child. We can safely assume that as the bestiary gained prominence thanks to its ability to spread moral Christian teachings, it would have also become an obvious candidate for illustrations.

As with their written entries, different bestiaries also shared elements of their illustrations. As observed by Benton in her detailed account of animals in medieval art, *The Medieval Menagerie*, illuminations in bestiaries were generally brightly coloured with reds, blues, and golds, colours not easily found in nature (1992, 70). Although in the case of tigers and other rare creatures, non-natural colours such as blue could be expected, the reason behind more common animals such as horses being coloured blue, as is the case with horses across several bestiaries, is less clear. Usually, the illuminators and artists who worked on bestiaries also worked in other media, and reproduced images by poking their outline with a series of tiny holes and then pushing charcoal dust through them (71). This meant that images could be standardized to a degree, rendering the represented animals more familiar.

The aforementioned phoenix entry, when contrasted with the phoenix entry in the Bodleian bestiary (ca. 1220), demonstrates that the *Physiologus*'s pagan nature became increasingly obscured under new societal demands.[7] The Bodleian entry contains two contradictory accounts on the phoenix, most likely because of an indiscriminate compiling of previously existing sources. This signals a change from authorship to medieval compilation practices. The first part of the entry is closely related to what was written in the *Physiologus*, with a few significant differences. The phoenix here is from Arabia, not India, and it derives its name because "its colour is like the dye from Phoenicia or because it is unique in the whole world" (Barber 1993, 141). The phoenix was a regal animal, as Phoenicians were famous for their purple of Tyre, a shade made from murex sea snails that ranged from red to purple and was a prized export to the Mediterranean and the Middle East (Jensen 1963, 104). This divergent information can be traced back to Isidore of Seville's account of the phoenix. The mention of Phoenician civilization, however brief, offers an entry point into a parallel myth of the phoenix worth pursuing. A possibility exists that associating the bird with Phoenician civilization served to sever its previous ties to the Egyptian city of Heliopolis,[8] and that the Bodleian bestiary represents one of many works shifting in content towards a hermetically Christian allegory.

Given that the only mention of Egypt in the *Physiologus* is the one made in the translator's introduction, it is worth entertaining the possibility that the Heliopolis that is mentioned may not have been in Egypt. There is another contender for the home of the phoenix, a different Heliopolis that bore that name for almost a thousand years, before the spread of Islam resulted in the city reverting to its Semitic origins in the seventh century. Previously known as Baalbek, Heliopolis was likely renamed during the time of the Seleucid Empire, around 198 BCE, and was usually distinguished from its Egyptian namesake by the epithet "in Phoenicia" or "in the Lebanon" (Ragette 1980, 17). The city then came under the rule of the Roman Empire during the Pax Romana, around 27 BCE, and it proved to be a key location due to the many tactical advantages it provided (Jidejian 1975, 21). When Constantine converted to Christianity in 312 CE, pagan practices began to be restricted (62). It was not until 440 CE, however, that the previously constructed Greco-Roman temples began to be actively destroyed; and in the place where the sanctuary of Balanios had once been, for example, Theodosius constructed a Basilica dedicated to St Peter (Ragette 1980, 69).

Mythology on the phoenix preceding the *Physiologus* is complex, with sources claiming various origins and defining characteristics, at times at the cost of chronology. The convoluted tradition allows for misunderstandings, making it difficult to point to any one trajectory of the myth as definitive. The argument for Egypt stems from Herodotus's description in the *Histories*, Book 2, which dates to the fifth century BCE. In his narration, he also describes the bird as partly red and partly golden. Ovid's account in the *Metamorphoses*, Book 15, from the first century CE, offers the earliest counterpoint, when it reads: "But one alone / A bird, renews and re-begets itself / The Phoenix of Assyria" (Ovid 2008, 363). This fact, together with Isidore of Seville changing the bird's plumage to the colours of the Phoenicians around 700 CE, favours a Phoenician-based myth. The alternative is worth exploring as a later-occurring parallel myth that offered useful reformulations of the text as ecclesiastical powers attempted to advance the Christian aspect of bestiaries and cast aside the pagan ones. The ambiguous, unidentified Heliopolis left room for more overt Christian connotations, which in turn produced more didactically useful bestiaries.

In addition to the geographical debate, other elements in the entry demonstrate increasing preference towards exclusively Christian content. Though the hermeneutics of the allegory remain mostly untouched in the entry's first account on the phoenix, the description of the bird itself and its characteristics are quite different from its source in the *Physiologus*: "If the phoenix has the power to kill itself and bring itself to life, why, O foolish man, do you grow angry at the word of God who is the true son of God. For our Saviour descended from heaven, and unfolded His wings, which were filled with the sweet scent of the Old and New Testament" (Barber 1993, 141). The priest described in the *Physiologus* is removed in this version of the text, as is most of the pagan imagery: "It lives for five hundred years, and when it feels itself growing old, it collects twigs from aromatic plants and builds itself a pyre, on which it sits and spreads its wings to the rays of the sun, setting itself on fire" (141). Though traces of sun worship persist, the phoenix of the medieval period is self-sufficient, a change that allows yet another trace of pagan worship to be erased.

As mentioned, this entry contains a second allegory of the phoenix, in which the creature is equally self-sufficient yet achieves its means differently by building a chrysalis of frankincense and myrrh, among other spices (142). As the elements necessary for the burning change from brushwood to frankincense and myrrh, the Christian allusion within the ritual is emphasized. The conflicting depictions and interpretations of the phoenix indicate a compiler's decision to combine two previous sources into one entry. This version of the resurrection of the phoenix is reminiscent of the one in the *Physiologus*, which explains the stages of the bird's regeneration. In this case, however, the allegory is quite different: "Oh man, make your chrysalis, and putting off the old Adam, and all his deeds, clothe yourself in the new man. Your chrysalis and sheath is Christ, who will protect you and shelter you in the evil hour" (143). The phoenix no longer symbolizes Christ, but rather the sinner who must bathe in Christ so that his soul may find protection from evil and temptation.

The passage which follows the above entry states: "The phoenix produces all the signs of the Resurrection; for the birds are there to teach man, not man to teach the birds" (142). As seen in the *Physiologus*, man is merely an interpreter of the archetypal doubles of heavenly affairs, bestowing a new dimension to the origin and purpose of animals in the book of Genesis: "Then God said, 'Let us make humankind in our image, according to our likeness; and let them have dominion over the fish of the sea, and over the birds of the air, and over the cattle, and over all the wild animals of the earth, and over every creeping thing that creeps upon the earth.'"[9] The Christian God gives humans power over all animals, yet the bestiary reminds the reader that though powerful over them, humans must look out to nature and animals, observing their patterns and dynamics as the keepers of secrets on higher truths. In the New Testament, animal is rendered equal to human in the following verses: "Look at the birds of the air, for they neither sow nor reap nor gather into barns; yet your heavenly Father feeds them. Are you not of more value than they? Which of you by worrying can add one cubit to his stature?"[10] As a trope, animals in the role of teachers is not confined to the medieval bestiary and resurfaces time and time again as the genre evolves.

Despite their immense popularity, bestiaries were not exempted from paradigm shifts. The Renaissance and its emerging preference for scientifically sound texts left less and less room for the allegorical beast, obscuring the literary genre. How the bestiary form first arrived on American soil thus poses an interesting albeit complex question. Different theories exist on the plausible reason for the continued survival of bestiaries in the New World. Luisa Fischer in "Zoológicos en libertad: La tradición del bestiario en el Nuevo Mundo" (1996) argues that elements of the bestiary survived by becoming parts of works such as fray Bartolomé de las Casas's *Historia de las Indias* or José de Acosta's *Historia natural y moral de las Indias*. In other words, Fischer holds that the survival of the genre is owed to its ability to blend seamlessly with other forms. She chooses not to explore the possibility of the genre surviving as a stand-alone work. Fischer's second claim regarding the expansion of the medieval genre into contemporary literature includes looking at one animal in particular, the axolotl, and identifying different literary instances featuring the salamander. This includes the work of Octavio Paz, specifically the entry titled "Salamandra" in his *Configuraciones*, and Julio Cortázar's axolotl in *Final del juego*, among others, with only one instance of the axolotl existing in a bestiary (Arreola's). The use of a specific creature has little to do with the form of the bestiary, and this argument is better suited as the analysis of a symbolic creature rather than as part of a study on the evolution of the bestiary. While the title of Fischer's work, "Zoológicos en libertad: La tradición del bestiario en el nuevo mundo," refers to the freeing of the bestiary from the tradition of animals, it is important to be careful and ensure that an argument is not made for a break in the tradition rather than a reshaping of it.

In his study "El bestiario medieval en las crónicas de Indias (siglos XV y XVI)," Marco Urdapilleta Muñoz seeks to understand whether the animal entries in explorers' diaries could be considered a new form of the bestiary. Among the chronicles, he analyzes fray Bernardino de Sahagún's *Historia general de las cosas de la Nueva España* (1499–1590) and Francisco Hernández's *Historia natural de la Nueva España* (1514–1587). The similarities found between the two genres, Urdapilleta Muñoz argues, have less to do with one form being heavily reliant on the other for models and information, and more to do with the fact that both belong to a greater zoological tradition that encompasses other works like the Bible, the *Natural History* of Pliny the Elder, and the *Etymologies* of Isidore of Seville. Although both the bestiaries and the *Historia de las Indias* belong to the same zoological tradition and draw from similar sources, the reports of the New World are not in fact based on the medieval bestiaries and thus cannot be considered part of their evolution.

A third theory exists that bestiaries, rather than transforming when they arrived in the Americas, arrived there unharmed. Irving Leonard's *Books of the Brave* (1953) holds that the encyclopaedias of Bartholomaeus Anglicus, Vincent de Beauvais, and Albertus Magnus were all transported to the Americas around the seventeenth century, as were Pliny the Elder's *Natural History* and Avicenna's *De animalibus*. Though Leonard does not explicitly speak of bestiaries, the works mentioned hint at beast-based literature being transported to the Americas. Demetrio Gazdaru speculated that some bestiaries would have likely been transported in the personal luggage of missionaries and Spanish authorities, though this remains hypothetical (2010, 273). Although these hypotheses contribute to the understanding of the zoological writing tradition in America, the idea of inconspicuous animal traces and a handful of antique books do not provide a definitive link between the genre's medieval origins and its contemporary proliferation. In the hopes of shedding light on centuries in which the bestiary did not appear, the next chapter explores a new theory behind the current proliferation of the Hispanic bestiary.

2

THE BESTIARY'S MIGRATION TO THE AMERICAS

La originalidad consiste en volver al origen.

Antoni Gaudí

As indicated in the last chapter, the Renaissance and Scientific Revolution largely rendered the bestiary obsolete – a superseded allegorical genre inhabiting a world rapidly coming to favour the scientific method. Despite the centuries-long hiatus, there is a growing number of original interpretations of the bestiary form over the past two decades, representing a proliferation of the genre in Hispanic literature. The bestiary's journey from its original medieval, European context to twentieth- and twenty-first-century Latin America, and eventually to Spain, remains obscured, as no clear means or mode of transportation has been identified. Despite the little information available, a series of significant publications point us towards a theory of how and why the bestiary might have been reintroduced and amplified in Hispanic literature. Six influential, acclaimed authors published bestiaries in the span of three decades: Jorge Luis Borges, Juan José Arreola, Augusto Monterroso, Pablo Neruda, Nicolás Guillén, and José Emilio Pacheco. Their activity merits attention as a crucial juncture in the evolution of the bestiary. This chapter thus argues that their six interpretations are central to the revival of the genre, each author marking a split from tradition, propagating possibilities and inviting experimentations that reverberate today.

CONTEMPORARY BESTIARIES AS PARODIES

As past and contemporary bestiary authors and illustrators manipulate the once restrictive medieval form, driving the genre well beyond its originally intended context, several questions arise: What characterizes the literary genre? How much can the boundaries of a literary genre be pushed before it becomes a different entity? Can the societal purpose of a genre shift over time? The previous chapter provided a brief overview of the origins of the bestiary, which serves as a foundation for the following remark: twentieth- and twenty-first-century bestiaries can be understood as postmodern parodies of their medieval counterparts. Parody, according to theorist Linda Hutcheon (1989), is a defining feature of postmodern art, as it embodies the complexity of a culture implicated by late capitalism and liberal humanism, one that questions the status quo from within the established system. The parody questions received traditions and histories, among other concepts that might have become accepted as natural. These bestiaries set out to undermine tradition, simultaneously using and abusing it (23).

The theoretical connection between parody and allegory proves useful when applied to the bestiary genre. Hutcheon equates her parody with the phenomenon that Craig Owens labelled allegory, presenting a centuries-old link between different generations of bestiaries. Owens holds that an allegorical image is necessarily appropriated, that the allegorist confiscates images rather than invents them (1980, 69). Whether labelled as allegory or parody, a parallel is evident in the bestiary's treatment of that which it allegorizes. The medieval bestiary allegorized the heavens and the sacred aspect of God's creation, including God himself. The postmodern, disenchanted, or, at the very least, secularized bestiary utilizes parody/allegory to explain, understand, and unknot the past.

It becomes necessary to outline the defining characteristics of the bestiary genre so that it is not conflated with other examples of parody, zoological writings, fables, and so on. Given the vast temporal and geographical differences spanned by the works of this book, one might wonder what ties a contemporary bestiary – parodic and postmodern, featuring only humans – to its medieval counterpart. The claim which underpins the corpus linking the remote past to the most recent publications is that twentieth- and twenty-first-century bestiaries can be called such because they maintain the *form* of the medieval bestiary: the division of creatures, usually the illustrations, the brevity of the text, and at times even the title. It is in the *content* of the works that these bestiaries innovate, playing with their respective zeitgeists, challenging the medieval Christian institution from which they were derived by merely existing as secular, subversive works. The only way to recognize a bestiary beyond the medieval, European canon is by its form. As the Christian dogma and references to antiquity are discarded, and the interpretation of "animal" is abstracted, the need for a new definition becomes apparent. All works explored in this investigation therefore conform to the following definition of the term: a collection of titled, independent short texts, largely descriptive but sometimes anecdotal, often accompanied by an image, about real, mythical, or implied beasts.

A curious series of publications, spanning several Latin American countries in the latter half of the twentieth century, shed some light on the transition of the bestiary from a largely obscure to bourgeoning genre. Despite bestiary-adjacent writing appearing sporadically before this period, such as Juan José Tablada's *El jarro de flores* (1922) and Jose Durand's *Ocaso de sirenas: Manatíes en el siglo XVI* (1950), it was after the 1950s that a cluster of bestiaries emerged, disrupting the scarcity of previous decades. In 1973, the critic Yulan Washburn noted these "surprising phenomena" of experimentation with ancient forms like exempla, parables, fables, and bestiaries by Latin American authors in the 1950s, 1960s, and 1970s. His study provides the foundation for the theory developed in this chapter, which holds that the six examined authors – Borges, Arreola, Monterroso, Neruda, Guillén, and Pacheco – are responsible for the current flourishing of the genre. The following pages examine the authors involved in the reappearance of the medieval form, and their impact on subsequent bestiaries. Both chronologically and thematically, the resurgence of the bestiary can be traced to a single work published in two editions, and the renown of its author: Jorge Luis Borges's *Manual de zoología fantástica* and *El libro de los seres imaginarios* (both translated into English as *The Book of Imaginary Beings*).[1]

Manual de zoología fantástica *by Jorge Luis Borges and Margarita Guerrero (1957), and* El libro de los seres imaginarios *by Jorge Luis Borges and Margarita Guerrero, illustrated by Silvio Baldessari (1967)*

Manual de zoología fantástica and *El libro de los seres imaginarios* are the two titles given to Borges's bestiary. The former was published in 1957 and the latter in 1967; the ten years between works allowed for an expansion of the first edition and the addition of illustrations by Silvio Baldessari. Though the book is a collaboration between Borges and Margarita Guerrero, her role in the work is unclear. In a well-researched and well-documented blog entry, Omar González (2014) recalls that Borges, in love with Margarita Guerrero, or Margot, as he affectionately called her, proposed the compilation of a bestiary as a way of holding her attention. Although her role has been under-researched, a piece of epistolary evidence written by Guerrero points to her administrative contribution to the book, and her potential hand in selecting the texts featured in the two bestiaries. Given that the topics henceforth explored are well-documented Borgesian idiosyncrasies, this question of co-authorship will not affect the overall argument.

Aside from his delving into Ultraism – a Spanish literary movement inspired by surrealism – the mature Borges famously revered literary tradition. Though his Eurocentrism has always been a point of contention among his critics, it was precisely the appeal of past and present European forms that led to his bestiary. Unlike the manifestos of the Ultraist movement, or the claims of creationist works, Borges was comfortable with the notion of literary unoriginality. He did not believe that inventing metaphors was possible; according to him, metaphors capable of forming intimate connections between one image and another have always existed (Borges 1960, 71). The prologue written for *Manual de zoología fantástica* references this idea: "Plato (if he were invited to join in this discussion) would tell us that the child had already seen the tiger in a primal world of archetypes, and that now on seeing the tiger he recognizes it" (Borges and Guerrero 1974, 13).[2] Beasts, sources of wonder for humankind, also incarnate the ubiquitous metaphors that Borges deemed worthy of writing and rewriting. Borges's encompassing mind culminates in an expression of a collective repertoire of creatures, through which the reader can compare the fears, hopes, light, and darkness of humanity. He draws from all corners of the world, displaying each culture's creation as part of a collective consciousness, accepting tradition as a necessary precursor to all "new" literature. This cabinet of curiosities is compiled much like the medieval bestiaries: a scrapbook of sorts, in which entries are supplemented by accounts like those of Conrad Gesner, or the remarks of Marco Polo.

Tradition strengthens when rooted in another notion central to much of Borges's work, the appreciation of religious and philosophical ideas for their aesthetic value. Perhaps the most famous example of this was Borges's obsession with Kabbalah, a school of Jewish mystical thought. In a lecture on the topic he stated: "The word Kabbalah means, if the texts I have read don't mislead me, something like 'received' or 'the received tradition,' and this etymology sends us to a fact far distant from us" (Borges 1988, 57). In the same lecture he underlined that, particularly during the Middle Ages, novelty was not held in high regard (57), highlighting the subjective value of originality – its dependency on context. Borges's reverence for literary custom and fascination by a mysticism rooted in tradition was the foundation for much of his writing. When this is considered, the bestiary emerges not as an anomaly, but rather an inevitability.

Borges's understanding of Kabbalah stemmed from a close reading of Gershom Scholem's *Major Trends in Jewish Mysticism*.[3] Despite studying the subject from what many consider to be its definitive scholarly text, Borges deviated greatly from what Scholem wrote was orthodox Kabbalism. To understand the extent of implicit Kabbalist elements in *Seres imaginarios*, it is important to qualify what Borges meant when he referred to Kabbalah. The first main deviance from an orthodox understanding of the tradition is Borges's literary and secular interest. In a 1982 interview, he stated, "it is the idea that the whole world is merely a system of symbols, that the whole world, including the stars, stood for God's secret writing. The idea is to be found in the Kabbalah, and I think that may be my chief attraction to it" (Borges and Barnstone 1982, 82). His interest was founded on the Kabbalist understanding of language, which reflects the fundamental spirituality of the world, in possession of its own mystical value (Scholem 1941, 17). Borges was interested in Kabbalah as a methodology for textual play. In addition to secularizing the practice, Borges attributed to Kabbalah many hermeneutical practices that belong to German

Hasidism (Gematria, Notarikon, Temurah). It is important, then, to recognize that Borges was not working with mysticism in the strict sense of the word, but more so adopting a notion of it. His interviews, lectures, and fictional elements on the subject reveal that what he meant by Kabbalah was a precise, Borgesian version of the subject.

Borges was interested in the main function of Kabbalah's classic texts, *Sefer Yetzirah* (*Book of Creation*) and the *Zohar* (*Book of Splendor*), elements of which are woven into *Seres imaginarios*. According to his reading of the works, their purpose was not to state or argue, but rather to suggest and inspire (1988, 54). He was attracted to the subtlety of alluding to an idea and engaging the reader as part of a text, allowing them to discover the hidden doctrine within the text (54–5). The allegorical, medieval bestiary also demanded this type of active reading, and Borges did not ignore this: "During the Middle Ages, for example, it was believed by Christians that animals had been created, like the creatures from the fables, with a moral purpose" (59). Both *Manual de zoología fantástica* and *Seres imaginarios* demonstrate the mix of religious elements beyond their intended context, allowing the works to function as intersections for Borges's interests in tradition and Kabbalah.

Another Borgesian element present in *Seres imaginarios* is infinity. His short stories brim with the theme, as they often require that readers retain the impossible in their minds. While critic Jaime Alazraki argues that the format of the short story reinforces the idea of infinity in Borges's narrative (1988, 30), the form of the bestiary proves an equally adept space in which to explore the theme. In the prologue to *Seres imaginarios*, Borges states: "The title of this book would justify the inclusion of Prince Hamlet, of the point, of the line, of the surface, of dimensional hyperplanes and hypervolumes, of all generic terms, and perhaps each one of us and the godhead. In brief, the sum of all things – the universe" (Borges and Guerrero 1974, 12).[4]

Despite the possibilities for inclusion, Borges amends and decides that animals alone suffice. For the reader, however, who may not have considered the sort of creatures one could include in this type of catalogue, a challenge ensues. With the mention of imaginary beings like the line, words, and Hamlet, Borges cracks open the door to the infinite, inviting the reader to imagine more. He makes this invitation explicit by stating, "A book of this kind is unavailable incomplete; each new edition forms the basis of future editions, which themselves may grow on endlessly. We invite the eventual reader in Colombia or Paraguay to send up the names, accurate description, and most conspicuous traits of their local monsters" (Borges and Guerrero 1974, 12).[5] Whatever edition a reader may hold in her hands, then, is but a mere fragment of a larger fractal structure that will continue to split and form as new names are given to old metaphors.

On the kaleidoscopic nature of the Jewish religion at large, Scholem (1941) wrote: "The more genuinely and characteristically Jewish an idea or doctrine is, the more deliberately unsystematic it is. Its principle of construction is not that of a logical system" (158). This characteristic, measured chaos, can be channelled into a methodology described by Borges: "These procedures, as is well known, include the vertical reading of sacred texts, the reading referred to as boustrophedon (one line from left to right, the following line from right to left), the methodical substitution of certain letters of the alphabet for others, the sum of the numerical value of the letters, etc." (1999, 83). Borges encourages the reader to frequent the bestiary in a nonlinear fashion, comparing it to the way that one might play with and reveal new shapes with a kaleidoscope (Borges and Guerrero 1967, 7). This thirst for the total meaning a text might offer presupposes that if an infinite intelligence writes, the work must be meaningful from every entry point. Nothing is by chance, and every minute detail, even the letter with which the text begins, must hold meaning (Borges 1988, 56). While it would be bold to assume that Borges considered his intelligence infinite, his request that the reader approach his text from different angles and as inexhaustible and endless is inspired by the sanctity of the *Zohar*. The lack of systematicity in *Seres imaginarios* is only furthered as Borges and Guerrero encourage the inclusion of more beasts and as the order of the beasts varies throughout different editions.[6] The nature of the bestiary, plotless and endlessly rearrangeable, offers both author and reader the freedom to approach literature in new ways.

Traces of the idea that all metaphors worth inventing have already been imagined can be found in the "A Bao A Qu" entry, the first creature to appear in most editions of Borges's bestiary. The A Bao A Qu has lived on the stairs of the Tower of Victory since the beginning of time. It lives in a lethargic state and is only visible when following a person in their ascent of the stairs: "At each level the creature's colour becomes more intense, its shape approaches perfection, and the bluish form it gives off is more brilliant. But it achieves its ultimate form only at the topmost step, when the climber is a person who has attained Nirvana and whose acts cast no shadows. Otherwise, the A Bao A Qu hangs back before reaching the top, as if paralysed, its body incomplete, its blue growing paler and its glow hesitant" (Borges and Guerrero 1974, 15).[7] The creature can be understood as a symbol of the journey towards purity, a theme that resurfaces in many cultural, religious, and historical contexts. Scholem (1941) himself could have dreamt the A Bao A Qu, as a way of encapsulating the soul of Hasidic literature: "Prayer is likened to Jacob's ladder extended from the earth to the sky; it is therefore conceived as a species of mystical ascent" (100). Borges plays with the creator-less creation. An afterthought in the abovementioned entry reads, "Captain Burton registers the legend of the A Bao A Qu in one of the notes of his version of *A Thousand and One Nights*" (Borges and Guerrero 1967, 12; my translation).[8] Norman Thomas di Giovanni's English translation contradicts this, stating: "this legend is recorded by C.C. Iturvuru in an appendix to his now classic treatise *On Malay Witchcraft* (1937)" (Borges and Guerrero 1974, 16). Perhaps the question prompted by the entry is not "Who authored, recorded, or transcribed the legend of the A Bao A Qu?" but rather "Does it matter?" If all worthwhile metaphors, including that of the A Bao A Qu, exist and have always existed, there is no harm in attributing to a metaphor one authorship instead of another.

Another characteristic of this bestiary is the insurmountable distance Borges seems to keep from the reader. The metaphor, although elaborate in content and form, ultimately feels impersonal. Borges was famously impermeable to social causes and disapproved of "the tendency of modern literature to reveal men's weakness and to delight in their unhappiness and guilt" (Alazraki 1988, 68). Gabriel García Márquez, for example, admitted he read Borges's work religiously to train his own prose, despite detesting Borges, calling his literature "a literature of evasion" (Kiely 1993, 83). Despite Borges's decision to write in Spanish, his beasts belong to the world, and have a distinct Borgesian flavour, less so a Latin American one.

Similarly, the illustrations by Baldessari in the first edition of *Seres imaginarios* maintain the reader in a space between formality and familiarity. Born in 1916, Baldessari is among the most prolific Argentine book illustrators, mainly active during the 1970s and 1980s until his death in 1987. Baldessari started publishing his comic strip *Tiro* in the magazine *Figuritas*, yet he remains elusive, almost mythical (Kearin 2012; Figueroa 2009; Del Popolo 2012). His work is ubiquitous and instantly recognizable: he illustrated all the covers for the publisher Losada's "Biblioteca clásica y contemporánea" and "Novelistas de nuestra época" collections, as well as countless covers for the publishing house Paidós. Informal sources state that he was the director of art and design in many publishing houses across Latin America (Figueroa 2009). Despite the pervasiveness of his work, the only information available on the artist can be found in blogs, with their respective authors also struggling to find further information. Baldessari's art is thus simultaneously distant and familiar. The compilation of beasts is meant to work as a depository of creatures suspended in a collective consciousness, temporarily misplaced, but never forgotten. Baldessari's images have a similar effect, for, though his name is not widely known, his art is ubiquitous in second-hand bookshops and used paperbacks, and instantly recognizable to book enthusiasts all over Latin America.

Baldessari's thick, almost clumsy black lines of ink summon shapes from their sleep, incarnating Borges's metaphors on monochromatic backgrounds. Blogger Quique Figueroa (2009) describes Baldessari's style as "Picasso-pop-expressionist." A single colour is bestowed upon each image, often aquas, oranges, light blues, and ochres. Baldessari's images play a role similar to that of the imagery in medieval bestiaries, as they support the textual claims on any given beast. Not all entries are illustrated, as is the case with the A Bao A Qu. An illustration of Abtu and Anet (figure 2.1), however, accompanies the following lines: "As all Egyptians knew, Abtu and Anet were two life-sized fishes, identical and holy, that swam on the lookout for danger before the prow of the sun god's ship. Their course was endless; by day the craft sailed the sky from east to west, from dawn to dusk, and by night made its way underground in the opposite direction" (Borges and Guerrero 1974, 16).[9] The banshee entry (figure 2.2), describing an Irish figure with a bloodcurdling scream that announces death, is also illustrated (Borges and Guerrero 1967, 64).

Together with the A Bao A Qu, these entries offer a sampling of Borges and Guerrero's encyclopaedic bestiary, vast and universal. In both illustrations, especially with Abtu and Anet, colour permeates the thick black lines, causing them to lose their sharpness. The

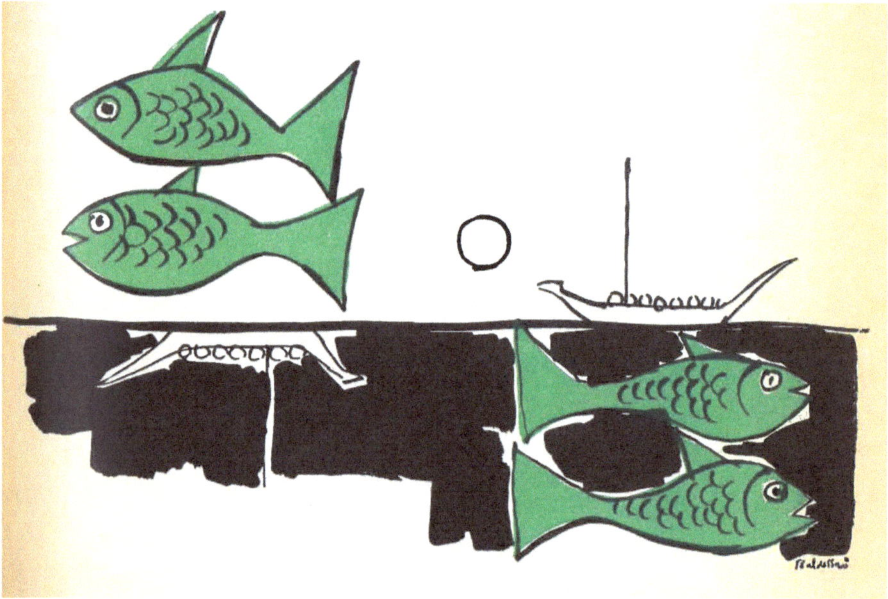

Figure 2.1 | Image of Abtu and Anet, depicting the two guiding fishes of the ancient Egyptian sun god Ra (Silvio Baldessari, 1967).

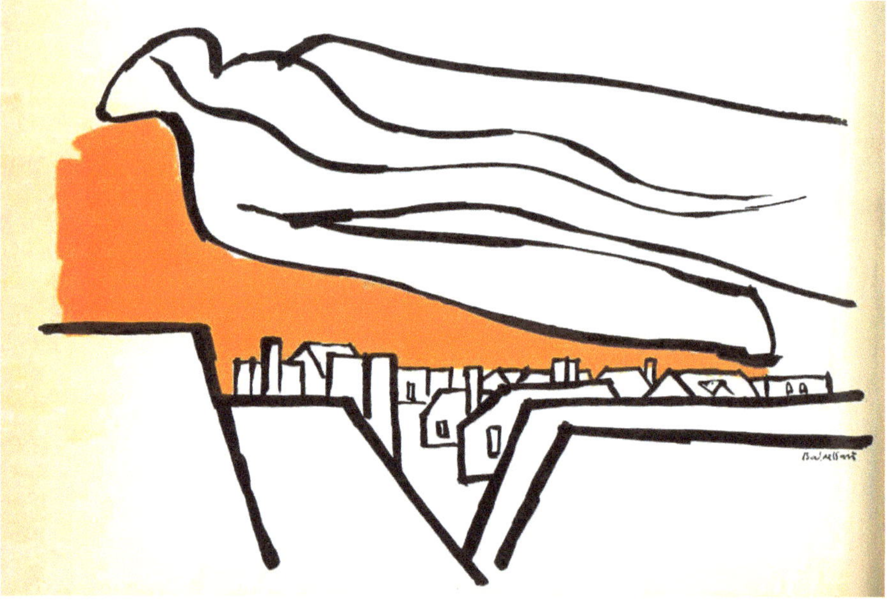

Figure 2.2 | Image of a banshee soaring over a neighbourhood, presumably in Ireland (Silvio Baldessari, 1967).

strokes, though masterfully revealing succinct, intentional shapes, look haphazard, as though they were taken from the illustrator's hands before the ink had dried. Abtu and Anet are placed in a mirrored landscape that parallels the circular nature of the entry's last sentence, static despite the aqua blue bestowed upon them. The banshee's ration of colour emphasizes her speed and freedom, as Baldessari's traces propel her awesome scream through the night. Ultimately, Baldessari's illustrations hint at forms, and thus the concepts fuelling his figures remain malleable, open to interpretation.

A line from *Manual de zoología fantástica*'s prologue reads: "Of course, we are fully aware that this book, perhaps the first of its kind, does not exhaust the sum total of imaginary animals. We have delved into classical and Oriental literatures, but we feel that our subject goes on forever" (Borges and Guerrero 1974, 14).[10] With these words, Borges simultaneously acknowledges the bestiary tradition and announces the course of the Hispanic bestiary.

Bestiario *by Juan José Arreola, illustrated by Héctor Xavier (1972), and* La oveja negra y demás fábulas *by Augusto Monterroso (1969)*

Juan José Arreola and Augusto Monterroso are difficult writers to classify. For the former, this challenge stems from the relative lack of critical attention he has received compared to his contemporaries Juan Rulfo, Agustín Yáñez, and José Revueltas. Arreola's decision to write short texts as well as his distinct prose stand outside the established tradition. During the time Arreola wrote short stories, the genre was viewed as drill work, a stepping stone towards a novel. Yulan Washburn (1983) holds that Arreola's use of the short text, along with the foundation established by Borges's and Julio Cortázar's short stories, pushed to legitimize the form (21). Arreola baptized his genre, a hybrid of prose poetry, short stories, and essays, "varied invention" (Garrido 1997, 15). He also advocated for fantasy and imagination when the Mexican literary landscape was interested in modern life, social justice, and the Revolution (Washburn 1983, 21–2; Garrido 1997, 14). Although Arreola shared these concerns for justice and ruminated on philosophical matters, he did not express his thoughts with a realist style. Given the reigning literary currents during Arreola's time, the dissonant elements of his writing are the key to understanding his interest in the bestiary.

A comedic tone links the writing of Arreola and Monterroso, as they belonged to a tradition characterized by its ability to employ irony, humour, and parody to unveil and destabilize a pre-established order (García Meza 2012, 16). Through this humour they destabilized the status quo, targeting the very core of the genre. The authors are the first to parody the bestiary for comedic purposes, using the form to convey messages vastly different to the intentions of the original medieval monks and authorities.

Arreola and Monterroso also contributed to a genre of Latin American literature that proved influential on their bestiaries, the microrrelato (flash fiction), with Monterroso's "El dinosaurio" serving as a most prominent example of the genre. Containing a strict internal structure, in which plot development is often secondary, the microrrelato's essence is best summarized by subject authority Dolores Koch (1981), who holds that it offers simple but zealously precise and bisemic prose; it is soaked in humour, be it through paradox, parody, irony, or satire; and it can rescue antique literary forms and insert non-literary formats from the media (124). As we will see with entries from both authors, and as is pointed out by Andrés Neuman (2001), a non-humorous paradox also exists between the form and content of the microrrelatos, which offer a plurality of narrative centres, which in turn create a highly interpretable space (146). Intertextuality, parody, linguistic conceptism (wordplay), transcendentalization of the everyday, and absurd humour, as well as irony, hyperbole, and an open or surprising ending, are also tools used in the microrrelato (Beneyto 1996). Neuman takes Beneyto's elements, and, adding Arreola's admission of a Kafkaesque love of hyperbole, carries out a comparison across three greats of the microrrelato: Arreola, Monterroso, and Virgilio Piñera (Neuman 2001, 146). He concludes that the elements proposed by Beneyto, along with the hyperbole, are mostly present in the authors' writing, and that the exclusion of some elements can be debated. These elements and the brevity of the text demand an invested reader, someone who Neuman approximates to the poetry reader (147) and who can also be compared to the medieval allegory reader. In his interpretation of Arreola's "La migala," Neuman states that while the contemporary short story often involves the unravelling and resolution of an enigma, the microrrelato is the revelation of the enigma's very existence (145). Because of this difference, the microrrelato must be seen as a text different from yet equal to the short story. Beyond being merely influential, microrrelatos will prove intrinsic to both canonical Hispanic bestiaries and contemporary works.

Arreola's *Bestiario*, illustrated by Héctor Xavier,[11] was initially named *Punta de plata* (*Silverpoint*) because of the silverpoint technique Xavier used in his illustrations, inspired by the beasts of the Chapultepec Zoo. Washburn (1973), a contemporary critic and acquaintance of Arreola's, revealed the writer's familiarity with the bestiary: "He knew its characteristics, its aims, its techniques, and its quirky personality, and chose the form because, somehow, its nature allowed him a perspective that permitted a communion with himself and his public that he felt he could not achieve with an exclusively contemporary form" (296). While the form being used remained medieval in nature, Arreola's tone and devices reflect the mid-twentieth-century context in which he wrote, complete with its crises and lack of conformity with daily reality. Arreola's words prove significant when considering the latent Christian tradition in the medieval bestiary: "I believe in matter animated by the spirit. I have come to believe that God is realized in his creation. I cannot believe that God existed before creation. God is because we are. Man is capable of intuiting and conceptualizing God – man is the indispensable creature" (1995, 23; my translation). Arreola states that without the human, God is null, an axiom shift that serves as the basis for the inversion present throughout these entries.

In the case of Arreola's giraffe, Arreola presents the reader with an ironic allegory. The giraffe's extreme proportions, which cause her to search in higher planes for what others can find on firm ground, are representative of the frivolities of her spirit. Though the term "ironic allegory" may seem contemporary, its origins are rooted as firmly in literary tradition as allegory itself, and both Isidore of Seville and Cicero saw the two elements as belonging to each other (Hollander 2001, 97; Tambling 2010, 21). Ellen Douglass Leyburn (1956) outlines the elements shared by allegory and irony: both are didactic, both simultaneously hide and reveal, they are often brief as to maximize their impact, and they represent a standard of judgment through which the reader and the allegorist agree on what "the right side," be it moral or not, is. They must find balance in the degree of similarity between truth and its representation, because if they overlap, the metaphorical aspect is lost, and if they are not similar enough, the reader becomes frustrated (5). Given the outlined parameters and Arreola's brief, poignant prose, the synthesis of both devices is particularly effective in the entries of *Bestiario*. The importance of a writer's ability to make the reader simultaneously conceive of the satirized human traits and the animal as animal, never letting them become entirely human nor entirely animal, is also indispensable (60). This notion is reinforced by Edwin Honig (1959) when he states in *Dark Conceit: The Making of Allegory*, that a good allegory does not explicitly state its intentions, but rather, it entices the reader with its constant play between subject and sense (5). Arreola is direct, but subtle. He suspends the reader, his prosaic poetry lets them know that something more can be interpreted, but he surpasses the medieval allegory aesthetically by not explicitly revealing his intentions. Arreola finds a balance between explicitness, subtlety, and his preference for brevity, maximizing the effectiveness of his entries.

When playing with giraffes, Arreola (2018) challenges not only medieval allegorical style in his prose, but its concepts as well. Firstly, his God has little in common with the all-powerful Christian God. God's mistakes when designing the giraffe's proportions lead to costly revisions: "Some biological problems had to be resolved for them, problems that are better suited to engineering and mechanics: a nervous circuit twelve metres long; blood that elevates against the laws of gravity thanks to a heart that functions like a well pump; and at these heights, a tongue that reaches higher still" (68; my translation).[12] The reader is left to wonder if Arreola's God would ever be so clever as to hide snippets of information about his celestial kingdom in creatures, as he seems to barely have a grip on earthly creation. Arreola's God did not make giraffes in his infinite intelligence but rather had to begrudgingly revise his work after realizing an error in calculation with respect to the animals' height and dietary preferences. Xavier's illustration presents an unimpressed giraffe reluctantly glancing back at the viewer, perhaps aware of its own ludicrous proportions. The mention of circuits and pumps blends creation and machine, elevating the trade worker to the same status as God, or making a mechanic out of the creator. Arreola oscillates between spiritual problems and plumbing problems, communicating both as equally important but the latter as more urgent. The blend of life and machinery is a recurring theme in the work, also seen in the entries on the rhinoceros and the elephant. The tone of the entry draws from the moralistic, authoritative voice of medieval allegory. The giraffe's height is in direct correlation with its moral extravagances, much like how the medieval beaver demonstrates piety through his lack of reproductive organs. Despite the moral message being rife with humorous inconveniences for God, it does not ring any less true, as the entry ultimately overlaps with the medieval bestiary in its didactic teachings about the human condition. The giraffe's lowering to the status of donkey serves as a warning for the spiritual letdowns of opulence. This entry exemplifies a modern allegory that forgoes a fear of God for a more reasonable critique of human nature. It promotes spirituality, not religion, and it wraps up its message in a humour that is only ever unintentional in medieval texts.

Beyond the obvious thematic similarities between the approaches of Arreola and Xavier, Xavier's choice of medium, the silverpoint technique, adds an enchanting layer to the work. Silverpoint, like the bestiary, originated in the medieval period and is seldom seen in contemporary art. While the technique is also called metalpoint, the availability, ease of use, and relatively competitive cost of silver has made the two terms, metalpoint and silverpoint, interchangeable (Burns 2012, 2). Silverpoint peaked in popularity – and beauty – during the Italian Renaissance (Sell and Chapman 2015, 5) and consists of leaving small deposits of metal on a coated surface, often gesso or primer, via a wire attached to a wood stylus (Burns 2012, 2–6). Like the microrrelato, silverpoint is an unforgiving medium; once a line is traced it cannot be undone (Burns 2012, 8), it demands precision and skill from the artist. It also has a limited tonal range, as it is always a pale grey, regardless how much or little the artist presses (10). As with any restriction, be it of word or medium, the creativity and skill of the artist shines despite the difficulties. Despite all the drawbacks of the medium, the skilful artist can create unified, delicate drawings – and in the case of Xavier's animals, lifelike features and textures (figure 2.3).

Xavier's giraffe betrays the same loving detail and eye as Arreola's prose. Here, critic Viktor Shklovsky's notion that "art exists so that one may recover the sensation of life; it exists to make one feel things, to make the stone stony. The purpose of art is to impart the sensation of things as they are perceived and not as they are known" (1965, 2) is pertinent. Through his skilful traces, Xavier makes the giraffe more giraffe-like: the tiny eyelashes and tufts of fur along her back are the product of engaged observation, and a veneration for the animal that moderates the unforgiving nature of the medium. She seems to have been caught unaware, as though the reader/viewer and their intrusive thoughts about

Figure 2.3 | Silverpoint sketch of a giraffe, inspired by those at the Chapultepec Zoo in Mexico City (Héctor Xavier, 1958).

her proportions and hydraulics are unwelcome. Much like how Arreola's entry on her seems to reveal information once known but forgotten, the oxidization process and its ethereal results unveil what has always existed.

Another innovation of Arreola's with respect to the bestiary is his assertion of a strong national identity, as can be seen in his entry on the axolotl, in which he attributes what he knows of the creatures to his mother and the Franciscan friar and missionary Bernardino de Sahagún (Arreola 1972, 40–1). The axolotl originates from the lakes Xochimilco and Chalco along the southern edge of the Basin of Mexico (Armstrong and Malacinski 1989, 13). Its name references the Aztec god Xolotl, god of surveillance over the dead and resurrected, monstrous beings, games, and twins (4). The Nahuatl word *axolotl* and its Spanish translation, *ajolote*, can thus mean "water slave, water servant, water sprite, water monstrosity, water twin, and water dog" (3). Its scientific name, *Ambystoma mexicanum*, references its national roots as well. In titling his entry "axolotl," Arreola marks a turning point in the tradition of the Hispanic bestiary. The featuring of an existing Latin American creature – to be differentiated from Borges's call for Latin American creatures – in a European form foreshadows a new order for an old genre.

By including Bernardino de Sahagún's words, Arreola (1972) inserts the historic collision of Europe and the Americas. His entry betrays amusement and perhaps fatigue at Bernardino de Sahagún's fascination with the axolotl, as can be felt in his mocking of the friar's Latin cry "¡*Simillima mulieribus*!" (Similar to women!) and his commentary "And again Bernardino de Sahagún" (25; my translation). Arreola works to demystify the axolotl, and by extension, his nation. His aside – "in a nearby town, my mother treated a woman mortally pregnant with axolotls" (25; my translation) – demonstrates familiarity with the creatures, particularly the position they hold in the Mexican literary tradition. Roger Bartra is another notable example of this phenomenon. In *The Cage of Melancholy: Identity and Metamorphosis in the Mexican Character*, he establishes axolotls as representative of the Mexican farmers and revolutionaries who fought to have things remain unchanged. Because the axolotl can procreate and live out its life in the larval state, without experiencing metamorphosis, Bartra (1987) found the comparison suitable: In this sense the axolotls are the same as the peasants of Morelos. The axolotls' resistance to metamorphosing into salamanders obliges them to undergo a marvellous revolution, to eternally reproduce their larval primitivism (61). By contrast, in the celebrated story "Axolotl" (*Final del juego*), Cortázar relays an infatuation with the creatures that denotes an exoticism incomprehensible to those who consider axolotls part of their daily affairs and identity. While Cortázar's narrator ogles and longs to know the axolotl, Arreola's mother helps get rid of the nuisance of an accidental pregnancy by them, signalling the use of an imported genre for local, quotidian purposes.

Unfortunately, the axolotl is not illustrated, as it was not originally included in *Punta de plata*. A significant parallel can be drawn, however, between Xavier's choice of medium and Arreola's axolotl, as the former also allows for the interpretation of a European form in a Latin American context. In *Punta de plata*'s prologue, Arreola highlights silverpoint's status as a curiosity, adding the detail that Xavier introduced a piece of Mexican silver into his mechanical pencil, which gave way to the illustrations upon which Arreola based his writings: "I saw the first drawing at his house: the image of the bison that looks like a graphite rock, and it was there that the old idea of a bestiary once again took shape" (2018, 8; my translation). Arreola's mention of Xavier's inspiration and medium – the Chapultepec Zoo, a recognized institution in the heart of Mexico City; and a piece of Mexican silver – highlights the fundamentally Mexican character of the collaboration, down to the employment of the very metals for which Mexico was plundered.

Finally, Arreola's musings on seals in "Las focas" present a playful, humorous entry of visceral prose: "Fleeting shuttles, seals weave and unweave the fabric of their endless erotic games. They hug without arms and slip off each other, improvising their rounds *ad libitum*. They spank the water with hard slaps; they clap themselves in viscous ovations. The pool seems made of gelatin. The water is full of lips and tongues, and the seals enter and exit, relishing themselves" (2018, 25; my translation).[13] Arreola incites the senses with grotesque imagery. The seals, incarnations of a libertine vogue, are so greedy with lust that they transform their environment into a deranged sexual paradise: "As is in the microscopic drop, the seals slide through the cool entrails of virgin waters with zoospermic flagellates, and women and children innocently watch the genetic pantomime" (25; my translation).[14] Arreola uses humour through the physicality of the seals, discrediting any creationist argument. If there is design behind seals' sexual shapes,

Figure 2.4 | Silverpoint sketch of seals, inspired by those housed at the Chapultepec Zoo in Mexico City (Héctor Xavier, 1958).

then many assumptions about God must be questioned. The viscous mess housed in this entry is more likely the result of a senseless world that offers no place for the meticulous medieval God. The entry is also not overtly didactic. Arreola's tongue-in-cheek chastising of animals serves foremost to entertain, and together with Monterroso, it makes way for a new type of bestiary, simultaneously far more and far less serious than the medieval sort.

The seals give the impression that while Arreola's form reflects a cohesiveness with Xavier's form, the content is entirely dependent on each reader's imagination (figure 2.4). Although Xavier's seals are far from lustrous and chaotic, a common thread of humour joins the work of the author and the illustration. This silverpoint drawing is unlike others; rather than regal and poised, it illustrates self-important, pompous creatures. Xavier's seals seem to hide that which Arreola claims they are, putting on aristocratic airs where deviant currents run deep.

Augusto Monterroso published *La oveja negra y demás fábulas* (*The Black Sheep and Other Fables*) in 1969, over a decade after Arreola's bestiary. The decision to include his work in this book was challenging, as many of its elements prove difficult to categorize, the most obvious one being the work's title. The second challenge was the inclusion of entries that were not strictly about animals, including ones titled "Good," "Evil," "parentheses," and "sleepless hand mirror." I have included *La oveja negra y demás fábulas*, however, because despite its ambiguous qualities; its style is congruent with contemporary bestiaries. Monterroso never finished primary school and was self-conscious about his lack of formal education. In an interview with Jorge Ruffinelli he confessed to approaching Aesop's and La Fontaine's fables as an adult to overcome the feeling of inadequacy before the genre (Monterroso 1981b, 21). Soon after, he realized "that that was silly, that I should not read them and do my thing as God led me to understand it" (21; my translation). Given the proximity between the fable and the bestiary, it is not outlandish to speculate that Monterroso, through autodidactic experimentation with one genre, came upon another.

Monterroso's awe of Borges also points towards the bestiary. His "Benefits and Curses of Jorge Luis Borges" (*Movimiento perpetuo*) appeals to the most celebrated themes of Borges, among them infinity and his fastidious, precise use of language. Though often an overlooked work of Borges, *El libro de los seres imaginarios* was likely added to the roster of descriptions and entries informing Monterroso's pen. *La oveja negra y demás fábulas* includes Kafkaesque animals and punctuation signs, the former present in *Seres imaginarios*, the latter hinted at in its prologue. Monterroso (1981a, 23–4) has also called his entire literary work an homage to Borges. Carlos Fuentes, in a blurb found on the back cover of the edition of *La oveja negra* referenced here, recognized its Borgesian influence and invited unfamiliar readers to imagine it as "Borges's

Figure 2.5 | Woodcut of an owl, from *1800 Woodcuts by Thomas Bewick and His School* (Thomas Bewick, 1962).

fantastic bestiary having tea with Alice." A further comment from the author also proves revealing. When talking about his love of classification and taxonomies, Monterroso wrote: "Even the chaotic ones cited or invented by Borges, whom I have classified together with Kafka as a humourist, are more or less hopeful attempts of organizing chaos" (1981b, 35; my translation). The Borgesian taxonomy is present in Monterroso's work. The varied categories included in *La oveja negra* are in closer proximity to Borges's kaleidoscopic archival entries than they are to the general predictability of fable plots. The entry titled "Los otros seis" (The other six) and its corresponding image (figure 2.5) exemplify this. In the text, Monterroso introduces a studious owl who acquires all human knowledge, is declared one of the "Seven Sages of the Country," and then is left to wonder who the other six sages might be (1969, 45).

The owl obsesses with the infinite knowledge of all knowledge, and the narrator compulsively lists his accomplishments. The owl sources its knowledge from coveted books, mixing infinity and bibliophilic tendencies in a manner that is reminiscent of Borges's "La biblioteca de Babel" (The library of Babel), and of Borges himself. The owl's status as one of seven sages or wise men of the country is reminiscent of Borges's "Lamed Wufniks," thirty-six righteous men who are unaware of their own identity and whose mission is to justify the world before God, appealing to the notion of unrecognizable and overlooked beings of great power existing amongst mortals.

The similarities with Borges are honed when in "Paréntesis" (Parentheses), Monterroso presents a literate flea with a familiar encyclopedic knowledge and lust for lists. At night, the insomniac flea ponders being more like Kafka, Joyce, Cervantes, Sor Juana, and Goethe, highlighting one feature or other of the mentioned figures (1969, 93). Though the entry displays Borgesian qualities, the introspection bestowed to animals is entirely Monterroso's. His sharp yet relatable tone contrasts with the grand scale and rather intimidating manner of Borges. Ruminating animals with literary aspirations and linguistic mastery fill the twenty-first-century bestiaries. In this aspect, Monterroso will rival Borges's influence on future bestiary authors.

Monterroso employs a humour that is sharper and more unforgiving than any other bestiary author until this point. His critical, sarcastic tone makes for a satisfying catharsis in the face of cultural and societal constriction. There is, at the heart of his pompous listings, a wink of awareness, an eye roll that forces the nomenclature to lower its brow and prostrate itself before bored indifference. Borges's fantastic, endless lists serve as indisputable inspiration, but *La oveja negra* dulls their shine with the wisdom of someone disillusioned by the quotidian.

Beyond the contextual elements and given that this investigation holds that the bestiary is defined by form, it is pertinent to consider Monterroso's prose and how it dissociates from the traditional fable as exemplified in the following two entries and their respective images: "La cucaracha soñadora" (The dreamer cockroach) (1969, 49), which tells a circular tale of a cockroach that dreamt its name was Gregor Samsa, and "El espejo que no podía dormir" (The mirror that couldn't sleep), in which a neurotic mirror is unable to fall asleep (29).

Admittedly, both entries commence in typical fairy tale or fable fashion, employing the Spanish translation of "Once upon a time": "Era una vez," or "Había una vez." They lack, however, the fable's characteristic plot-driven narrative. Both texts remain descriptive, rather than pushing forward any action or narrative. In addition, the Spanish uses the imperfect tense, which, as the name denotes, communicates the unfinished. It is used to describe, to present ongoing events in the past, and to establish context. The preterit composes the nodes of action that drive a story forward. To write exclusively in the imperfect is to focus on description, to remain stagnant in the past, relaying the qualities of a certain topic, but not following the narrative pattern of "beginning, conflict, resolution, moral" that is intrinsic to fables. The tense, when combined with Monterroso's characteristic brevity, blends more effectively into the current of new bestiaries than into the format of traditional fables.

The first edition of this work also complies with the illustrative requirements of the genre. Its images are taken from *1800 Woodcuts by Thomas Bewick and His School*, a collection curated from the works of eighteenth-century English wood engraver Thomas Bewick and his apprentices, first published in 1962. Bewick, much like Monterroso, innovated on an old genre. He perfected an art that many considered obsolete and consequently reshaped book production and illustration for the next hundred years (Hutchinson 1962, vi). The depth and sentiment of the stories Bewick told on a small square of wood are no less astonishing than the worlds Monterroso opened with fewer than two hundred words. Bewick's scenes foreshadowed the Romantic Revival (vi), capturing the essence of his time. Like Monterroso, he was at his best when depicting what he knew best, like the birds of Northumberland he sketched from life.

The illustration choice reveals much about Monterroso's intentions as an author. Bewick's woodcuts are a nod to the lavish imagery that once accompanied medieval manuscripts, but their context honours the text and its reality, not God. The woodcuts are of interest because they hint at the true fibre of Monterroso's literary fabric. In an interview with Rafael Humberto Moreno-Durán, Monterroso confessed identifying as a realist, not a humorist. If reality resulted in something that was entertaining or comical, he believed, that had little to do with his intention and most likely reflected the tragic, comedic aspects of daily life (Monterroso 1981b, 94). The sober images acknowledge Monterroso's desire to be seen as a realist author, as he poignantly bares his prose in this niche between reality and its absurd projections. The imagery reminds the reader that, despite Monterroso's oscillation between laughter and tears, he ultimately seeks to convey societal truths. With this tone, wit, and bite, Monterroso's entries become the beasts they describe, for as Isaac Asimov stated: "These small texts, seemingly inoffensive, bite if one approaches them without due caution, and they leave scars, and it is precisely because of this that they are rewarding" (C. López 2003, 14; my translation).

Monterroso's desire to write about reality leads to another junction between him and Arreola. As seen, Arreola explores elements of the human condition in an allegorical, removed manner. His philosophical rumination contrasts with Monterroso's half-veiled approach to denouncing his societal context. The namesake of his book, "La oveja negra" (The black sheep) (figure 2.6), reads: "In a far-off country many years ago there lived a Black Sheep. They shot him. A century later, the repentant flock erected an equestrian statue of him, which looked very good in the park. From then on, every time Black Sheep appeared they were promptly executed so that future generations of common, ordinary sheep could also indulge in sculpture" (1971, 29).[15]

Though sometimes denied by Monterroso, who throughout the interviews transcribed in *Viaje al centro de la fábula* contradicts himself many times, his writing betrays unmistakable political undertones. Isabel Jijon states, "When Monterroso explains that his work 'is concerned with social dilemmas, but not with politics in the strict sense of the word,' he is talking about his literary creations, and not about himself as author. The responsibility of questioning oneself ethically belongs to the reader" (2011, 69; my translation). Teresa Sadurní argues that Monterroso accomplishes his astounding brevity through leaving aside all that can be constructed or imagined by the reader (2005, 106). In Monterroso's defence, he tries to warn the reader by quoting K'nyo Mobutu: "So much are animals like man / that at times it is impossible / to distinguish between them" (1971, 11).[16] Some effort will reveal that these lines are darker than they initially appear, as the index of Monterroso's book labels Mobutu as "Anthropophagite," or, in

Figure 2.6 | Woodcut of a sheep, from *1800 Woodcuts by Thomas Bewick and His School* (Thomas Bewick, 1962).

plain terms, "cannibal." This required involvement on the part of the reader, typical of the microrrelato, leads to endless interpretations, as the reader is invited to fill in what Monterroso has omitted with their own sense of the world.

Monterroso's significance lies in his work's undeniable influence among other bestiary authors. Clearest of all is Monterroso's pioneering of the books that will be explored in chapter 3, which discusses insecure, introspective creatures preceded by those in *La oveja negra*. The space Monterroso creates between what is written, its image, and the reader's interpretation is a resource that bestiary authors will use time and time again. Addressing pressing metaphysical issues and playing with the human/animal dynamic are also key developments that usher Borges's bestiary to a new stage. The brevity of the prose and the works' humour, along with other elements of microrrelatos, will become a golden rule for future bestiary writers. Monterroso and Arreola, separately moulding similar bestiaries, set up much of what the genre would become in the years that followed.

Bestiario *by Pablo Neruda, with woodcuts by Antonio Frasconi (1965)*

The medieval bestiary and its interpretations by Borges, Arreola, and Monterroso share prose as a common element. Many contemporary bestiaries, however, choose verse, and Pablo Neruda distinguishes himself as one of three pioneers of the style. Neruda, a prolific portent whose verses transcended his native Chile to represent Latin America internationally, proves difficult to classify due to the constant evolution of his poetry. In *The Poetry of Pablo Neruda* (1979), René de Costa identifies facets of the poet: the erotic, neo-romantic Neruda of *Veinte poemas de amor y una canción desesperada* (*Twenty Love Poems and a Song of Despair*) (1924); the vanguardist tones of *Tentativa del hombre infinito* (*Venture of the Infinite Man*) (1926); the hermetical, obscure verses of *Residencia en la tierra* (*Residence on Earth*) (1933), the epic lyricism of *Canto general* (1950), and the anti-poetics of *Estravagario* (*Extravagaria*) (1958). Despite the fluctuating tones of his verses, animals are a constant for Neruda, sometimes varying in their style of representation but nonetheless always present in his works.

The most obvious contender of Neruda's publications for inclusion in this book, *Bestiario* (2007, originally published in 1965), cannot be considered canonical. Although it conforms to the definition of a bestiary, this work was compiled and published posthumously by Neruda's editor, Giuseppe Bellini. *Bestiario* did not circulate as a bestiary for the same amount of time, nor have the same impact as previously examined bestiaries, and is therefore not a referent through which the course of the genre can be better understood. Neruda, however, foreshadowed his posthumous work with a poem also titled "Bestiario." Initially published in *Estravagario*, "Bestiario" was reprinted in 1965 as a stand-alone, bilingual work translated by Elsa Neuberger and illustrated by Uruguayan artist Antonio Frasconi's woodcuts. Unfortunately, no information exists on the rationale behind the work being produced bilingually, nor about the translator. We do know that Frasconi was an admirer of Neruda's work and illustrated the original poem, so it would be safe to assume that the English translation was meant to broaden its audience, especially given Frasconi's residence in the United States. Beyond bibliographical reformatting – that is to say, "Bestiario" becoming *Bestiario* – the poem was divided into subsections, moulding itself to the bestiary's

Figure 2.7 | Woodcuts of various animals, including a horse, chicken, and fox, enclose Pablo Neruda's verses (Antonio Frasconi, 1965).

short text requirements. Frasconi's orange-and-black woodcuts are essential and play a role beyond the descriptive, transforming the verses into self-sufficient or self-contained entries. Because there are no subtitles labelling the animal or topic of each entry, the woodcuts announce the content of the section before the words can be interpreted. At times, image and text are altogether impossible to separate, as is the case with the opening entry (figure 2.7).

Animals encase, and at times dwarf, the bilingual verses. Neruda's poetry in this work is one of curiosity, of a desire to learn from the most minute of creatures. His romanticizing of animals in this poem is subject to much commentary. Martha Paley de Francescato claims: "In Neruda everything is a fervent desire to get closer to the most minute of existence on the planet" (1977, 35). Bernard Schulz-Cruz supports this idea and holds that Neruda passes no judgment on the beauty or worth of the animals, and in

Figure 2.8 | Woodcut depicting four large rabbits, jumping over verses by Pablo Neruda (Antonio Frasconi, 1965).

opposition to Borges's erudition, he resolves to accept and admire animals as they are (1991, 25). Neruda's longing negates the medieval practice of imposing moral views onto the animals. In this instance, the creatures are not jailed by words, but rather *they* surround and define words. Both the medieval and the Nerudian animal teach, but the latter instructs with no ulterior motives and does so through innate behaviour rather than contrived messages.

The animal, liberated from religious, political, and social agendas, carelessly jumps on the verses, and in the entry in the rabbit, does so quite literally (figure 2.8). The rabbit ignores Saint Francis – among the most venerated saints and of particular importance to animals – and the poet himself, charming Neruda with its rowdiness. Unlike the medieval perception of a rabbit's fertility, the animal condemned and chastised as a cause of famine, the natural drive of Neruda's rabbit is celebrated. Some medieval bestiaries, based on Pliny the Elder's account of the beasts, described rabbits' fertility and reproductive rate as harmful to societies, as their ravenous eating led to human famine. Neruda is not preoccupied with past notions of the animal, and asks to speak to the rabbit, just as he asks to speak to the birds, oysters, little lizards, foxes, penguins, horses, and dogs. All these creatures prove common, distinctly unremarkable when compared to what the fantasy worlds of the griffins and A Bao A Qu's offer. His request to speak directly with the animals underlines the idea that no other interpreter, mediator, or ambassador will do – they might corrupt the message. The choice in illustrator solidifies this position of dignified simplicity. Known for their beautiful, clean images, all accentuated by a potentially limiting medium, Frasconi's illustrations provide the sort of approximation Neruda longs for, simple and direct. The rabbit's and by extension the other animals' versified praise are better contextualized by Neruda's own childhood reminiscences: "I always loved these zoological and botanical books. They extended my childhood. They brought me the world of the infinite, the unparalleled world of nature. These books of terrestrial exploration have been my favourite and I rarely fall asleep without looking at the effigies of adorable birds or stunning insects, as complex as clocks" (1972, 537; my translation). Neruda's words reveal nature as an object of fascination, endlessly renewable. Arnaldo Donoso Aceituno and Juan Gabriel Araya Grandón attribute the labyrinth metaphor to "An ecological thought that includes all imaginable forms of coexistence" (2016, 33; my translation). As the authors state, there is a clear disdain for an anthropocentric perspective, and Neruda explicitly foregoes the creation of humans for the wisdom of animals: "and I will not leave this planet without knowing what I came to seek, / without investigating this matter, / and people are not sufficient for me."[17]

The woodcut profile accompanying these verses illustrates the labyrinth of nature, which includes the human mind and its pathways. This human brain simultaneously mirrors nature's labyrinthine appearance and acts as a model that facilitates comprehension of a larger whole. At the centre of the woodcut is an ambiguous shape that could be a stylized ecosystem, surrounded but not subjugated by the ego. Natural entities are at the centre of Neruda's mind, and his words "I have to go much further / and I have to go much closer"[18] underline the need for introspection and exploration, as he is a part of – and contains – the whole as well.

Figure 2.9 | Woodcut depicting a large cat, standing atop the final line of a poem by Pablo Neruda (Antonio Frasconi, 1965).

Human activity and that of animals are parallel poles in these verses. The Marxist undertones later associated with the author have not yet turned his animals into emblems for a socialist cause. Rather, nature is simultaneously an escape and a totality, untouched by Neruda's mistrust of capitalism, alienation, and rationalization. The fixation on the animal world leads to a distancing from self-consciously nuanced human activity and a striving towards an idyllic state with and within nature. His escapism culminates in a complete eradication of the person. The poem concludes with Neruda's demands to speak to the cat and the faceless cat, the every-cat roaming freely, all over his words and work (figure 2.9).

Frasconi's deliberate divisions force the reader to consider each sub-entry on its own, revealing the small challenges to and advances in the literary tradition of the Hispanic bestiary. When read all the way through as a single poem, however, the message is simple and consistent: Neruda wants to talk to animals, at any and all costs, a sentiment that renounces an anthropocentric bestiary and favours one that partakes in nature, being edified by it instead of employing it. Neruda's animal poetry is foremost an act of love towards all animals (Neruda 2007, 15), and it represents the clearest act of love to arise in the bestiary tradition thus far.

The examined *Bestiario* is but a sample of Neruda's poetic treatment of animals. His influence on writers' approaches to animals goes beyond this single work. His *Odas elementales* (1954) (*Odes to Common Things*) and *Nuevas odas elementales* (1955), for instance, contain homages to the birds of Chile, lizards, sea gulls, hummingbirds, and, among more abstract creatures, a clock in the night and to a spool of thread. The odes teach the audience to observe carefully, mindfully, lest the regal nature of everyday objects be ignored (Neruda 2007, 8). Such is Neruda's apology of fauna that his epic advocates for the humane treatment of animals: "You question me about the wicked tusk of the narwhal, / and I reply by describing / how the sea unicorn with the harpoon in it dies" (1971, 131).[19] The anger towards senseless ivory harvesting and animal suffering is a first in the bestiary's canon, a visceral response to unjust treatment. This liminal juncture of theory and praxis, of denouncing precise practices through art, will resurface in bestiaries that take stances on critical issues, such as Gabo Ferro, Christian Montenegro, and Laura Varsky's *200 años de monstruos y maravillas argentinas* (2015) and Carlos Ferrándiz and Carlos Baonza's *Bestiario médico* (2000).

Neruda's legacy where the bestiary is concerned can be traced to his 1965 *Bestiario*. His use of verse in a space formerly reserved for prose established a tradition from which later authors drew inspiration, a phenomenon that will be explored in the chapters that follow. Neruda's romantic attitude towards animals will at times blend with Monterroso's ruminating humour and give way to a branch of poetic creatures who defend their desires and views directly to the reader. The new use of imagery to complete the text and not merely accompany it makes way for dynamic bestiary entries, in which the artwork becomes more stylized and relevant than ever before. The dismissal of an anthropocentric agenda, the humble and uncomplicated approach to interacting with nature, is perhaps Neruda's most significant contribution of all, as it presents a major shift in the core message and purpose of the genre.

El gran zoo *by Nicolás Guillén, illustrated by Fayad Jamís (1967)*

Nicolás Guillén's *El gran zoo* (The great zoo), illustrated by Fayad Jamís and published in 1967, is also a verse bestiary. The Cuban writer, poet, and journalist is best known for his verses, which concern racial dynamics, particularly the question of negritude (Blackness) in Caribbean and American contexts, with *Motivos de son* (Motives of son) (1930) being his most celebrated work. Despite this notorious and acclaimed early work, Guillén's poetry goes beyond a focus on the strictly racial; according to Stephanie Davis-Lett, Guillén's work can be roughly divided into three periods: 1927 to 1934, the period that focuses mainly on Black poetry; 1937 to 1964, dominated by a focus on the social, political, and revolutionary; and 1968 onwards, a period defined by the variety of themes and experimental techniques that Guillén explored (Davis-Lett, quoted in Jackson 1988, 111). *El gran zoo* falls mainly on the cusp of his socio-political phase but also demonstrates an undeniable amount of what Davis-Lett recognizes as experimental poetic technique, with occasional avant-garde flairs. While all three of the author's phases are evident in *El gran zoo*, Guillén's bestiary betrays foremost a humour and wit often neglected in his oeuvre. The humorous unorthodoxy of this work is hinted at in the first poem, "Aviso" (Notice), which doubles as the zoo director's announcement. In it, the poetic voice describes some of the beasts that the visitor/reader will encounter, including the Aconcagua mountain, live clouds, and a lecturing monkey (1967, 7).

"Aviso" functions as a prelude to the rest of the collection. The Cuban cry "¡Patria o muerte!" ("Homeland or death!") (7) at the end of the poem points to the revolutionary and socially critical current that underpins *El gran zoo*. Clouds, monkeys, a cyclone, and a guitar are part of the wide array of entities included in this bestiary. Guillén calls it *The Great Zoo* as opposed to *A Great Zoo* or a variation of an undefined institution because of its all-encompassing nature. Unlike Borges's A Bao A Qu, or Arreola's highly metaphorical seals and giraffes, Guillén opts to anthropomorphize the Caribbean, hunger, and the KKK, among other entities, forgoing the metaphor in favour of a direct, clear voice.

The director responsible for the announcement lists several entities before arriving at a (professor) monkey, letting the public know that animals are not the main attraction, as they are visiting no ordinary zoo. Clouds, for instance, have been captured

Figure 2.10 | Sketch of clouds joined to abstract shapes by black wires or strings (Jamís Fayad, 1967).

for the benefit of zoo-goers, and they reside in "El nubario" (The cloudhome). Guillén's entry "Las nubes" (The clouds) foreshadows his later avant-garde stage, including the presence of some of the movement's main themes, including space and skies. Guillén's writings on non-human beings in part take up Borges's proposal of including more than just fantastic creatures. He compiles a wide range of clouds, upon which he bestows qualities ranging from the imaginary, reminiscent of the shapes sought out in clouds, to the strictly geographical and climatic. Some are given human qualities, like the matronly midday clouds, or black, big-breasted storm clouds, and others are entrusted with angelic precious cargo. All clouds, however, are displayed in one *nubario*, in which all are invited to enjoy their delicate form. Putting behind bars entities too great for human conquest is a constant in Guillén's bestiary. His poetic feats mock humans' impulse to capture, conserve, and display bigger and bigger hauls. While comical, his account of attempting to bring live clouds from Greenland, Norway, or Newfoundland is not far from contemporary inhumane practices that seek to force wild beasts into a display. Guillén's awareness and criticism of a modern practice, as well as the transcendent, persistent nature of the problem, is in part what gives this work an avant-garde flavour. Although the bestiary is scarcely illustrated, the clouds entry boasts an impressive image (figure 2.10).

The image recalls a paper construction, a sketched assemblage, with many of its components hinging on each other as would the limbs of a paper doll. Fayad Jamís was a Mexican-born Cuban artist who also wrote modernist poetry. Supported by André Breton during his stay in France, Jamís's surreal, futuristic influences are palpable in the image, for instance in the children's windmill on one side, or the birds or fallen angels originating from and tethered to the cloud material on the other. The trace of thin lines accentuates the ethereal yet mechanical nature of the drawing.

Guillén's mockery of human aspirations to cage what is impossible to be caged finds its flipside when humans become the subject of curiosity. Furthering the trend introduced with Monterroso's bestiary, Guillén erases the line between animal and human by giving animals human qualities and describing humans as the worst types of beasts, as seen in the entry titled "El chulo" (The pimp) (1967, 65).

The poem exemplifies the socio-political focus that Davis-Lett has argued was characteristic of the years in which Guillén wrote *El gran zoo*. Guillén tells a cautionary tale of a pimp nearing the end of his life, locked up with his emaciated prostitutes. Keith Ellis explains that Cuban pimps liked to wear buttoned undershirts, with the most prestigious pimps bearing golden buttons. These golden buttons, paired with the H.R. brand logo as well as a Rabocolt 38 revolver, made for an impressive, authentic "chulo"

(Ellis, interview by Ailén Cruz, 2019). Contrasted with the pimp's incarceration, his past glory only highlights his fall. Guillén's critical placement of humans in a space traditionally reserved for animals is arguably the first to do so, and it is a decision that has greatly influenced many contemporary authors. This criticism relies on an *a priori* assumption that animals are inferior to humans, and that to be compared to an animal is an insult, a concept that will be further explored in chapter 6.

"El chulo" also presents a fascinating case study on censorship. When *El gran zoo* was published in the 1970s in Spain, many of its poems were censored. Some, like "Policía," were altogether removed (Ellis 1973, 92). Among other censored passages, Ellis states that a reference to the street called San Isidoro in Havana was omitted. He attributes this to San Isidoro's patronage of Madrid, and the fact that the street was a centre for prostitution in pre-revolution Havana (92). It is unsurprising that censorship should be reserved for the human figures in Guillén's work, as they represent explicit instances of social criticism. Guillén's "Aviso" and "El Caribe" (The Caribbean) are as critical as "El chulo," and yet they remained untouched. The trend hinted at in the censorship of explicit, human-based entries and the allowance of less literal criticisms, meanwhile, points to a potent political use of the bestiary.

A different sort of revolution, less critical and more prideful, is uttered as a warning in the poem "El Caribe." The description of a stunning creature, "Marine and enigmatic / possessing a crystal crest / a blue spine, green tail, / and compact coral belly,"[20] is offset by the warning on its aquarium: "Careful: it bites" (Guillén 1967, 9; my translation). The revolutionary, socio-politically active Guillén is evident in its verses, along with streaks of his modernist background and upbringing. In "El Caribe," revolution is advocated for in unity, and the verses are consistent with a sentiment often expressed by the poet. In an address he gave in December of 1974 to the Department of Spanish at the University of the West Indies he urged for unity among peoples of the Caribbean, denouncing the fact that they had been "kept separate by the evil imperialist faith that divided them, that confronted them, face to face, like quiet ghosts. Mr. Haiti, Mrs. Jamaica, the Misses Guadalupe and Martinique, Mr. Barbados, Mrs. Cuba ... What can they say to each other in their English, in their Patois, in their French, in their Spanish, in their Papiamento?" (Guillén and Irish 1975, 79). "El Caribe" represents Guillén's political call to unity, a unity that, especially before imperial powers and their remnants, is a revolutionary act. By personifying the Caribbean Sea and its islands, its maritime life, its natural disasters, and warning of its bite, Guillén proudly communicates the existence of a dangerous creature. His poem describes the Caribbean as a whole, united against potential threats.

The warning included in the above verses demonstrates a combative nature unlike anything seen in previous bestiaries. Guillén's influence can be seen in subsequent bestiaries, especially those analyzed in chapter 4, which largely assume a rebellious stance that challenges the didactic, homogenizing tradition of the genre. Guillén's rebellious poetic voice, along with his inclusion of humans and non-animal entities in his poetry, set a precedent for a significant number of contemporary authors to be explored in this study.

Álbum de zoología *by José Emilio Pacheco, illustrated by Alberto Blanco (1985), and* An Ark for the Next Millennium *by José Emilio Pacheco, illustrated by Francisco Toledo (1993)*

Álbum de zoología, written by José Emilio Pacheco and illustrated by Alberto Blanco, was published in 1985. In 1993 the University of Texas Press published a bilingual edition of the book under the name *An Ark for the Next Millenium*, translated by Margaret Sayers Peden and illustrated by Francisco Toledo. Two main differences exist between the original and the bilingual editions, aside from the latter containing poems in English and Spanish. The first is that the two books are not a one-to-one mirror of one other. *Álbum de zoología*, for instance, is divided into three sections (water, air, and earth), while *An Ark for the Next Millenium* is divided into four (water, air, earth, and fire). This latest category in the bilingual edition only contains one beast, the salamander. Some poems, such as "Cat" can only be found in the Spanish version, while "Live Bait" exists only in the English version. The second difference is that *Álbum de zoología* only contains three illustrations, functioning as title pages for each of the categories. *An Ark for the Next Millenium* instead contains Toledo's images throughout the work. Since the two works overlap in nearly all of the poems, and were published within very few years of one another, for the purposes of this chapter they will be treated as one work and will be addressed by the original title of *Álbum de zoología* unless otherwise stated.

Widely regarded as one of the major Mexican poets of the second half of the twentieth century, Pacheco received the prestigious 2009 Cervantes Prize for his literary oeuvre. Characterized by his accessible language and questioning of life in the modern world, Pacheco dedicated much of his work to the animal kingdom. With a unique perspective in which he attempts to inhabit the animal experience, differentiating him from all other canonical authors, Pacheco has influenced a distinct branch of contemporary bestiaries. *Álbum de zoología* was not the first of Pacheco's work to heavily feature animals. Writing about Pacheco's 1963 *Los elementos de la noche*, Michael Doudoroff identified the presence of "animals, later to populate many of Pacheco's most memorable indictments of man, lurking in these opening lines" (Doudoroff 1989, 265). Pacheco builds upon this in *No me preguntes cómo pasa el tiempo*, published in 1969, which features the section "The Animals Know," comprised of thirteen animal-centric poems that would later become *Álbum de zoología*. After the publication of *Álbum de zoología*, which took place in the same year as the devastating earthquake that killed at least five thousand people and caused hundreds of buildings to collapse in Mexico City, he published *Miro la tierra*, in 1986, which in keeping with his previous work offers the readers moral lessons derived from his observations of animals.

Álbum de zoología, like much of Pacheco's work concerning animals, possesses a style not yet seen in the writings of the canonical authors included in this chapter. Borges's bestiary amasses and collects; Neruda's and Arreola's observe, admire, and describe; and Monterroso's and Guillén's use animals as metaphors and to make implications. Pacheco instead blends the allegorical, moral tradition of the bestiary with a desire to communicate the perspective of the animal. Rather than observing the beasts featured in his work, he relays their possible concerns, attempting to inhabit their consciousness and to offer the reader a new perspective. The shift from an anthropocentric perspective to an animal-centric one is a departure from the canon thus far, influenced by an interest in animal consciousness that began with philosophical and cultural currents in the 1970s and 1980s, and that still reverberates today.

Many of the qualities, themes, and language found in the poems in *Álbum de zoología* reflect the "nonhuman turn," a term popularized by Richard A. Grusin in his 2015 book of the same name. Broadly speaking, the movement, which began in the second half of the twentieth century and continued into the twenty-first century, argued for redistributing both agency and the power over delineating and enforcing hierarchies away from humans. This shift was based on a variety of approaches such as new materialism, new media theory, systems theory, and, most relevant to the analysis of this book, animal studies. The push to dismantle human authority and acknowledge the agency that is often overlooked in animals is palpable in Pacheco's poems. Scholar Randy Malamud states that "Pacheco's animal poetry is keenly attuned to the featured poetic animals themselves: predicated upon a deep appreciation of a dignity that is independent of and apart from humanity" (2000, 6), adding that "Pacheco's poetry addresses how non-human animals and people share the world: how our own species is inextricably connected with all the others" (7). The poem "Pez," for instance, offers a depiction of existence as a fish:

> You were born
>   for the net
>   for the harpoon
> For hooks
>   asphyxiations
>   and frying pans
> We infect your sea by usurping it
> Now you ensure justice
>   poisoning us (Pacheco 1993, 21)[21]

Pacheco tries to capture the fish's experience, beginning with the varied indentation among the lines, which imitates the back-and-forth flow of a school of fish. Admittedly, Pacheco attributes vengeance, typically thought of as a human practice, to the fish, which are acting as vessels for mercury poisoning. Despite the use of a metaphor and slight anthropomorphizing, Pacheco offers a possible perspective and highlights how, as a creature gets further away from humans, it becomes more likely to be treated as non-living entity – be it as a resource, nuisance, etc. The nonhuman turn questions the relegation of living beings to object status, especially through the concept of an "insuperable line," introduced by utilitarian philosopher Jeremy Bentham, which "with conscious irony ... divides beings that count from those that do not" (Garrard 2023, 124). It would be, of course, impossible to draw a line that includes all humans and excludes all animals. Even if reason were the measure behind the division, we would need only compare an adult dog to an infant to see the difficulty in deciding which should go where (124). The impossibility in carving out and controlling these ontological categories, of bestowing agency and sovereignty to some beings and not to others, is further explored in chapter 6.

In his book *Ecocriticism*, Greg Garrard presents a helpful typology to analyze how animals are represented in various media, which tend to highlight either their otherness from or likeness to humans (131). Neither category is "good" or "bad," as there is nuance in each potential representation. In the category in which animals are depicted as Other, there exists the denigration and reductivity of the animal, as well as mechanomorphism or Cartesian anthropodenial, which encourages the view that animals are to be seen as machines, their cries of pain nothing more than the misfirings of a radio or alarm clock. Garrard adds a third term to this category, coining the word "allomoprhism," which rather than deny or draw discriminatory conclusions regarding the differences between species, seeks to celebrate these differences. In the latter category, likeness, there exist both crude anthropomorphism, or the disnification of animals, which threatens the sovereignty and autonomy of animals altogether by making them overly palatable to human understanding, as well as critical anthropomorphism, which, as seen in the case of Pacheco's poem "Pez," attempts to imagine the perspective of the creature in question.

Though the work contains a good amount of critical anthropomorphism, *Álbum de zoología* can be classified as an allomorphic work. This category argues not for the erasure of the differences between humans and animals, but rather an acknowledgment that humans and animals are different from one another, as are all species, because differentiation is a fact of evolution (126). When describing the neologism, Garrard gives the example of Australian poet Les Murray, whose book *Translations from the Natural World* he calls a "vivid testament to the difficulty, if not impossibility, of the representational work it undertakes" (143). In Murray's book, elements such as phonetics, syntax, and lexicon are dense and strange, paying tribute to the way in which different aspects of nature communicate and emphasizing their unfamiliarity to humans (144). The poem "Two Dogs" is a wonderful example of Murray's attempt to translate the natural world into words: "Enchantment creek underbank pollen, are the stiff scents he makes, / hot grass rolling and rabbit-dig but only saliva chickweed. / Road pizza clay bird, hers answer him, rot-spiced good. Blady grass, / she adds, ant log in hot sunshine. / Snake two sunups back. Orifice?" (1992, 19). The conversation between the two dogs is interlaced with the various scents they pick up, and Murray succeeds in both making the difference between human and animal apparent and bringing the reader closer to a possible animal experience.

This same allomorphic literary current runs through *Álbum de zoología*, in which Pacheco also grapples with the difficulty of representing the natural world, and of depicting the difference between human and animal, sitting in the discomfort of the unknown and the beauty of its mystery. Let us take, for instance, the entry "The Whale" as an example of this literary style:

Large floating tribes
    migrations
icebergs of flesh and blood
    doleful islands

Through the sad night of the deep
    resounds
their elegy and farewell
    because the sea
has been dispossessed of its whales

Survivors from a different apocalypse
    they adopted the shape of fish
without becoming like them

They must surface to breathe
    covered with millenary algae
and then
    the cruel, explosive harpoon
gluts itself on them

And all the sea becomes
    a sea of blood
as they are towed to the factory ship
    to make lipstick
    soap   oil
    and dog food

His eyes [are] like the eyelids of the morning.
Out of his nostrils goeth smoke,
like that of a pot heated and boiling.
In his neck strength shall dwell,
*and want goeth before his face.**
**Based on Job 41:18–22 (King James Version)* (Pacheco 1993, 25–7)[22]

The attempt to depict a more realistic animal experience is brought into relief when the poem is contrasted with a medieval work. In *The Medieval Castilian Bestiary*, a book out of Brunetto Latini's thirteenth-century *Tesoro*, we encounter the echinus, more commonly known as the sea urchin. In the entry, the echinus is called "wise" for superstitious reasons, since it knows when a storm is looming and intelligently prepares for it. Steven Wagschal in *Minding Animals in the Old and New Worlds* (2018) points out that the treatment of animals in medieval entries was both inaccurate and done to serve human purposes. He states that the "echinus is, thus, symbolic in the sense that it is a sign for humans that helps them anticipate a real threat about the awesome deadliness of nature, allowing them some measure of control (however fictitious or self-deceptive)" (43). The echinus, like so many other animals, is treated anthropocentrically only, existing to placate human concern (39).

By contrast, Pacheco's poem on whales seeks to understand their plight: "Through the sad night of the deep / resounds / their elegy and farewell." The poem is based on observation and knowledge of the natural world, as Pacheco acknowledges whales' evolutionary history, their terrestrial past, and communal pods when relays that "they adopted the shape of fish / without becoming like them" and calls them "large floating tribes." Pacheco then imagines possible concerns or important matters for the whales, as opposed to moulding imagined qualities for the purposes of human edification. He paints a vivid description of a crimson sea that ends with the whale becoming several different everyday products, losing both life and dignity. There is no explicit moral lesson in this poem, nor the sort of allegorical teaching that medieval bestiaries included, but as pointed out by Malamud, in Pacheco's intersection of aesthetics, ecology, and ethics exists the potential to educate and reform readers (2000, 5).

Pacheco's version of a bestiary also offered a hybridity that would influence later authors. Despite reading like a modern ecological text, there is a double cosmogeny at play in Pacheco's verses. The influence of Judeo-Christian faith is evident throughout, both in explicit references to the book of Job and in the inclusion of the bestiary tradition, with its moral teachings and warnings. The quoted verses from Job in "Whales" are a part of God's reminder to Job of his insignificance and impermanence before creation. The strength of the whale reflects both God's omnipotence and a sad irony as pointed out by Malamud: "humanity has humbled and vanquished this noble animal, which once seemed as omnipotent as the Creator. Modern people have subdued God's majesty" (12).

The Christian elements are clear in *Álbum de zoología*, as are Mesoamerican spiritual traditions such as animal souls, which offer a possibility for complex, respectful animal–human relationships, as identified by Malamud. In this tradition, human souls originate outside the body, often in animals (Gossen 1996, 81–2). This is based on Gary Gossen's studies of the Chamula Tzotzil, a community descendant from Mayans and occupying Southern Mexico, and their concepts of *nagualismo* and *tonalismo*, with the former referring to the transformation of a person into an animal, and the latter a person's companion animal or destiny, something that is bestowed upon everyone. According to Gossen, the common thread joining these different expressions "focuses on the predestination and life history of the self that lies outside the self and is thus not subject to individual control" (83). The dual inheritance is visible in the tension between *Álbum de zoología*'s moralistic tone and its departure from depicting man as the keeper of creation. The medieval bestiary was a medium through which humanity's stewardship and superiority over the rest of creation was reinforced. In Pacheco's work, the hierarchy of man above all else is dismantled and questioned, and a new type of bestiary that seeks to represent animal language, movement patterns, and possible thoughts is created. In this, Pacheco's bestiary would come to influence a non-anthropocentric take on the genre that will be further explored in chapter 3, with Javier Tomeo's *Bestiario* (1988), and in chapter 6, with Carlos Ferrándiz's *Bestiario médico* (2000).

Only three images attributed to Alberto Blanco appear in *Álbum de zoología*, and, unfortunately, not much information is available on them. The style of his images, however, closely resembles that of the images found in *A Year of Kindness* (1978–89), a book listed in the 2011 artist catalogue produced by Athenaeum (Blanco 2011, 20). Comprising fifty-four collages made from nineteenth-century

Figure 2.11 | Collage composition of an elephant inside palatial surroundings, carrying a gazebo on its back (Alberto Blanco, 1985).

engravings, the book celebrates the practice and history of the collage. The image for the "Earth" section (figure 2.11), for instance, recalls the Hindu belief that the Earth was held by four elephants standing atop a turtle. The elephant depicted here, both standing inside a building and holding one on its back, unites an unlikely

Figure 2.12 | Painting of a spectral elephant (Francisco Toledo, 1993).

scene, as it steps on a garden contained within a palatial building with vaulted ceilings. Blanco's collages reflect the spirit of *Álbum de zoología*; as Pacheco uses a medieval form to relay new messages, so Blanco uses centuries-old engravings to relay new messages.

The images by Francisco Toledo in *An Ark for the Next Millenium* are instead of a visceral nature, underscoring some of the more difficult themes in the book. Toledo's images mirror Pacheco's hybridity. Cynthia Steele points out that while Toledo displays a "remarkably broad grasp of contemporary Western aesthetics," his work is also "heavily colored by the magical thinking and Zapotec mythology of his native Oaxaca (1995, 91). Though the book is printed in black-and-white, muting the earth tones distinctive to the artists of (and representative of) rural Oaxaca, Toledo accepts and depicts the omnipresent death and destruction that Pacheco finds so disturbing (91). Toledo's elephant (figure 2.12) has a spectral appearance, as opposed to Blanco's formidable albeit crazed form of expression. Its hind legs seem to be evaporating, wasting away, and its head has the appearance of a cadaver outlined by barbed wire. Rather than standing among palatial surroundings and lush vegetation, it seems bereft, traversing arid terrain. The formidable creature here could be reduced to dust at any moment, carrying with it an ephemeral quality. Toledo's use of circular movement and repeated figures and geometric lines reinforces Pacheco's continual refashioning of themes and imagery associated with egotism, cruelty, and decay, occasionally attenuated by humor and beauty (92).

In the closing of her book review, Steele states, "I can think of no more original and important pair of talents to steer us into the next millennium than those of José Emilio Pacheco and Francisco Toledo" (92). Steele's words became prophetic, as Pacheco and Toledo are the final author/artist duo to have been placed among the cluster of canonical authors, and thus the pair closest to the twenty-first-century resurgence. Published during the early decades of the nonhuman turn, Pacheco's interpretation of the bestiary offers a hybrid model for authors to follow, especially those to be examined in chapters 3 and 5. The model uses the form of the bestiary genre, a traditionally anthropocentric enterprise, to try and convey nonhuman concerns and perspectives.

CONCLUSION

Although the trajectory of the bestiary from medieval Europe to the twentieth- and twenty-first-century Spanish-speaking world cannot be traced with certainty, the experimental character of the Latin American avant-garde and Boom periods offers significant insight into the current proliferation of the genre. Because of the status of their authors, the parodic works of Borges, Arreola, Monterroso, Neruda, Guillén, and Pacheco can be considered canonical, a cluster of works representing the revival of the genre in Latin America and, eventually, Spain. Many of the stylistic choices made by these five authors were the seeds of trends found in more recent bestiaries. These trends include, but are not limited to, ecocentric bestiaries, themes of deception, ironic allegory, humans in animal spaces, and purely ludic works. In light of the five authors' stronghold on contemporary interpretations of the bestiary, evidenced by the propagation of the topics and themes they explore, it is not too bold a claim to state that, without the experimentation of the mid-twentieth century, there would have been no resurgence in the twenty-first.

The works presented in this chapter also revolutionized the dynamic between text and image. While in some cases, illustrators replicated the use of medieval imagery by having it support the text, the plurality of illustration styles nonetheless point to increasingly individualized ways of understanding the genre. Whatever role images play in these canonical works, the visual takes centre stage, encouraging readers to observe as carefully as they read. As with the canonical works, all bestiaries have henceforth exhibited a relationship between text and image in which the latter no longer functions as a didactic support, but possesses its own power, at times holding the key to understanding the entry.

The seemingly curious decision made over half a century ago by six of the most prominent authors of Hispanic literature reverberate today in the resurgence of a once extinct genre. In following chapters consider these works to be the inspiration for dozens of others and attempt to map the most relevant and innovative interpretations of the bestiary form.

3

ANIMALS BEYOND MORALITY

I have studied many philosophers and many cats.
The wisdom of cats is infinitely superior.

Hippolyte Taine

Animals have no unconscious, because they have a territory.
Men have only had an unconscious since they lost a territory.

Jean Baudrillard

The interpretations of the bestiary genre by Borges, Arreola, Monterroso, Neruda, Guillén, and Pacheco resonate in various ways across a wide corpus of contemporary works. This chapter explores one of the trends exhibited by contemporary versions of the genre: ruminating bestiaries, in which the animal's perspective prompts reflections and meditations, conserving the poetic flair characteristic of Arreola, Neruda, Guillén, and Pacheco especially. *Bestiario* by the Aragonese Javier Tomeo (1988; 2000; 2007), written in prose, and *Bestiario* by the Barcelonian Carlos Pujol (2012), written in verse, exemplify this trend. Their entries offer the reader insight into the animal psyche, allowing them to observe its fears, insecurities, and hopes. As opposed to the medieval tradition, in which animals acted as vessels for Christian moral teachings, the beasts in the works of Tomeo and Pujol look inward and grapple with matters of the human condition. By focusing on the animal perspective, these works shift away from the anthropocentric and theocentric nature of medieval bestiaries and move towards a more inclusive, ecocentric cosmovision. This chapter examines the mechanics of this shift as devised by the authors, as well as their impact on the reader.

READING PRACTICES IN MEDIEVAL SOCIETY

The first chapter of this book traced the most relevant characteristics of medieval bestiaries, as well as their history. To better understand the changes undergone by the genre, it is essential to observe the changes in readership as they pertain to the two eras covered here. The lion entry in *The Aberdeen Bestiary* (ca. 1200), for instance, summarizes the qualities of the lion and draws parallels between the beast and Christ. The entry blends etymology, pseudoscience, and theology into a prototypical account that encapsulates the mission of the bestiary: to provide moral teaching and guidance.

Often a bestiary's first creature, the lion serves as an allegory for both Christ and God in his entirety, educating medieval society about the nature of God and reinforcing the Catholic trinity. All claims are made explicit by the explications that immediately follow the allegory. According to the entry in *The Aberdeen Bestiary*, the lion sleeps with his eyes open, paralleling how Christ's divine nature remained awake as he was crucified and buried. As discussed earlier, the animal in this context was but an entity through which humans could better understand celestial and spiritual affairs. The elements of this entry reflect the philosophy of their time. With faith as knowledge, God and subsequent king as authorities, a predetermined position in society for each being, and the established dualism of the earthly and the heavenly, the lion entry – and by extension bestiaries in general – is a neat literary cutaway of the medieval philosophy and worldview.

Reading bestiaries in the Middle Ages was an allegorical affair, one which reflected heavenly archetypes. This approach largely contrasts with contemporary reading. Aside from content and the medium itself, the concrete aspects of reading, including methodology, have also transformed over time. Medieval readers approached a manuscript in a different way than do contemporary readers. Marshall McLuhan's *The Gutenberg Galaxy* (1962) discusses the shift in both what is read and how it is read, and presents a series of cultural events that are linked to the world both before and after the invention of the Gutenberg printing press. His theory on both the reader and reading material throughout human civilization proves a useful tool with which to analyze the context, content, and form of both medieval and contemporary bestiaries.

The source manuscript for the lion entry illustrates the significant changes in reading practices (figure 3.1). Latin aside, the modern

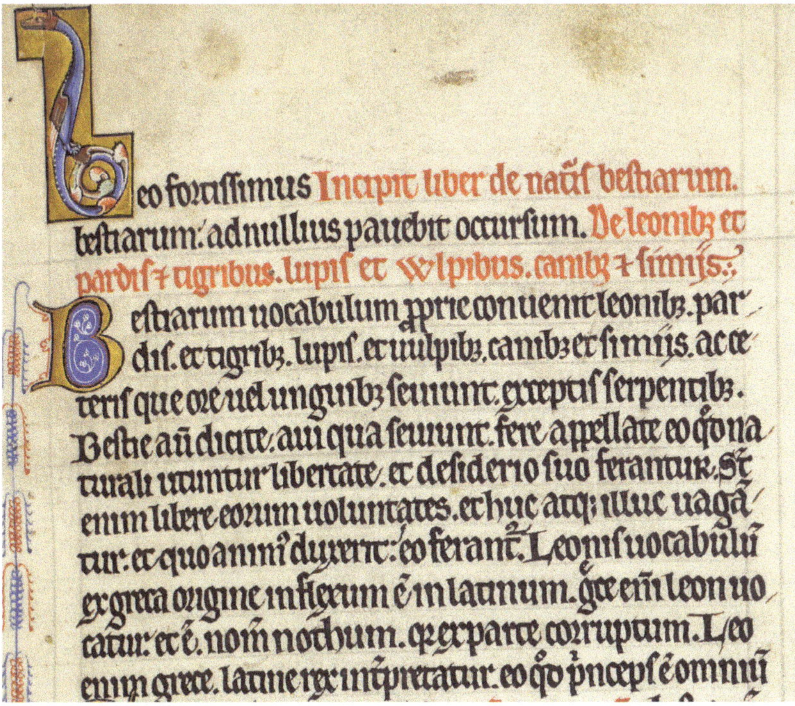

Figure 3.1 | A section of *The Aberdeen Bestiary* manuscript showing an illuminated "L," as well as irregularities in spacing, spelling, and other aspects typical of medieval manuscripts (*The Aberdeen Bestiary*, ca. 1200).

reader would find the entry challenging to read, even in translation, and especially out loud. McLuhan's book argues that the technology available in a particular era dictates its sensorial equilibrium: certain types of media will appeal to or require the involvement of one sense more than another, making an era predominantly visual or auditory, and so on. The medieval manuscript was not subject to the consistent spelling rules, grammar, punctuation, and word separation now considered indispensable, transforming each word into "a separate entity and at times a problem which he [the reader] whispered to himself when he had found the solution" (McLuhan 1962, 88). These textual irregularities added to low literacy rates, and the prohibitive costs of books resulted in few readers and many listeners. This pushed the act of reading toward what would today be better recognized as public recitation, which helps explain why texts tended to be of a rhetorical rather than literary nature (89). This rhetorical characteristic is evident, for instance, in the urgent explications offered at the end of every allegory, as seen with the lion. Reading aloud was thus an auditory endeavour in which listening played as important a role as seeing: "It is a real acoustical reading; *legere* means at the same time *audire*; one understands only what one hears, as we still say '*entendre le latin*' which means to 'comprehend it'" (Jean Leclerq, quoted in McLuhan 1962, 89). The institution of medieval literacy and writing meant that reading, far from being the silent, visual ritual it is today, was mostly an auditory practice (McLuhan 1962, 28). Furthermore, reading was, with few exceptions, a communal activity, sharing little with the individualistic practice of today, a consequence of the contemporary book's portability, affordability, and availability.

Relying on aural as opposed to visual stimulation when reading literary texts differentiates the medieval reader from the contemporary reader. This reign of sound over all other senses meant that people's perception of the world was different from that of the current visually governed society. The aural allows for simultaneity; different sounds can flood the ear at once, while vision, especially when reading, is restricted to a linear, successive intake of information (Ponzoni 2015, 3). Humans attuned to multiplicity can accept the world as magical, which McLuhan takes to mean inhabited by obscure, unpredictable forces (2). In fact, reading itself is likened to muttering a spell: "There is no lack of indication that reading throughout ancient and medieval times meant reading aloud, or even a kind of incantation" (McLuhan 1962, 84). In part, the difficulty one experiences when encountering medieval bestiaries is that, like myths, which are also the product of oral societies, "they do not exclude any facet of experience as literate cultures do. All the levels of meaning are simultaneous ... all the meanings are right there in the verbal statement" (72). The significance of oral societies' simultaneity, and its consequences, will be revisited later in an examination of contrasting bee entries from medieval and contemporary bestiaries. We have already encountered another aspect of medieval writing and reading in the phoenix entry discussed in the introductory chapter. As seen with the phoenix, maintaining a consistent tone or attitude in prose was not a priority during that time (135). As discussed in the first chapter, the two unconnected, contradictory origins attributed to the phoenix exemplify this heterogeneity.

Now that we have established how the reading of bestiaries has evolved, let us turn our attention to the changes undergone by their content. Pujol's and Tomeo's treatments of the literary beast marks a change in the bestiary's trajectory, as the animal is not considered a mere narrative tool, but rather an autonomous being able to exist beyond Christian philosophy. Admittedly, the medieval bestiary did not altogether deny the wild nature of animals. The introduction to *The Aberdeen Bestiary* states: "Here begins the book of the nature of beasts. Of lions, panthers and tigers, wolves and foxes, dogs and apes ... They are called 'wild' because they enjoy their natural liberty and are borne along by their desires. They are free of will, and wander here and there, and where their instinct takes them, there they are borne."[1] These lines acknowledge the limited freedom that beasts have. It is a physical, territorial, biological freedom rather than a metaphysical one. While the medieval animals wander at their leisure, their symbolic weight remains unchanged, turning them into roaming referents. This mental inactivity is not shared by the animals in contemporary bestiaries, as their thoughts roam freely, signalling a new type of bestiary in which the animal supersedes anthropocentric constraints.

The change in the treatment of the animal, from vessel to agent, brings forth an obvious problem. Certainly, the argument can be made that an animal written by humans is still an animal written by humans, and that, regardless of intentions, it still functions as an anthropocentric tool. The reality, however, points to a paradigm shift in how humans think about the animal, and in their interaction with it. An attempt to think vicariously through another is, at the very least, an acknowledgment that this other deserves attention, and empathy. The shift from cramming a beast into a convenient lesson to searching for its identity as a being demonstrates that the bestiary as a literary genre can be adapted to communicate new ideas in a new era, providing a reason for its current resurgence in Hispanic literature.

Bestiario *by Javier Tomeo, illustrated by Natalio Bayo (1988), and* Bestiario *by Carlos Pujol (2012)*

Both Pujol and Tomeo chose to write *through* the animal, as opposed to *about* it. In some cases, this manifests as entries written in the first person, while in others, it translates into an attempt to understand what the animal might feel or think. Tomeo, born in 1932, lived through Franco's dictatorship, which heavily influenced his political stance and work. He was certain that literary forms other than the social realism prevalent during his time could contribute to the eradication of Franquismo, so he opted for an obscure literary path that avoided censorship and led him to become "a marginal, somewhat odd writer, something that made the publication of my first works all the more difficult" (Molinaro 2002, 598; my translation). He believed that an author was to be a witness of their time, that their job was to identify where change was required, without the obligation to provide solutions (604). Tomeo did not aim to moralize, but rather to provoke reflection. Less is known about the life and intentions of Pujol, a literary critic, translator, and author born in 1936. His poetic bestiary is peculiar, as all of the animals featured in it are objects: a stuffed bear, a porcelain steed, a wooden duck. These animal-objects suggest that, perhaps, proximity to people is dangerous, as the human condition might prove contagious. Both authors critique the treatment of animals at large with the implicit question: Why include real animals when humans are more comfortable with their objectified presence? While the medieval beast was granted mobility in exchange for disseminating a message, Pujol's animals dream up worlds from their static inertia.

Tomeo and Pujol were transparent in their adoption of the medieval bestiary; they chose to keep its name intact, acknowledging the centuries of tradition spanned by the genre, as well as its brevity, subtitles, and, in Tomeo's case, images. They also write their bestiaries as parodic works for a visual audience. This claim, perched between Linda Hutcheon's and McLuhan's theories of contextualized artistic production, benefits from further clarification. Hutcheon argues that the period in which parody can exist must necessarily be reactive to the form of modernism that came before it. McLuhan viewed Western society as closely related to the manner of disseminating and consuming information. The chronological flagstones of the theorists are not immediately compatible, nor are the catalysts to which they attribute the realities that they identify and describe. Yet both portray a highly individualistic society and its interaction with an authoritative centre. Furthermore, modernity, and subsequently postmodernity, would not have existed without the Gutenberg press, as "[p]rint created national uniformity and government centralism, but also individualism and opposition to government as such" (McLuhan 1962,

Figure 3.2 | Sketch depicting two men staring at scarab-like insects (Javier Tomeo, 2000).

236). The two lines of thought are interlaced, and the parodic bestiaries betray many of the changes McLuhan attributes to the shift in the dissemination and consumption of information.

The 2000 edition of Tomeo's bestiary features drawings by Tomeo, and the 2007 edition contains images by Zaragoza native Natalio Bayo. In the case of Tomeo's illustrations, two elements are immediately evident: the child-like quality of the drawings, and the dissociation between text and image. Tomeo's illustrations have little unity with their corresponding texts; as often, no relationship exists between them. The bee entry, for instance, depicts an image unrelated to any subject matter covered in the text (figure 3.2), as do the entries "Hormiga reina" (queen ant) and "Ballena azul" (blue whale).

Because no consistent connection exists between the entries' text and images, what follows is a commentary on the overall style of the drawings. To highlight his creatures' tone of resignation and their reflections, Tomeo's images often include a humanizing element. A mirror, poison bottles, and books are some of the objects that reinforce the animal–human link and deepen the simultaneously humorous and poignant effect of the entry. The use of these objects and the doodle-like quality of the images are misleading of the bestiary's true intent.

The contrast between the childish drawings and the sharp criticism gives the overall entry a jaunty self-awareness, as if the insects know they are perceived as lesser beings and therefore exploit this to underscore their delivery. Tomeo, who lived through Francoist Spain, believed that his work continued to be published despite the censorship of the dictatorship because it did not explicitly mention things like freedom, human rights, labour strikes, justice, elections, or democracy (Molinaro 2002, 598). His illustrations aid the illusion of an innocuous work, allowing it to pass unperceived by those who were looking for overt, obvious challenges to the Francoist regime. A similar phenomenon was seen in Guillén's *El gran zoo*, as its symbolic, allegorical nature allowed it to mostly avoid censorship, despite its stinging social commentary. These authors' ability to communicate political and social realities during dictatorships highlights the genre's ability to incite, an aspect that relies on the seemingly inoffensive form of the bestiary to bypass suppression.

Bestiario's 2007 edition, featuring images by Natalio Bayo, is more traditionally linked to the medieval bestiary, as there are images for most entries, and they correspond to the creatures described in the entries. Bayo's illustration for the bee entry, for instance, depicts a series of bees collecting pollen from a flower (figure 3.3). Whether directly linked to their respective entries or not, both sets of illustrations underline the importance of the visual, something that is present in the totality of what the bestiary genre sets out to accomplish.

Tomeo's bee inaugurates the individualistic beast for a contemporary bestiary by addressing the reader directly, employing a haughty tone: "I could have also been queen, for the record. For that to happen, I would have only needed to have been fed royal jelly during my larva stage" (Tomeo 1988, 45; my translation).[2] Illustrating a stark departure from didactic entries like that of the lion in early bestiaries, this bee is consumed with her internal monologue. Her obsession, evident through her ruminations, is the consequence of an individualistic era in which the advancement of literacy makes the separation between thought and action possible. More specifically, this literacy refers to that obtained

Figure 3.3 | Painting depicting three bees clustered around a flower (Natalio Bayo, 2007).

through the phonetic alphabet, as hieroglyphs and ideographs do not demand the level of abstraction that an arbitrary symbol attributed to a phoneme does (McLuhan 1962, xvii–xviii). This split between thought and action, McLuhan argues, is a consequence of the shift from the auditory to the visual that accompanies the growth of a literate civilization. He partly bases his claims on the psychiatrist J.C. Carothers's study "Culture, Psychiatry, and the Written World." Like McLuhan, Carothers correlates a lack of literacy with a reliance on listening: "the nonliterate rural population lives largely in a world of sound, in contrast to western Europeans who live largely in a world of vision. Sounds are in a sense dynamic things ... of movement, events, activities, for which man, when largely unprotected from the hazards of life in the bush or veldt, must be ever on the alert" (1959, 310). Free from immediate danger due to living in urban spaces, the Western individual routinely disregards surrounding sounds. The literate person's intentional silence demonstrates that the skills required for living in the Western world and for reading are one and the same: both require a well-developed sense of spatiotemporal relations, a habit dependent on visual synthesis (310). This trend in literate societies is relevant when observing changes in how the literary animal is presented, as, according to both McLuhan and Carothers, the auditory-driven way of life (be it of the non-literary rural population of Carothers's study or the medieval audience of bestiaries) does not separate thought from action.

While all societies seek conformity, in those in which the verbal carries more weight, no clear distinction exists between action and verbal thought (312). Where thought and action are one, the need for uniformity encompasses both, and detrimental thoughts must be constrained as much as detrimental action. Because these are strict societies, all conflicting individualistic thought is shunned. This, coupled with the possibility of magic, makes it so that when such thoughts do occur, they are perceived as derivative of external evil forces, to be rejected in oneself and others. Alternatively, societies in which verbal thought is somewhat separable from action are less likely to constrain thought, if they do so at all. The trade-off of thinking of oneself as a self, of being an individual person, is that the individual person finds themselves responsible for their thoughts, "with all that this entails – in the way of rationalization, self-denigration, and so on – in mental health and illness" (312). The difference between the two societal models is well illustrated by the bee entries in both *The Aberdeen Bestiary* and Tomeo's *Bestiario*.

The medieval bee embodied the externalizing manner of life. *The Aberdeen Bestiary* praised the bee's virtuous behaviour, highlighting its reverence for received social order, along with its industrious nature. Above all, the medieval bee functioned as an exemplary part of a whole, working alongside her community to achieve stunning feats of architecture and to create honey. The illustration accompanying the bee (figure 3.4) supports the pleasant orderliness attributed to the insect, as it depicts symmetrical, tidy lines of worker bees flying into their respective hives.

This harmonious way of life can be juxtaposed with the account of the bee written by Tomeo (1988, 45–6). Tomeo's bee belongs to a beehive much like the one depicted in *The Aberdeen Bestiary*. Both entries reference worker bees, drones, a sovereign, and the impressive architecture of the beehive. The decision by Tomeo to place an ambitious, individualistic bee in a pre-Gutenberg hive heightens the contrast between the medieval and postmodern entries. Where the medieval bee is praised for her conformity, Tomeo's bee

Figure 3.4 | Image painted atop a burnished gold background, showing three neat rows of bees entering their hives (*The Aberdeen Bestiary*, ca. 1200).

resents not being queen. The hive or backdrop remains the same in both the contemporary and medieval entries, despite the centuries that have passed between them. It is thus left to the narrative shift to hint at the change that has transpired. The medieval entry's narrative does not single out any bee, save the sovereign bee, as being in compliance with the natural order. The regent/subject dichotomy was an acceptable one during the medieval period, as the single regent and the collective implied in the word "subject" was an apt analogy of appropriate population subjugation, be it before a regent or God. In Tomeo's bestiary, however, an ordinary worker bee has broken free from the Leviathan, eclipsing the queen and usurping the reader's attention, thus upsetting the anonymous and collaborative dynamic of the hive. She resents not having been fed royal jelly, a fact that cemented her ordinary existence. Drones of the hive mock her wish to be fertilized and advise her instead to return to her work. The open and dissonant desires of the worker bee introduce a pivotal shift in messaging.

The bee's final words, uttered moments before her death, prove enlightening: "Customs and traditions don't matter when one is born with the senses in revolt" (Tomeo 1988, 46).[3] She is indeed revolutionary; she cannot harmonize with her auditory hive because she is of a visual age. To argue that she is no different from the queen, she relies on the ability to see ultraviolet light and to differentiate colours. McLuhan and Carothers argued that the reign of the visual was synonymous with the literate being and that as a result of this literate/visual existence, one gains the ability to split the self from thoughts and loses the capacity to attribute dissonant thoughts to an outside source. The containment of the cacophony, representative of a level of abstraction only possible after the invention of the phonetic alphabet, causes the "trauma of literacy," and it results in "a split man, a schizophrenic" (McLuhan 1962, 20). This bee seems, at the very least, aware of the power of literature and narrative control, as she presents the reader with a version of hive life according to her perspective. If the trauma of literature isolates a person in a society largely afflicted by it, the bee, alone in an auditory hive, becomes an outcast beyond any hope of redemption.

As virtuous creatures, medieval bees revered their sovereign. While the *Aberdeen* entry mentions only that "[t]he bees who do not comply with the laws of the king, repent and punish themselves and die by their own sting," it can be assumed that, due to the auditory society in which these bees existed, this compliance included that of their thoughts. There is no mention of thought, as thought and action were one. The presence of this pious, cooperative nature in all aspects of the bee's existence is what has made them such extraordinary behavioural examples for humans. Tomeo's bee, however, is the heiress of a literate, visual mode of thinking that allows her to separate her thoughts from her actions. She disdains the very existence for which her medieval sisters were praised. While her medieval counterparts manufactured a democratic product enjoyed by all, she describes her tasks as menial, recalls her days as dark, and highlights her perfection against a drab, ordinary background. Her ability to carry out the tasks expected of her while resenting them betrays a duality in character that would have been inaccessible, or useless, to medieval bees.

This ability to camouflage in action but diverge in thought becomes more acute as she cultivates treasonous opinions about the queen. Her defiant attack of the centre resides in the claim that she could have easily been queen had she been fed the appropriate jelly. She is not mistaken, but, unlike the medieval bee who readily died by its own sting at the mere thought of treason, Tomeo's bee promotes her claim to the throne, reducing divine right to a matter of nutrition. Her reflection and study of her own thoughts reflect a Cartesian, consequential manner of thinking, out of place in her hive.

The narrative demonstrates how the bee's thoughts gradually translate into action. Because she has allowed her thoughts to roam so far from her actions, however, once she acts, her behaviour proves wildly dissonant from the expectations of her hive. While the medieval bee reproduced without intercourse or lust, and thus laboured with no pain, Tomeo's bee longs to be fertilized, to become acquainted with the "nuptial flight," provoking the mockery of the drones. Her wants, misplaced in her hive, alienate her. The bee's refusal to accept a role that is expected of her puts her at odds with all her surroundings, and the hive must ostracize her to ensure their own survival.

The end of the entry makes it clear that the bee will die, unfulfilled and shunned, as her outlook on the world and manner of perceiving it are simply not compatible with those of her hive. Her discontentment, which would have been better suited to psychoanalysis, or feminist theory, belongs to contemporary Western society, leaving her alien to her conformist sisters. While the medieval bestiary communicated the nature of bees with the mission of spreading the example of an obedient, laborious, and pious community, Tomeo's bee falls prey to the more seemingly disturbing trends in contemporary thought, forcing her to accept her role of "revolutionary" as a consolation prize.

Although the entry initially reads as an upsetting, contemporary interaction, it partly honours the medieval moralizing tradition. Despite not donning an explicatory coda, Tomeo's entry delivers a pertinent moral lesson. Bees' shared preferences with and importance to humans emphasize the effect and relatability of this particular bee's condition. Like humans, bees enjoy colourful flowers, prefer sweet to other tastes (unlike flies or dung beetles), and spread a form of culture among their hive members. Their pollination is critical to human survival, and their cooperative hive dynamics encode as many lessons today as they did during the Middle Ages. Tomeo's entry seems to push for a balanced settling of the historical dialectic. He acknowledges the contemporary individualistic trend, as well as the split between a person's thoughts and actions. Through the bee's lonely death, however, he warns that regardless of how idiosyncratic thoughts may become, humans are still dependent on larger networks and communities.

The entries in Pujol's *Bestiario* also demonstrate elements of the shift from an aural to a visual perception of the world. Pujol alludes to the shift through transitions from noise to silence, from a fragment of a whole to individual existence. His entry on a dog exemplifies this approach: "I'm not sure what it is I guard, the invisible air / I caress nightly ramblings, / and I store loneliness in my memory, / of a stray dog" (2012, 17; my translation).[4] The dog, which, considering its immobility, can be assumed to be some sort of figurine, is in anguish because of its lack of identity: "Afraid of asking questions / I interrogate the silence and obtain no answer. / Unsure if I am imaginary, if I manage to remember, I exist" (17; my translation).[5] Its instinct, relayed in the first verse, is to search for something over which to watch, but the air's invisibility frustrates its efforts. When its first effort to visually relate to the world fails, it tries to access ancestral, auditory knowledge. This attempt also fails, as it finds the contemporary home to which it belongs silent, presumably due to the dog's anesthetized sight and hearing. "I store loneliness," it laments, longing for a past in which it wandered as a vagabond. The trajectory that has led to the dog being left on a shelf is revealed as he sighs a variation on *cogito, ergo sum*: "If I manage to remember, I exist." Its utterance reveals that this dog has inherited the memories of a vagabond time past, of a world likely filled with sound and images. As it sits unable to interact through any senses, a glimpse is offered into a potential next stage of existence, a reified existence in which all action and thought are internalized and made imperceptible.

A similar phenomenon occurs with the elephant, who grapples with the contrast between its past as a giant of the jungle and its present as an ivory miniature, a bibelot (20). Tomeo's bee suffered because she was unable to attribute her dissonant thoughts to external forces. This trend is furthered in Pujol's dog and elephant entries, as the animals not only internalize thought, but are also immobile, and consequently thought is all they are reduced to. The elephant is acutely aware of its gradual demotion from portent of the jungle to household trinket. For each of them, the only mode of interaction with their surroundings resides in their minds, taking the separation of thought and action to a virtual, sedentary place, where action is null. Longing for their mobile, flesh-and-blood past, these creatures are the antithesis of the roaming medieval beasts. While the latter were laden with Catholic allegory but free in their movements, Pujol's creatures are untethered in their thoughts but bound in their actions, leading to a frustrated existence.

The unfolding of McLuhan's theory is challenged by these contemporary beasts. While he foresaw the stage after the visual one as a return to the aural, predicting that the world would function as a global village with one common brain supported by technology (1962, 31–2), Pujol's and Tomeo's creatures predict a trajectory that better represents what has occurred. Indeed, because Tomeo and Pujol, respectively, wrote in the late 1980s and at the beginning of the twenty-first century, the societal changes that they foresaw were imminent, and arguably easier to predict, unlike for McLuhan. Regardless, the exponential growth of the pace of inventions and technological developments and the introduction of social media in 2004 makes their predictions nonetheless impressive.

The contemporary creatures, especially Pujol's, are not too radical a metaphor for the consequences of current social media use. Unlike McLuhan's prediction of a somewhat idyllic, space-defying village, these animals are hostages within their bodies, anxious and longing for a different existence, more compartmentalized than ever before. An ivory elephant is not much different than a sedentary person exclusively interacting with others through a glowing screen. The isolation, desperation, and existential angst palpable in these bestiary entries are paralleled by rising rates of anxiety, depression, and suicide, particularly among the digital natives that do not remember life before social media platforms. McLuhan argued that the emphasis on the visual forced other modes of experience to become covert, driving them into the realm of the subconscious. Not only has the separation between a person and their subconscious not reversed in the electronic age, it has accelerated, splitting into as many social media images, witty posts, or accounts as one might have. These beasts, unwilling or unable to cross their literary thresholds, are an apt analogy for the isolation that the Internet age produces. Pujol's bestiary offers an array of melancholic creatures that, despite residing near one another, cannot leave their designated space to interact with others and potentially improve their state. As the beasts expose aspects of contemporary reality, their introspection prompts the reader's own, drawing out similarities between human and animal.

Tomeo's bee and Pujol's elephant and dog explore the shift in the sensory intake that McLuhan attributes to a pre- and post-Gutenberg world. They act as a bookend of the bestiary genre, and apt indicators of their era, from Catholic allegory to digital, virtual identities, providing a reason for their unchanged form despite the centuries spanned by the genre. The next few paragraphs evaluate why the bestiary proves an excellent candidate for the subversive parody that Hutcheon attributes to postmodern art. Tomeo's and Pujol's works are decidedly postmodern, as indicated by their strong ideological position in the use and abuse of tradition, as well as in their acknowledgment of inner contradiction and their self-aware admission of their provisional existence (Hutcheon 1989, 13). They mix fact and fiction, as seen in the medieval bestiary. While the medieval bestiary indiscriminately blurred the real, the imaginary, and the theological, the postmodern bestiary establishes the borders between fact and fiction to deliberately cross them at will (35).

The following entries by Tomeo and Pujol demonstrate the interaction between modern, empirical scientific observation and postmodern subversion. Tomeo's entry "Búho" (owl) describes an indecisive owl, burdened with centuries' worth of symbolism: "Some say that I bring bad omens, that my squawks announce death. Yet, in other times, there were poets that revered me as king of all nocturnal birds and consecrated me to Juno, wife of Jupiter. Some even saw me at the feet of Minerva, the goddess with the fiery stare, guardian of artists. I live then, with that uncertainty" (1988, 68; my translation).[6] The owl is uncertain as to which superstitions and mythologies he represents, torn between being Minerva's companion and avatar, and the spiritual representation of intelligence and light. Pujol's salamander expresses similar sentiments in verse, longing for the days in which it could withstand the heat of flames without being burned: "Present day science prohibits us / Believing things like this, / Beautiful and impossible" (2012, 22; my translation).[7] Denied the abilities it was once bestowed by scientific discourse, the salamander "limits itself to being a urodele / a mere common beast, / without a single privilege" (2012, 22; my translation).[8] Both entries incorporate facts archived in human systems of knowledge to undermine received tradition. The owl is a nocturnal bird with large, sharp eyes, just as the salamander is scientifically categorized as a urodele. With positivist parameters established, however, the animals start to usurp the place traditionally reserved for a human agenda. The salamander, for instance, interrogates the bestiary content to undermine it. In keeping with the Plinian current, bestiaries have often mentioned the salamander's ability to survive in hot flames. For instance, *The Book of Beasts*, a translation of a twelfth-century Latin bestiary, states: "The *salamandra* has its name because it prevails against fire" (White and Davies 1955, 182). Pujol's nostalgic creature sighs and reminisces about a time in which these qualities were permitted by human knowledge. Perhaps, the revoking of the salamander's powers is merely a consequence of a world now predominately visual and which no longer allows magic. McLuhan and Carothers, after all, attributed simultaneity and thus magic to the unliterary self. In a world ruled by what can be seen and what is, as opposed to what might be, the salamander is forced to adapt. With its ability to survive fire revoked, the salamander must endure the almost bureaucratic process of huffing in line and updating its credentials.

Like the salamander, the owl carries the weight of associations accumulated over time. The owl must interpret the myriad of significations attributed to it, wondering how much of his identity crisis is owed to his status as an emblem or metaphor. Both animals are overwhelmed by their symbolic burdens. Defined by external discourses, they sift through externally attributed characteristics to arrive at a concept of self. The maddening consequences of humans' tight grip on animalia are taken to their absurd extreme by the salamander's claim that an external belief dictates its characteristics.

With these creatures especially, Pujol and Tomeo refuse the idea of victimized animals, as their owl and salamander defy restrictive traditions with their manipulation of language. Unlike the prototypical medieval beasts, these animals have mastered the human codes that once caged them and use this proficiency to hollow the monolith that threatens to crush them. The owl's colloquial language, "I'm still not very sure however, what it is exactly that I represent" (Tomeo 1988, 68; my translation),[9] betrays a creature that, rather than awed by human ingenuity, is weary and annoyed at the influx of contradictory information. While the salamander's self-esteem initially comes across as battered ("it limits itself to being a urodele / a mere common beast, / without a single privilege"), the pejorative in the Spanish original, *bestezuela*, seems directed at changes in societal currents instead of the creature. What in medieval bestiaries was a sacred blend of scientific, pseudo-scientific, mythological, and literary elements is here presented as an ordinary superstition. The owl and salamander's casual use of information shrugs at and undermines the systems of knowledge that restrict them. Pujol's and Tomeo's employment of a medieval form highlights the destabilization of this classical and medieval knowledge. Through their attack on the discursive centre, the entries embody the skepticism of a contemporary audience, spurred by the decision to use the name of the genre as the name of the work, strengthening the reference to the tradition in question.

The works examined in this chapter maintain the bestiary form – in the case of Pujol's non-illustrated bestiary, it is worth mentioning that not all medieval bestiaries were illustrated – drawing attention to changes in content, to a contemporary mentality residing where a medieval one once did. As the dialectic that frames societal change advances uncertain, the bestiaries demonstrate inharmonious outlooks through their disjointed tones. While the rebellious bee found herself suffocated by the rigidity of the hive, Pujol's owl and Tomeo's praying mantis are free from the infrastructure of the medieval allegory. Pujol's owl-object ruminates, "It seems as though I ask myself: And who are you? / Nobody answers – does wisdom / consist only in asking? / They interrogate me and I keep silent" (2012, 21; my translation), before finally confessing that he remains silent for fear of betraying his ignorance.[10] Tomeo explores a similar preoccupation with the praying mantis, who is distraught at the possibility of ceding to the wrong part of her anatomy: "More than once, contemplating my reflection in the mirror of the tank, I ask myself: And what if I am the cruel insect I think I am? What if I were a flower?" (1988, 19–20; my translation).[11] The bee would have rejoiced in such freedom; however, for the next two creatures, it reflects a complete loss of structure.

Rather than the daunting freedom that the medieval praying mantis enjoyed, European society was built on clear paths and expectations. Johan Huizinga presents a snapshot of this existence in the introduction to his work *The Waning of the Middle Ages*: "Every event, every action, was still embodied in expressive, and solemn forms, which raised them to the dignity of a ritual" (1924, 1). Certainly, the great occasions of life, including birth, marriage, and death, were celebrated, but also lesser events like journeys, tasks, and visits. Formalities abounded, and "[o]ne sound rose ceaselessly above the noises of busy life and lifted all things unto sphere of order and serenity – the sound of bells" (1924, 3). Rituals like the ones described by Huizinga, punctuated by elements such as bells and pomp, created a more purposeful, spiritually secure existence than that of today.

Along with this depiction of a society that is more clearly defined than contemporary Western society, Huizinga examines the notion of everything and everyone existing in their place by naming groupings, known as "estates" or "orders" in the Middle Ages: estates of the realm, trades, matrimony, virginity, sin, the ecclesiastical estates of sacerdotal and monastic orders, the different orders of chivalry, and so on (1924, 47). Without reducing medieval life to its general trends, a stark difference between contemporary and medieval life emerges. McLuhan (1962) discusses this difference in the first pages of *The Gutenberg Galaxy*. He begins with an analysis of *King Lear*, suggesting that the play is representative of the transition from a world of defined roles (all-encompassing identities such as a member of a religious congregation) into one of jobs (a fragmented part of an identity, such as an accountant or sales clerk), and claiming that in the play the characters Kent, Edgar, and Cordelia "are 'out of phase' in the language of W. Yeats. They are 'feudal' in their total loyalty which they consider merely natural to their roles ... *King Lear* offers a complete demonstration of how it felt to live through the change from medieval to Renaissance time and space, from an inclusive to an exclusive sense of the world" (14). Whereas Tomeo's owl ridicules the nomenclature imposed upon it, his praying mantis and Pujol's owl fervently long for it, as they have fallen prey to a world in which jobs have replaced roles. The loss of referents leaves a vacuum of identity as acute for these animals as it is for humans. Aided only by the accounts of ancient scholars and philosophers, the creatures are left with the daunting task of constructing an identity.

Pujol's owl grapples with insecurity, unsure of whether he is worthy of the owl's reputation as a sage creature. He is presented as a kitschy trinket, recognizable only by its form, with no vestigial remnants of an owl's predatorial prowess. The owl imagines a conversation that never takes place and, afraid of being discovered to be a fraud, perches frozen and silent. Unlike Tomeo's owl, he does not verbalize the endless array of qualities attributed to him, rendering them meaningless through monotonous repetition. Instead, he sits still, unable to speak.

In these entries, both the bestiary genre and humans are parodied. The idea of a praying mantis paralyzed before the choice of deciding to live for its top or bottom half is both entertaining and encapsulates a dilemma symptomatic of contemporary society. Humans are in part differentiated from animals by their ability to suppress instinct. It seems that in the absence of instinct or a role, one must select a job and thus open oneself up to endless choices. Ashley Montagu's *Man: His First Two Million Years* argues that the increase in material dissemination and literacy is positively correlated to the detachment people feel in the world (1969, 76). The more "literate" people become, the more detached they are from the world in which they live. For the non-literary, however, what happens *is* reality: "If the ceremonies calculated to increase the birth of animals and the yield of plants are followed by such increases, then the ceremonies are not only connected with them but are part of them" (199–200). The practical logic Montagu attributes to the non-literary person is denied to the literate. Similarly, the mantis of the literary age has allowed thought to override instinct, has paused to ruminate for too long, and now stands frozen. The representation of this phenomenon is made more acute because neither creature – owl or praying mantis – seems interested in connecting with reality. The crystal owl does not speak out of fear of another, confirming the deepest fears of its imposter syndrome. The praying mantis ends its soliloquy with two questions in which the main idea is expressed with the imperfect tense of the subjunctive, cementing the distance between the praying mantis and reality.

Despite Pujol opting for poetry and Tomeo for prose, the writers share a stylistic cohesion that is in stark contrast with the medieval prose entries in two ways. The first can be observed in the lion and bee entries, quoted earlier, though perhaps the clearest example is that of the phoenix from the Bodleian bestiary (ca. 1220), introduced in the first chapter. In that entry, two different tones and conclusions are simultaneously attributed to the same animal. This lack of cohesion was common in medieval literature, as the notions of a single author – and consequently, attribution, rights in a text, and even plagiarism – did not exist. Whereas in the medieval period bestiaries were most heavily based on an anonymous compilation and were nourished through acceptable authorities (Saint Isidore of Seville, Saint Ambrose, etc.), contemporary bestiaries reflect a tone made possible only through the contemporary notion of the author. As books became commodities and individual portable objects, as opposed to common goods, and as the concept of authorship began to be concretized with the British Statute of Anne, or the Copyright Act, in 1710, the idea of the individual author grew. This, in turn, eventually allowed for the types of entries found in Pujol's and Tomeo's bestiaries and the remaining corpus. The control over tone, and the maintenance of the same throughout an entry, is in part what makes these animals poignant and compelling. Whatever stylistic or character decisions Pujol or Tomeo make are maintained, transforming the animals into relatable slices of the condition of being, as opposed to distant, wild creatures. Although all entries belonging to the *Bestiarios* are characterized by this cohesive, compelling tone, it is most entertaining when employed by animals who readily use it for mischief, as is the case with the horsefly.

Tomeo's bee entry demonstrated the adverse effects of the separation of verbal thought and action consequential of a society that relies on the abstract phonetic alphabet. This divide, however, can provide an opportunity, as "in a highly literate society, then, visual and behavioural conformity frees the individual for inner deviation. Not so in an oral society where inner verbalization is effective social action" (McLuhan 1962, 20). The literary society, coupled with the parodic, postmodern impulse, gives way to devious animals that enjoy tormenting humans. The horsefly entry in Tomeo's *Bestiario* introduces an insect that is all too happy to give the entomology enthusiast a grim ultimatum. It relishes in announcing that the beauty of its eyes disappears in death, making its species a poor addition for the collector's pin. The horsefly thus enumerates the lepidopterist's choices: "a) annihilate us, despite the incomparable beauty of our eyes," or "b) allow us to live, and enjoy that beauty, at the price of suffering our painful bites and that, in spite of everything, we remain alive" (Tomeo 1988, 18; my translation).[12] The horsefly is one of the few cohesively illustrated entries, although Tomeo's style makes it difficult to discern whether the image actually depicts a horsefly. The spots on the insects wings and the suggestion of a ribbed body could well match a real horsefly; however, the body is too long. A glimpse of the horsefly's anarchist spirit, however, is visible in the bombs it drops on the countryside over which it flies.

This insect weaponizes its sophisticated knowledge of biological functions and formal logic to threaten the collector. The horsefly understands its inner workings better than the average human might understand their own anatomy. Aware that beauty is of the highest value in the visual era, and of the mechanisms behind the specific, ephemeral beauty of its eyes, the horsefly exposes its argument with ruthless precision. It uses modern methods that assume human superiority as an axiom (bureaucracy, lists, syllogisms, etc.) to place the human collector at the mercy of an insect, at the end of a lose–lose situation. Thus, any decision made by the collector will prove dissatisfying in one way or another, and, in true Kafkaesque fashion, makes them a victim of both bureaucracy and their own circular logic. Pujol's next entry, however, features a human-ridiculing monkey, taking Kafka's Red Peter to its own postmodern limits and presenting the happy, silly predisposition traditionally attributed to the mammal as a farce. Pujol's monkey disdains zoo visitors, revealing that he is mocking humans, not entertaining them (2012, 23). Humans, fatuous and vain according to the monkey, interpret his gestures and faces as silly amusement, unable to see their own nature reflected in his movements.

The monkey, more overtly than the horsefly, undoes another medieval bestiary trend. Although no bestiary contains monkeys, some do feature apes that are described as belonging to different groupings. Bestiaries, particularly those partly comprising Isidore of Seville's *Etymologies*, did not depict apes favourably. Despite their similarity to humans (hence the taxonomical name "simian"), they are ultimately used as a metaphor for the devil, with copious detail about their hideous faces and backsides. Not only does Pujol's monkey not accept the dogma or the insults of humankind, he outright makes fools of his visitors. He plays with human assumptions, aware that humankind, contrary to research, imagines the separation of thought and action as an exclusively human enterprise. The zoogoers in Pujol's entry vainly assume that monkeys imitate human actions, interpreting the monkey as a failed human, as having lost in the evolutionary game by a negligible percentage of DNA, and not as a creature simply amused with ridiculing us. The utterance of the term *monerías* (monkey business) by the monkey reveals its understanding of what is expected of him and ridicules humans by playing his "part" as a mockery. Imitation here is not a replica of human gesticulations, but rather a subversive, transgressive act that questions who truly deserves to be labelled a self-aware being.

CONCLUSION

Bestiario by Tomeo and *Bestiario* by Pujol represent the most pervasive contemporary bestiary trends in relation to the genre's medieval roots, as well as the changes in ideology between historical contexts, as reflected in their content. Whether images are present or not, the notion that form defines a bestiary will continue to ring true throughout *From Griffin to Axolotl*. It is because of this solid structure that the genre was able to revolutionize its content but remain unchanged in its essence. Different ways of understanding the world translate into different ways of writing this genre, as the tone, subject matter, uniformity, and morals shift to address the contemporary reader. The remainder of the corpus, to be examined in subsequent chapters, engages with the contextualization and theory explored in this chapter.

The ruminations and the focus on animal and insect subjectivity in their works establish Tomeo and Pujol as early pioneers of a larger trend that continues to grow exponentially. Today, the bestiary is only one of many genres that explore animal subjectivity, the novel being perhaps the most recognizable. In his article "El gran zoo de papel," published in *El país*, Jacinto Antón reports on the phenomenon, highlighting the general volume of works produced with the animal as a literary subject. The new "stampede," as he words it, is characterized by an emphasis in the personal and literary that goes beyond the scientific, and offers profound empathy with the animal subjects upon which the writings are based (2018).

Most of the works that Antón lists were published between 2012 and 2018. The bestiaries featured in this chapter, published between 1988 and 2012, are at the threshold of this new way of thinking about the animal. As seen in Neruda's and Pacheco's bestiaries, as well as the ones visited in this chapter, positioning the animal at the centre of literature becomes crucial as global warming, pollution, and biodiversity loss continue to advance. The inclusion of animals and their intelligence, as well as their subjectivity, is both necessary and overdue, adding to the complexity and reality of earthly existence. Furthermore, the recent boom in bestiaries demonstrates that these bestiaries are not anomalies or curiosities but rather an organic development of human concern and interest, as are the rest of the bestiaries to be examined in subsequent chapters.

4

APPROPRIATING THE BESTIARY

The previous chapter introduced and contextualized contemporary Hispanic bestiaries, contrasting them with their medieval counterparts. This chapter will examine a grouping closely related to the bestiaries featured in the previous chapter. Both categories are characterized foremost by their postmodern flair, but while those in the previous chapter reveal this character through a ruminating, contemplative tone, the bestiaries in this chapter present it through combative social critiques and the subversion of the genre's history. The bestiaries included in this chapter are divided into two categories: those that implicitly challenge the medieval canon and those that do so in an explicit manner. The first category includes *Bestiario de seres fantásticos mexicanos* (Bestiary of fantastical Mexican beings) (2016), written by Norma Muñoz Ledo and illustrated by Israel Barrón. This work is rebellious in its inclusion of beasts that belong to the Latin American tradition in a genre that originated in a Christian, medieval European context. In the second category are *Bestiario de seres prodigiosos*[1] (Bestiary of prodigious beings) (2001), written by René Avilés Fabila and illustrated by José Luis Cuevas, and *ABC de las microfábulas* (ABC of microfables) (2018), written by Luisa Valenzuela and illustrated by Lorenzo Amengual. Avilés Fabila's entries present sharp criticisms of everything from the reification and subsequent capitalization of the mythical, to the state of freedom in current society, while Valenzuela's work challenges the traditional hierarchy of dogma over form. Before delving into these new interpretations, however, it is worthwhile examining medieval prototypes to look for hints of the subversive in an otherwise conformist and moralizing genre.

We have thus far been examining the medieval bestiary as a moralizing, strict, and didactic enterprise. Despite these characteristics, and however antithetical the following might seem, subtle instances of subversion did exist in the medieval texts, and contemporary works with their rebellious character can be placed within this larger tradition. According to Debra Hassig in *Medieval Bestiaries: Text, Image, Ideology*, subversion in the medieval prototype was pornographic in nature, with art commissioners and illustrators making the most of the scarce opportunities to depict genitalia (1995, 109). Hassig holds that, through these images, the bestiary undermined celibacy and the liberation from sexual desire (109). This is relevant because few other forums allowed for such representations, especially in religious contexts. In chapter 1 we met one scandalous creature, the beaver, usually illustrated with male human genitalia. Other beasts portrayed with prominent genitalia or with illustrations involving nude human figures are the siren, hyena, unicorn, bonnacon, and wild boar (88). In a quantitative study of the images and texts corresponding to siren entries in medieval bestiaries, for instance, Hassig notes that only six out of twenty-two images match their textual entries; despite most sirens being described as half-woman, half-bird by the entries, the images depict a half-woman, half-fish creature, allowing for the possibility of drawing female breasts (105). Although the counterargument exists that the nakedness of the siren is representative of the negative associations held in the West with respect to nudity, and that such illustrations are intended to heighten sinful qualities, the depiction of a naked siren is undeniably dissonant in its context (109). An entry from *The Worksop Bestiary* (ca. 1300) (figure 4.1) showcases artwork bridging the two depictions of the siren, the half-bird and the half-fish, yet retaining the element of nudity not expressed in the text. This play of media and the space between them will be further discussed in chapter 6. For the purposes of this chapter, however, the artistic decision to depict unnecessary nudity in an otherwise conservative Christian genre can be interpreted as an injection of rebellion in a sea of conformity.

Another significant connection between the contemporary and the medieval is the evolution of morality in the genre. Sarah Kay, among other medieval bestiary scholars, indicates that the genre loses its sermon-like tone, becoming more secular as time passes (2017, 12). While this is true if one understands the bestiary genre

Figure 4.1 | Image depicting three half-woman/half-fish creatures, with bird's feet and with wings around their waists (*The Worksop Bestiary*, ca. 1185).

as ending with the medieval bestiaries, some (if not most) contemporary works do communicate a moral message, as illustrated by the works examined here. Certainly, most are not authoritative, but rather ludic, as Hispanic society has moved toward secularism and away from sermonic tones. Its didactic core, however purged of Catholic traces, is ever present in rebellious bestiaries.

Bestiario de seres fantásticos mexicanos, *by Norma Muñoz Ledo, illustrated by Israel Barrón (2016)*

Bestiario de seres fantásticos mexicanos contains an implicit subversion of the European bestiary tradition, as it foregoes the expected beasts and favours creatures autochthonous to Mexico. Where the phoenix or the blackbird once resided, now a reader can expect to find the *cholito de la suerte* ("good luck cholito") or the *burro que se alarga* ("self-elongating donkey"), creatures from the states of Hidalgo and Sonora, respectively. Keeping the name and form of the genre results in a simultaneously utilitarian and provocative text; it establishes the tradition, leaving no questions as to what the work's entries are modelled after. *Bestiario de seres fantásticos mexicanos* lacks no component of a traditional bestiary: whereas bestiaries such as the ones featured in chapter 5 truly challenge the form, this work is an exemplary bestiary, establishing the undeniable form of the genre that recalls its Christian, European roots in order to disseminate the very cultures that the colonizers who first arrived in America sought to negate.

In their work, Muñoz Ledo and Barrón elegantly avoid a common postmodern trap, what George Yúdice calls the exploring of, sometimes exploiting of, the marginal without the capacity for any solidarity with it (1991), fetishizing or gawking at the Other of Latin American society. The bestiary presents and questions mythologies long denied, striking the elusive balance between introducing marginalized narratives and neither marvelling at nor reducing them. This is achieved partly because the work can be classified as children's literature. Rather than detracting from the significance or "sophistication" of the bestiary, this presentation of the work amplifies its impact.

Aimed at children, this bestiary introduces a mythology often overlooked even by Latin American schooling. Muñoz Ledo adapted her more extensive, adult bestiary, *Supernaturalia* (2012), for the sake of familiarizing Mexican children with their own mythology. She holds that Mexican children's familiarity with films like *Frozen*, Disney characters, or Celtic mythology points to a loss in cultural identity, claiming that an effort must be made to hold on to the songs, games, and creatures that belong to Mexico (Kadner 2017). Press for this bestiary advertised it as a teaching tool, making constant reference to ensuring that children would know their *own* fantastic beings, and encouraging intergenerational conversation on the topic. Muñoz Ledo knows that the stories with which children are raised become a much more intrinsic part of who they are than whatever they might curiously pick off a bookshelf as adults. This points to a dichotomy: a cultural centre and a periphery, held on individual and societal plains, with the centre subjugating the margins. Nelly Richard states that the privileged or authoritative position of the centre "proceeds, above all, from the investiture of authority that allows it to function as a focus of endowed meaning. The symbolic advantage of the Center is a result of its monopoly over the resources to negotiate the power–discourse relationship through unequivocal processing and manipulation of the equivalencies of signs and values"

(1992, 58). To disrupt this privileging of the centre, and for this disruption to become more than a mere "stated disposition," "it becomes necessary to decentralize the symbolic power of cultural representation and pluralize the socio-institutional mechanisms of critical participation and debate" (1992, 5). This kind of disruption can take place when a medieval European genre is used to feature indigenous Mexican beasts.

The relationship between text and image aids this mission, as it reflects the work's didactic objective. At risk of stating the obvious, the effects of canons, cultural baggage, the colonialist agenda, Eurocentrism, or whatever we call the phenomenon whereby children learn about another continent's beasts before learning about their own, are not easily overturned. As a result of the difficulty of its task, the relationship between the work's texts and images are perhaps the most uncomplicated feature of the books examined here. Images accompanying these entries are exclusively supportive of their textual counterparts. Because of the underrepresentation of this folklore, there is a need to showcase it while the author holds the reader's attention. It is important to highlight once again the decision to keep the form as is, because if the genre of the bestiary cannot be assumed to be neutral, neither can the contemporary interpretation by Muñoz Ledo. In replacing European beasts with indigenous and Mestizo ones, the author questions what Richard refers to as "the equilibrium dictated by habit or convenience" (2004, 1). This is furthered by the work's inclusion of two of the forces that can exert pressure on the limits of social inclusion/exclusion and divide cultural power. The first force is a new group of actors, like women, youth, Indigenous peoples, and so on. The second is "transcultural and multicultural forces of the Latin American periphery that revise and critique the metropolitan synthesis of the center's modernity" (2–3). These are the very forces existing *a priori* in Latin American society – the naturally occurring synthesis of pre-Hispanic, European, and African elements. In the context of these bestiaries, the reader can see their presence in Indigenous names like Dtundtuncan, and Zux Coosyat, all followed by descriptions in Spanish. These "transcultural and multicultural forces" of the periphery maintain a margin and a centre that are in constant oscillation, forcing the reader to reflect on the history and the implication of this intermixing.

As previously mentioned, *Bestiario de seres fantásticos mexicanos* is the children's edition of a different bestiary-type book that

Muñoz Ledo wrote titled *Supernaturalia*. While *Supernaturalia* is not featured in this chapter, for it cannot be fully classified as a bestiary, we can look at the information it offers to supplement our understanding of the creatures featured in *Bestiario de seres fantásticos mexicanos*. Muñoz Ledo's works are the result of a seven-year investigation: such a lengthy project is required given that information on folkloric creatures tends to slowly disappear, as a result of the decreased use of the oral tradition on which it depends. In the 1990s, the National Council for Education Development (CONAFE), a Mexican institution that works with the secretary of education to improve education for marginalized groups and for rural communities, compiled oral testimonies from all corners of Mexico. Muñoz Ledo extracted her beasts from the CONAFE archives, which also included recipes and accounts on how electricity and water had been brought to one town or other (Kadner 2017). Because no single work exclusively dedicated to Mexican magical beings existed, she gathered information through interviews conducted across the country, as well as anthropological or philological recompilations (Mendoza Hernández 2016). Given the volume of creatures that Muñoz Ledo covers, and the fact that the only origin information she provides is the name of the states from which they originate, the contextualization of this work will be limited to a generalized Mexican culture, not focusing on any single region.

The mission of this bestiary's artwork is to illustrate beasts forgotten by the national consciousness. Israel Barrón revealed in an interview that the lack of knowledge about these beasts allowed him great artistic freedom. While creatures like La Llorona or the sirens are present in the Latin American imaginary, less celebrated creatures allowed him to freely interpret their appearance, and with his chosen colour palette (Goldman 2017). Barrón, from Xalapa, Veracruz, describes his process as an enthusiastic, marathonic endeavour, filled with sleepless nights that left him exhausted but filled with joy (2017). He considers himself a traditional painter, and although the exact medium of choice is left unspecified, it can be appreciated in the fine textures that characterize his work. In 2017, Barrón was the only Latin American illustrator to be celebrated with a Gold Plaque by the Biennial of Illustration Bratislava. This award, among the oldest and most prestigious in children's illustrations, recognized the illustrator's promotion of Mexican folklore.

Figure 4.2 | The Junchoo, a man-eating beast, has razor-sharp teeth and backwards-facing feet (Israel Barrón, 2016).

Despite being contained within a children's book, most of Muñoz Ledo's creatures are violent and dangerous. Like with any cosmogeny, Mexican mythology serves to understand the Mexican world: "[Muñoz Ledo] thinks about the violence that shakes large parts of her country. 'I think about the worst and most soulless of creatures' ... Mythology also exists to explain, in some way, the tens of thousands of disappearances, the thousands of femicides, or, in a different category altogether, the sensation of being watched in the Yucatecan jungle" (Kadner 2017; my translation). The entry titled "Junchoo" features one of the violent creatures of the children's rhyming bestiary.[2] Belonging to the states of Veracruz, Puebla, Oaxaca, and Tabasco, the Junchoo has a taste for human flesh, and his feet face backwards when he walks: "Terrible and powerful / Dreadful elf / For him human flesh / Is tastiest of all" (Muñoz Ledo and Barrón 2016; my translation)[3] (figure 4.2). Barrón's colour palette for the bestiary is filled with natural greens, earthy reds, terracottas, and dusky blues, offering slices of the Mexican landscape. The Junchoo's carnivorous teeth and its meal of human bone broth are contrasted by its friendly demeanour. The creature embodies a danger that is ubiquitous in society, despite friendly appearances.

To be able to escape this malevolent creature, Muñoz Ledo advises: "Before its white, jaguar teeth / Your fear you will have to dominate / Just laugh / And you will see him fall dead."[4] It is no coincidence that the way to survive an encounter with the Junchoo is through laughter. The relationship between the Mexican people and death has been the focus of significant scholarship. According to Octavio Paz, among the writers to theorize about this connection: "The Mexican, in contrast, is familiar with death, jokes about it, caresses it, sleeps with it, celebrates it; it is one of his favorite toys and his most steadfast love. True, there is perhaps as much fear in his attitude as in that of others, but at least death is not hidden away: he looks at it face to face, with impatience, disdain or irony. 'If they are going to kill me tomorrow, let them kill me right away'" (1961, 57–8). Mexico does indeed depart from the prevalent reaction to death: fear. Most famous are the internationally known Day of the Dead celebrations and the character of Catrina, as Mexico exports its relationship to death, spreading a different outlook on an otherwise often taboo and feared topic. As already mentioned, Muñoz Ledo sees her beasts as mythical representations of the violence that has come to penetrate all aspects of Mexican daily life. This relationship to violence is closely related to the perspective on death held by the country at large. Paz further explains that the Mexican indifference towards death derives from an indifference towards life: "the reason death cannot frighten us is that 'life has cured us of fear.' It is natural, even desirable, to die, and the sooner the better" (58). This indifference towards both life and death renders the fearlessness less of a state of valour and more of a tragedy. The songs, parties, and popular sayings that Paz mentions belong to the same family as the laughter necessary to survive a Junchoo encounter.

This purgatorial indifference is demonstrated in the following verses in the entry on "La Llorona": "Everything is encompassed in her lament, / Sadness, angst, and suffering, / Oh woman whose pain spills over!" (Muñoz Ledo and Barrón 2016; my translation).[5] La Llorona's tragic figure embodies Paz's comment, "life has cured us of fear." She is infamous across Latin America, with each country attributing different stories and qualities to her melancholic cry. In an interview, Muñoz Ledo recalls the two origins of La Llorona in Mexico – the tragic Indigenous woman, Malinche, who fell in love with a Spanish man, and the Aztec goddess Cihuacōātl, who foresaw the loss of her children, the Mexicas – when she states: "I think it's a representation of the Latin American woman up until a certain moment in history, and, in some cases, a current representation: that of the selfless woman, able to erase herself through the masculine figure" (Kadner 2017; my translation). The double heritage of Mexico, the state of being "sons of la Malinche," can thus be read as a "cure for fear." The raising of women to a metahuman plane is what renders La Llorona subhuman in this one, and she is left to wander in the in-between of laughter and death as punishment for her failure to uphold her role and know her place as a mother, wife, and, in some versions of the story, Indigenous person.

La Llorona is not the only creature of Mexico to betray the feminine condition. The Cihuatlaco, who belongs to the regions of Morelos, Nayarit, and Aguascalientes, lures in drunk men with her feminine figure, and enjoys a good laugh at their expense when they discover she is half-woman, half-horse. "Cihuatlaco o Cihucahuatoyl" means "horse woman" in the Nahuatl language, and many drunk men report her being the cause for their sobriety. In *Supernaturalia*, Muñoz Ledo cites the account of Valerio Marcos, a man from Nayarit who had lost his wife and children, and whose restaurant was suffering as a result of his excessive drinking. One night, returning from a friend's house, he saw a woman with a beautiful figure and decided to follow her, certain that she would also have a beautiful face. He asked her, "Why don't you answer, mamacita?" and touched her shoulder, so she turned to reveal the head and neck of a pinto horse. Marcos never drank again, and he joined Alcoholics Anonymous, where, between much laughter on account of his cowardice, other men told him that if you pray in front of the Cihucahuatoyl, the horse woman will disappear (Muñoz Ledo and Hernández 2012, 235–6; my translation). The Cihucahuatoyl serves as a fantasy of sorts, bringing comedic relief to an all-too-common reality in Mexico. There is power in being able to laugh at a drunk man's harassing, but because doing this in an everyday situation would prove too dangerous, the Cihucahuatoyl's account proves cathartic. There is satisfaction in the thought of a poorly intentioned person not only being conned but also being scared away from vices that could lead to further harassment or violence.

Because of the book's esoteric nature, and its use of creatures excluded by national narratives, *Bestiario de seres fantásticos mexicanos* provides insight into those who are marginalized by the centre. The work faces a challenge highlighted by Fredric Jameson, which is the inclusion of a different, long-silenced discourse without it being fetishized or treated by empty theorization. Since the book is not a postmodern theorization, but rather a dissemination of various creatures without pretense, it reaches a balance, and, as Jameson puts it, "neither reduces the 'Third World' to some homogenous other of the West, nor does it vacuously celebrate the 'astonishing' pluralism of human cultures" (2003). Rather, the bestiary presents the creatures as part of quotidian life, and as part of global contexts like capitalism and colonialism, complete with their gravity and defects. Barrón has given a face to the creatures and contextualized them in recognizable Mexican settings and landscapes, using the entire page to promote the richness and complexities of Mexican folklore to children.

The communicative aspect of the bestiary is strengthened by its affinity with the oral traditions from which the beasts originate. These beasts are Mexican, *mestizas*, belonging neither to the pre-Columbian nor to the Spanish. Little information is available on these beasts through contemporary widespread sources, even on the internet. Muñoz Ledo has made a wealth of beasts that were otherwise unknown widely available through the transcription of oral discourse and interviews. In the bibliography of her *Supernaturalia*, for instance, each chapter has a section titled "Oral Tradition Authority," in which a long list of interviews is cited. These works have much in common with the way in which the *Physiologus*, for instance, was compiled, as many sources came from oral tradition. Unlike many of the bestiaries examined in the following chapters, which are of a decidedly literary character, these works, above all, convey the stories traditionally common to other languages than Spanish, seeking to rescue and share traditions, past battles, idiosyncrasies, and losses, among other things.

This first bestiary represents an implicit subversion to the canon. It respects the form of the medieval bestiary entirely, without any changes to the relationship between text and image, the inclusion of subheadings, or the purpose to simply communicate the existence, characteristics, and allegory implicit in a given beast. The challenge it presents lies in its introduction of the margins to a genre that, for centuries, was only second to and shared its mission with the Bible, thereby exclusively communicating the perspective of the powerful centre.

Bestiario de seres prodigiosos *by René Avilés Fabila, illustrated by José Luis Cuevas (2001)*

Bestiario de seres prodigiosos by René Avilés Fabila and, as will be seen shortly, Luisa Valenzuela's *ABC de las microfábulas* (2009) depart from the bestiary tradition overtly. Rather than veiling their work in the subtleties and implications of Mexican beasts appearing in a European canon, Avilés Fabila and Valenzuela deliberately set up the European genre's mythology to reconstruct it with contemporary preoccupations and contexts. Avilés Fabila offers sharp criticism on inherited Romantic and Classical ideals and deconstructs much of what contemporary Western society considers to be normal. Valenzuela's challenge to the tradition is found in a reinvention of the relationship between language and morality. In her work, based on a genre in which language was traditionally used to communicate a didactic message, the roles are reversed and language triumphs over content, leaving moralistic teachings scrambling to keep up.

The intertextuality in *Bestiario de seres prodigiosos*, as well as its dialogue with other works of the genre, must be underscored to appreciate Avilés Fabila's interpretation of the bestiary as a contemporary genre. His work is replete with the influence of the works introduced in chapter 2, supporting the notion that the Hispanic bestiary is largely, if not completely, indebted to the canonical works of Borges, Arreola, Monterroso, Neruda, Guillén, and Pacheco. Avilés Fabila begins his work by quoting the epigraph in Borges and Guerrero's *Manual de zoología fantástica*. At the beginning of the section titled "Serpentarium," Avilés Fabila also quotes Guillén's celebrated poem "Sensemayá," which evokes an Afro-Caribbean chant that accompanies the killing of a snake. He borrows from Guillén when using the image of a zoo cage as an entry point for his bestiary as well, as will be seen in his phoenix entry. Monterroso's influence is also present, palpable in entries such as "Penélope and Aracne," as Monterroso also wrote an entry in his *La oveja negra* titled "La tela de Penélope, o quién engaña a quién" ("Penelope's tapestry, or who is fooling whom"). His work displays a constant theme of animals as being closer to their own nature than to that of humans, a topic already explored in the second chapter.

Dolores Koch claims that Avilés Fabila's work, like that of Arreola and Monterroso, aims to open the reader's consciousness to new perspectives (1981, 129). In truth, Avilés Fabila's entries above all highlight what is already present. It is not a metaphysical, spiritual awareness that Avilés Fabila is after, but rather a sharp incision into the fabric of contemporary society, a purpose largely alien to medieval works. His phoenix entry, for instance, signals a stark secularization in society, reflected by the changes in the treatment of the bird from the medieval period to now. His entry neutralizes the sacredness of the bird's ritual. Unlike the medieval phoenix, surrounded by myrrh and religious authorities, Avilés Fabila's phoenix in "Aviso en la jaula del ave fénix" (Notice on the phoenix cage) finds itself in an ordinary zoo, with his sacred immolation reduced to a matter of logistics:

> Funeral and rebirth schedule:
>
> Every 100 years, at approximately 12:30 in the afternoon, the cinnamon, nard, and myrrh that comprise the nest of the bird are set on fire (which, according to Ovid's words, is the bird's crib and the burial place of its father). At 1:30, after the aromatic flames have subsided, the Phoenix resurfaces triumphant, with his stunning golden and crimson feathers, out of its own ashes.
>
> Please be punctual. (Avilés Fábila and Cuevas 2001, 37; my translation)[6]

The tongue-in-cheek entry nods to enough of the traditional beast's mythology (Ovid's authority and traditional spices are mentioned) that the phoenix's fall from grace, so to speak, is all the more clear. The reader is reminded of the awesome nature of an immortal creature that can be reborn, and lest they miss the event of a lifetime, they are told to be punctual in a tone best suited to dental appointment reminders. The exact date and approximate time of the event is significant, given that sources around the world disagree on the number of years between the phoenix's immolations. With the mystery solved and a date set, the phoenix is stripped of any remaining mystique or aura. Though it is less obvious than his Ovid reference, here Avilés Fabila brings up Guillén, introducing the Hispanic canon alongside the European one.[7] Guillén's entry "El fénix" in *El gran zoo* reads similarly to Avilés Fabila's: "This is the cage selected / for the resurrection of the phoenix. / (Its ashes will arrive in December)" (Guillén 1967, 45; my translation).[8] Because Guillén is included rather than disqualified through a remark that places a structure on the infinite, Avilés Fabila inadvertently nods to the latest form of the bestiary as the more pertinent model to follow in a secular, disenchanted world. This tone, belonging to magical realism, is perhaps the only magic or wonder that the contemporary reader is comfortable with; the reader can accept that which is awesome, but only if they may visit it on their terms, and only if it is safely housed behind bars. By adopting Guillén's tone, Avilés Fabila chooses which of the incarnations of the bestiary will serve as the inspiration for the latest evolutions of the genre. The inclusion of non-European sources provides a glimpse into future bestiaries that may forego the expected sources altogether, representing a radical undermining of tradition in and of itself.

Avilés Fabila's references to his sources in his entries also constitutes a drastic change in the genre. Originally, bestiary entries were relatively self-sufficient, with text, image, and allegorical explanation all present in the same work, maximizing their teachability. In the entries "La verdadera esfinge" (The real sphinx) and "Sobre sátiros, una precisión" (An aside on satyrs), however, the information necessary to understand the beast is missing, and any further reading is an extra textual endeavour, made optional to the reader. "La verdadera esfinge" invites the skeptical reader to find Gustave Moreau's rendering of the sphinx at the New York Metropolitan Museum of Art, claiming that the artist's interpretation is the truest to life (80).

Avilés Fábila employs a similar tactic after pointing out that in the mythology, satyrs are thought of as exclusively male: "At the Frick Collection in New York, there is a stunning bronze sculpture depicting a female satyr carrying her child. Half goat, half woman, it suggests the possibility of a race that mysteriously vanished. For this reason, it is preferable not to imagine satyrs brutally possessing women but rather courting beings of their own kind with elegance" (81; my translation).[9] Both entries rely on an arduous reading dependent on access to endless information and a playful relationship between text and image. They mention an image that is central to the text yet is nowhere to be found in the book. This thus presents a subversion of what a bestiary has long been expected to do and deliver. If a bestiary's images were once used as a mnemotechnic device to ensure the retention of all taught material, references to an external image nullifies this original purpose. The intertextuality is essentially outsourced, mimicking contemporary economic practices.

The sphinx entry is not the only one to combine a capitalist reading of past mythologies. In a series of entries titled "Mitología publicitaria" (Mythological advertising), the author more explicitly employs the bestiary to critique current society. The chilling series describes a publicity campaign that employs harpies to sell appetite-stimulating pills. The campaign having proved successful, those in charge soon see a rise in cannibalism as food supplies dwindle. The practice is quickly spread to ensure population control, and the Catholic Church supports the practice for two reasons: "First: there is no longer any need for contraceptives, abortions, and other sacrilegious practices. Second: it fulfills an ancient Christian precept: eat, for this is my body; drink, for this is my blood" (90–2; my translation).[10] This entry, along with the others under "Mitología publicitaria," is perhaps the most significant example of the rebellious nature of this bestiary. Explicitly, Avilés Fabila turns his bestiary's mission into one of criticism and undermining the status quo, whereas the medieval works were, above all, an edification of the soul, a manner of ensuring the very conformity in society that Avilés Fabila seeks to undo. With the help of mythological harpies, mediocre advertising normalizes the horrifying potentiality of cannibalism. Public debates on something as private as abortion are a thing of the past after Harpy Pills are released. Media outlets' endorsement of cannibalism turns a widespread taboo into an everyday practice, even attaining the approval of the Vatican. Avilés Fabila's final line equates the most sacred of sacraments, eating and drinking Christ's flesh and blood, with cannibalistic practices.

In the entry featuring Cerberus, the legendary dog is placed at the entrance of a restaurant named El Averno ("The Underworld"). Despite the restaurant being modelled after a Dantean hell, complete with insufferable heat and torture devices, people readily submit themselves to its sadistic practices, entranced by the clout of the establishment. As Guillén does with the phoenix, Avilés Fabila disenchants the sacred and mythological, consequently forcing the reader to reflect on what is valued and encouraged in their culture.

Although the significance of the connection between bestiaries and the animal skin they were originally written on will be further explored in chapter 6, medievalist Sarah Kay's theory on the matter is pertinent for this entry. In *Animal Skins*, Kay states that medieval bestiary teachings are reliant on what Julia Kristeva has called "the powers of horror," since "they are as much experienced through visceral affect as taught through theological tenet" (2017, 5). Kay in this case references the uncanny feeling that arises when encountering animal skin as vellum, complete with its sutures and human skin–like appearance, and how the effect of this experience aids in imprinting the lesson on the reader-viewer's mind. While bestiaries are no longer printed on animal skin, Avilés Fabila brings a visceral quality to his entries that aids in the creation of his lesson. Though belonging to a secular world, Avilés Fabila's entries are no less didactic than the medieval ones, demonstrating that while the medieval bestiary became more secular over time, the Hispanic canon has merely shifted in terms of what it chooses to disseminate.

The final paragraph in Avilés Fabila's "Las quimeras del siglo XXI" (Chimerae of the twenty-first century) entry can be read as a commentary on the state of the bestiary genre, given Avilés Fabila's demonstrated familiarity with canonical Hispanic authors, as well as his knowledge of the traditional sources and general trajectory of the bestiary genre: "The new chimerae, fantastical beings that can be purchased in curiosity shops, at most provoke curiosity or an irresistible desire to keep them as pets. The fear of the unknown, of the supernatural, has unfortunately been banished in this century where everything is possible thanks to science" (2001, 104; my translation).[11] Chimerae are no longer a source of fear and wonder, and neither are the new bestiaries. Contemporary bestiaries can be found in niche bookshops, and though the impulse is not entirely understood, they are often subject to the same desire to be possessed as with Avilés Fabila's chimeric curiosities. Bestiaries are often constructed with an "anything goes" approach, with Avilés Fabila's bestiary being a prime example. The complement of different sources – arts, historical accounts, and narrative approaches, all moulded into a medieval genre – certainly shares the qualities of Dr Frankenstein's creature, sutured together and having a life of its own. Bestiaries have also similarly been cast aside, demoted from a prestigious genre to bookstore rarity, in favour of best-sellers, or, more pertinently, streaming services and video games.

Continuing with the notion of a mashed-together creation, *Bestiario de seres prodigiosos* features the work of José Luis Cuevas, a prominent figure of the Mexican Generación de la Ruptura, or the Breakaway Generation. Although Cuevas's images are not allocated to any one entry, the artist's reputation and corpus of work, focused on drawings and sculptures, are impeccably suited to Avilés Fabila's tone (figure 4.3, figure 4.4). La Ruptura was composed of young artists who, without the economic support enjoyed by a chosen few during the muralist movement, developed distinct, individual styles. Breakaway artists offered an alternative to the style and mission of the Escuela Mexicana, which doled out contracts for painted murals – contracts mainly reserved for the "great three": Diego Rivera, José Clemente Orozco, and David Alfaro Siqueiros. Resulting partially from the Cold War, which led to a general international expansion of trends and styles, and the fact that the state stopped being the sole promoter of culture, art began being sponsored by individual people, giving way to experimentation and furthering the abstractionism and geometries typical of the time (Feria and Campillo 2010). Fernanda Feria and Rosa Campillo write that the youth belonging to La Ruptura organized informally and spontaneously, disseminating cosmopolitan, abstract, and apocalyptic values (2010). Cuevas's reputation expanded beyond his role in a breakaway movement that challenged a national cultural mission. Cuevas is, in other words, a polemical artist for a polemical bestiary. He publicized his opinion of world-renowned artists such as Diego Rivera and Salvador Dalí, calling the former a meritless fraud and holding that the latter lacked imagination (E. López 1966, 20). He preferred the creation of new plastic forms, as demonstrated by Picasso, whose influence over Cuevas's work is evident.

In his article "José Luis Cuevas: Un animal impuro," Alberto Blanco calls Cuevas's creations "impure animals" (2008, 3). His art is full of distorted, agonizing dark figures, painfully mashed together. Blanco's observation is in reference to a passage in the Old Testament that reads "These are unclean to you among all that creep" (Leviticus 11:31; King James Version) when describing which animals should and should not be eaten by the Jewish people. This reference recalls the medieval purposes of the bestiary and situates Cueva and Avilés Fabila's work in clear opposition to the genre's original intentions. If the medieval bestiary represented all that was good, or the good that could be attained through avoiding evil, the inclusion of impure art and animals makes for an unkosher genre that strays from "good," acceptable

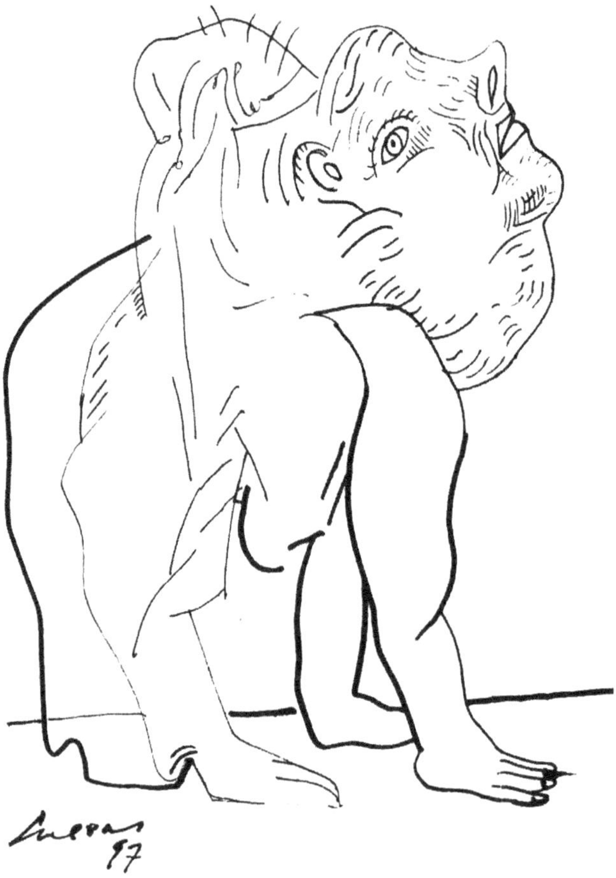

Figure 4.3 | José Luis Cuevas's figures, inspired by Cubism, convey a painful discomfort (José Luis Cuevas, 2001).

tradition. The link between animals' didactic qualities and the wretched human nature they reveal is further explored by Blanco when he baptizes humans as the only impure, imperfect animal, as well as noting that humans are the central focus of Cuevas's art (2008, 5). Blanco then compares the human to the minotaur, half-man, half-quadruped, unable to escape its own labyrinth (6). The difficult, winding path navigated by Cuevas's human is present in each entry of Avilés Fabila's work through its grotesque, absurd images and perversion of the original bestiaries.

Figure 4.4 | Ink on paper (José Luis Cuevas, 2001).

Whether Cuevas created art specifically for Avilés Fabila is unclear, yet Cuevas's amalgamated images perfectly mirror the variety of sources, canons, styles, and philosophies that Avilés Fabila mixed together and united with a dark, ominous undertone. The media that Cuevas used for these illustrations is uncertain, but the favouring of clean black-and-white lines, as opposed to his muddier lithography, suggests ink on paper. His monochromatic, cross-hatched, enmeshed creatures support Avilés Fabila's mission to communicate simple yet challenging

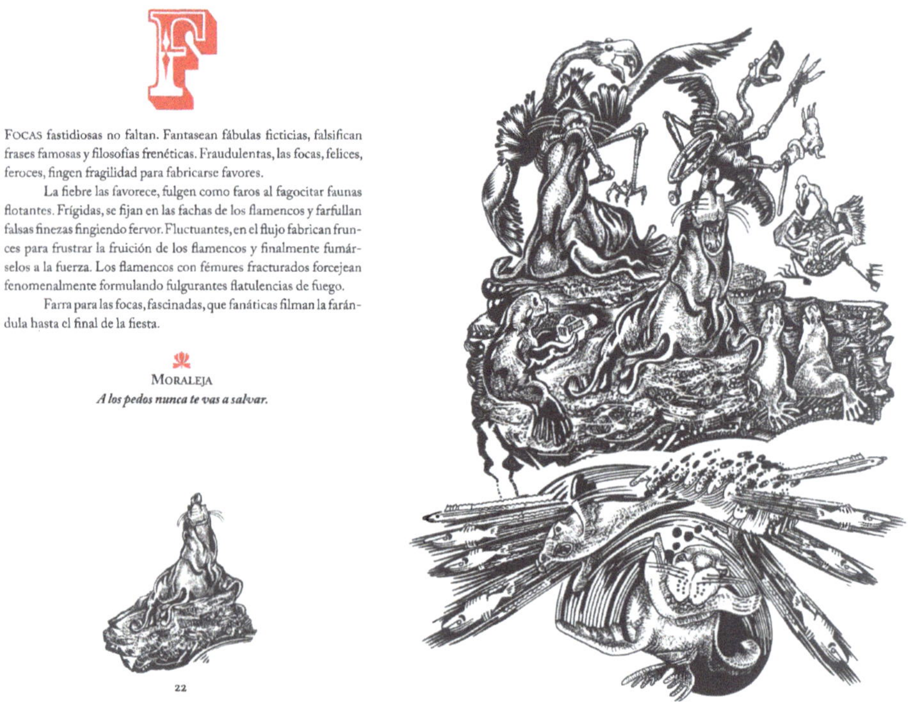

F

Focas fastidiosas no faltan. Fantasean fábulas ficticias, falsifican frases famosas y filosofías frenéticas. Fraudulentas, las focas, felices, feroces, fingen fragilidad para fabricarse favores.

La fiebre las favorece, fulgen como faros al fagocitar faunas flotantes. Frígidas, se fijan en las fachas de los flamencos y farfullan falsas finezas fingiendo fervor. Fluctuantes, en el flujo fabrican frunces para frustrar la fruición de los flamencos y finalmente fumárselos a la fuerza. Los flamencos con fémures fracturados forcejean fenomenalmente formulando fulgurantes flatulencias de fuego.

Farra para las focas, fascinadas, que fanáticas filman la farándula hasta el final de la fiesta.

Moraleja

A los pedos nunca te vas a salvar.

22

Figure 4.5 | Ink on paper (Lorenzo Amengual, 2018).

truths. The dark twist of harpies being used to promote dietary pills, or the maddening of a man who discovers after a lifetime of searching that mermaids are hideous – massive fish heads mounted onto beautiful, feminine legs – is reflected in these multi-headed, multi-limbed creatures. The rebellion against the message of a traditional form, coupled with the rebellion against an art internationally associated with "Mexicanness," gives shape to this interpretation of the bestiary. This departure from the expectations one might traditionally have of the bestiary is only made more clear with the reference to the genre itself in the name and form of Avilés Fabila and Cuevas's work.

ABC de las microfábulas by Luisa Valenzuela, illustrated by Lorenzo Amengual (2018)

A similar rebellion takes place in the pages of *ABC de las microfábulas*,[12] written by Luisa Valenzuela and illustrated by Lorenzo Amengual. The work is a fascinating subversion of the moral allegory and language hierarchy commonly found in bestiaries. Although Valenzuela titles her work a series of "microfábulas" (microfables), her form is closer to that of a bestiary, as each brief entry is followed by an explanation of that text's allegorical aspect, accompanied by an image. The descriptive tone of the entries as well as their present tense make the book much more of a bestiary than a collection of fables. Curiously, Monterroso also labelled his bestiary entries as fables, and Valenzuela cites him as the inspiration behind her microrrelatos.

Save for prepositions and articles, every word of Valenzuela's entries begins with the same letter as the animal's name. Although at first glance the title announces a rather orthodox bestiary, the form quickly dispels this assumption. First, the teachings allocated to various beasts are different from the ones explored thus far in medieval bestiaries: "Morals are usually very brief and to the point; however, the one you are reading goes against the grain. It is a macro-moral with far-reaching ambitions, conceived around the idea of complicity" (2018, 7; my translation).[13] The moral teachings vary from reflecting their medieval origins ("Sweetness is the most direct path to happiness" [54; my translation], "Foolish self-confidence often keeps you from seeing traps" [41; my translation]) to humorous teachings and those that border on the frivolous ("It's not worth it to act all macho when genetics are not on your side" [62; my translation], "Macrobiotic food isn't for everyone; it's better to not insist" [64; my translation]).[14]

Second, and most importantly, the moral, didactic aspect of the book is a by-product or happy coincidence of a language experiment. What really matters to Valenzuela is word use, and the substantial challenge that ensues from writing a book of entries that can only commence with a specific letter.[15] She encourages the reader to let go of everything and let themselves be led by language, carried away by word play and semantic constructions, to be delighted by any and all discoveries (6). The letter "F," for instance, belongs to seals (figure 4.5):

> Annoying seals are never in short supply. They fantasize fictitious fables, falsify famous phrases and frenzied philosophies. Fraudulent, the seals – happy, fierce – feign fragility to self-fabricate favours.
>
> Fever favours them; they shine like lighthouses as they devour floating fauna. Frigid, they focus on the flamingo's appearance, muttering fake compliments while feigning fervour. Floating in the current, they craft frowns to frustrate the flamingo's enjoyment and eventually give up and endure them. Flamingos, with fractured femurs, struggle phenomenally, unleashing fiery, furious flatulence.
>
> A party for the seals, fascinated, who fanatically film the spectacle until the end of the feast.
>
> Moral: Rushing won't save you. (22; my translation)[16]

Here, with the moral, Valenzuela plays with the expression "a los pedos," which literally translates to "by the farts," meaning "quickly," or "in a hurry." A close English translation with a similar tone and register would be "hauling ass." The play on words leads to a colloquial, vulgar teaching that contrasts with the skilful use of language. Here, it is worth recalling Richard's words that the centre can be challenged by new actors, a category to which Valenzuela as a Latin American and woman who lived and worked as an academic in the United States would certainly belong. Her manner of interacting with the centre, however, is what makes her work most appealing. By playing with the centre, by moulding it as she does in this entry, she, without any explicit politics, turns it into a game. She reverses the order of what is important and uses what once ruled supreme over acceptability, turning it into a liberating game. Her use of language and her playful tone is more reminiscent of avant-garde poetry than that of dogmatic authorities, laying bare her true intentions, which are far from moralizing. Because the Rioplatense dialect is insufficient to encompass the volume of vocabulary she is after, Valenzuela includes a glossary in the back of the book. In the glossary, all the terms taken from different countries' use of the Spanish language – not a small feat, given the immense regional variation found across the Hispanic world – are explained in order to facilitate the understanding of her work. While superficially this seems a kind gesture on the author's behalf, it necessarily brings up the fact that she has chosen to not write in "neutral" Spanish, which is so often preferred to ensure as wide a distribution as possible. It is more so a boast, given that her glossary reveals her substantial knowledge of different dialects of Spanish. These bragging rights become more evident in the tone she takes on in the glossary, where she defines "*Ñuñoa*" as "[a] place where ñuños flower, of course. Suburb of Santiago de Chile"[17] (73; my translation), "liquid letters" like "L" as "a liquid, it's enough just to hear it. Careful not to spill it"[18] (72; my translation), and "Iguazú" as an "Argentine national park with important cataracts that don't affect eyesight, on the contrary" (72; my translation).[19]

Amengual's illustrations seamlessly accompany Valenzuela's literary mission. Although his art is not the only example of playful art included in this study, his images have a cathartic quality that suit the self-indulgent character of *ABC de las microfábulas*. His crosshatching, the amassing of animals, and use of contrastive shades present themselves as visceral reactions to an idea – mental images imprinted directly onto paper. Black pockets of ink punctuate sections within the image, mirroring the staccato cadence of the alliteration in Valenzuela's text.

While the "F" entry is entirely playful, "G" offers a more traditionally didactic tone, more closely comparable to the didactic, political bestiary entries seen thus far (figure 4.6):

> Gorillas and worms enjoy globalization. People groan, beaten by the clubs of gorilla generals, tough and coarse men who gallop to the beat of "Great!"
>
> Great gymnasts, the gorilla generals and worms gratify themselves, with their grating throats. Woe to the kid who challenges them! They are handsome, gelatinous, gigantic. Grandiose screamers like macaws glorify war, gladiators, the blue-gray gendarmes, prison guards, and they enjoy the honking of geese. In groups, these lazy men pelt cherries at the people.
>
> They govern with guards and sentinels. The managers pay them big numbers, but greedy, they don't spend on union stews, they aren't communal, they are greasy scoundrels guarding the guillotine.
>
> Moral: A small step to the left often improves both your own life and others'. (24; my translation)[20]

In this entry, the author betrays her political affiliations through wordplay; the moral emerges from a prolonged play of double entendres. Words like "gorillas," "*gusanos*," "*gurí*," and "*garpan*" lend

G

Gorilas y gusanos gustan de la globalización. La gente gime, golpeada por garrotes de generales gorilas, guapos guarangos que galopan al grito de «¡Genial!»

Grandes gimnastas, los generales gorilas y gusanos se gratifican en grado gozoso, con el gaznate gárrulo. ¡Güai del gurí gay que los gaste! Son guapos, gelatinosos, gigantescos. Grandiosos gritones como guacamayos glorifican la guerra, los gladiadores, los gendarmes glaucos, los guardiacárceles, y gozan del graznido de los gansos. En grupo, los muy gandules le granizan las guindas a la gente.

Gobiernan con guardias y guaruras. Los gerentes les garpan grandes guarismos, pero golosos no gastan en guisos gremiales, no son gregarios, son grasientos granujas guardianes de la guillotina.

Moraleja

Un pasito a la izquierda
suele mejorar la vida propia y ajena.

24

Figure 4.6 | Ink on paper (Lorenzo Amengual, 2018).

themselves to different meanings in different Hispanic contexts (for instance, *gusano* can be a worm or an unpleasant person, without any political connotation), and the final product is above all loyal to the work's aesthetic mission. This aesthetic play does not negate the political underpinnings of the entry, and there is a strong argument to be made for the strengthening of a political message through its veiling. Valenzuela's affiliations, however, are obscured by the alliterations, making this form a poor carrier for mass moral teachings. If the political message is strengthened in the likening of certain characteristics with unpleasant animals, limiting of the number of readers who can understand the conclusion only serves to undermine the entry. Form trivializes the political, even for those who are able to read past the alliterated veil. The preference for the aesthetic over the prescriptive is also present at the beginning of the "*moraleja*" (or "moral"), which reads like a song lyric inciting a dance step, rather than an authority on how to live a good life.

A halfway point is reached between the playful and the serious in the "LL" entry, in which the reader receives sound yet tongue-in-cheek advice:

> Lluisa Llorent, the flame of Port Lligat, cannot find the key. Full of rain, a wound, she calls out to her lover, who does not arrive.
>
> Lluwellyn Llorent, her master, does not bring her the key.
>
> In the plain of Llobregat, the tires full, a flame on his key-chain, reading Vargas Llosa, Llinás, and *El llano en llamas*, Lluwellyn cries just to cry. Everything rains down on him.
>
> Moral: Never depend on intellectuals, no matter how close a relative they may be. (36; my translation)[21]

"LL" approximates the giving of advice, resulting in a surreal, nonsensical entry. While the reader might be tempted to understand her advice to mean something along the lines of "do not trust canons," or "not all that glitters is gold," the sole reason for these authors' presence in the entry is the sound of their names. Valenzuela's retelling of her process is significant here: "In the half-asleep state of the morning I would shuffle words that started with identical letters, based them on the names of animals, of course, and the microfables would start to take shape" (8; my translation). She offers further hints of this preference for the nonsensical with clear images of Salvador Dalí and his melting clocks, and architecture reminiscent of Port Lligat, Spain, where Dalí lived for years. As the product of pure authorial enjoyment, *ABC de las microfábulas* challenges the European canon. There are no reverent references nor paraphrasings of authoritative sources, as was once expected. There is barely a didactic or moralistic message to be passed along, a trend that, though altering through the centuries, has remained consistent in the genre. Valenzuela and Amengual's loyalty is to an aesthetic mission, a self-imposed challenge that they share with the reader, nothing more. The enthusiasm for the project spills into the glossary, where the author cannot help but continue to make fun of and have fun with the reader. *ABC de las microfábulas*, ultimately, does not seem to care whether it is read or not. It seeks to influence no one, and to change nothing. It is a playful literature for its own sake, accompanied by art that follows suit, without compromise or obligation.

CONCLUSION

Bestiario de seres fantásticos mexicanos, *Bestiario de seres prodigiosos*, and *ABC de las microfábulas* display implicit and explicit modes of subversion. This category of bestiaries challenges the European Christian tradition and deviates from the bestiary trajectory. The books aim towards new cosmogonies, canons, and aesthetic purposes, the formation of a tree with a common trunk, despite the differences between its branches.

It is worthwhile noting that these works' subversive or experimental qualities are possible only because of the relative lack of popularity of the contemporary genre. As the awareness of the bestiary has drastically fallen from its long-past status as second to the Bible, the need for the works to adhere to any one agenda has also gone by the wayside. This "fall from grace," this new, lower plane of existence for the bestiary, is a space in which, free from expectations and untethered from tradition, the genre can be reconfigured and redefined without ramifications or consequences. It allows for a democratization of the genre that in turn enriches it beyond measure, inviting authors to dream up their own beasts and idiosyncrasies, to come up with their own incentives and reasons for taking up the medieval form. The now marginalized bestiary invites other marginal texts to occupy the space once reserved for elitist purposes, redefining it and turning it into a transcendent genre.

5

BLURRING THE CONFINES OF THE GENRE

The trajectory of the bestiary from medieval to contemporary came with a gradual secularization that has shifted the meaning and judgment applied to common themes of the genre. Deceit, for instance, so rashly condemned in the original bestiaries, has metamorphized into accepting and encouraging "simulation" in contemporary works. A deceitful nature and deceitful actions, initially categorized as undesirable, came to be applied as an occasional, thought-provoking literary device, and finally became a defining characteristic of some contemporary bestiaries. This chapter traces a brief history of the concepts of simulation and dissimulation in medieval and early twentieth-century bestiaries in order to contextualize and deepen the understanding of the concepts in postmodern bestiaries: in particular, *Animalia exstinta* (2010), written by Esteban Seimandi, illustrated by Hugo Horita, and designed by Juan Cruz Bazterrica, and *Informe sobre ectoplasma animal* (2014), written by Roque Larraquy and illustrated by Diego Ontivero.

Before delving into the mechanisms of each work, we must define and contextualize the concepts central to this chapter. Simulation and dissimulation are defined by Jean Baudrillard as follows: "To dissimulate is to pretend not to have what one has. To simulate is to feign to have what one doesn't have" (1994, 3). The two terms thus recognize both processes and invite the reader to vacillate between them while reading these two works. Baudrillard further defines simulation as the generation of copies without an original, as well as this process's consequential production of the simulacrum – the imitation of a thing (1). Unlike some of the parodic bestiaries examined thus far, the ones featured in this chapter are beyond imitation, duplication, or parody, for simulation is

Figure 5.1 | Painting depicting a fox, mid-rouse, pretending to be dead atop its nest to more easily catch birds (*The Aberdeen Bestiary*, ca. 1200).

ultimately a matter of substituting the signs of the real for the real itself (2). In other words, the simulacrum is detached from the "real" and takes on its own dimensions, unrelated to previous reality. This culminates in a hyperreality, a blurring of any lines between fiction and the real – a world of signs without referents, present in the curated lives one might display on social media, product marketing, or sensationalized news. *Animalia exstinta* and *Informe sobre ectoplasma animal* signal the real yet rely on the most minimal amount of reality necessary to uphold their simulacrum, their hyperreal existence.

Figure 5.2 | Image depicting a hunter tricking a mother tiger with reflective spheres and stealing her cub (*The Aberdeen Bestiary*, ca. 1200).

Baudrillard's theories of simulation belong to a postmodern context, making them an unsuitable lens for medieval literature. The theme of deceit, however, a precursor of the simulacra, is readily found in medieval bestiary entries. During the period of the bestiary's proliferation, the doctrinal tenets of the bestiary manifested into a categorical allocation of "good" and "bad" qualities, virtues, and sins, attributed to animals. The fox of the medieval repertoire, for instance, represented deceit: a cunning beast, he was not to be trusted. When hungry, the medieval fox rolled itself in red earth to mimic blood, and then lay on the ground holding its breath, feigning death. Birds, believing the rouse, swopped down to perch upon him. Seizing the opportunity, the fox leapt up at once and devoured every last one. Even the fox's gait announces his devious nature, "for it is fleet-footed and never runs in a straight line but twists and turns."[1] The fox represents the devil, as its deceptive ways do not embody the Catholic doctrine. The image accompanying the text (figure 5.1) depicts the fox mid-hoodwink, seconds away from devouring the birds foolish enough to approach him. The fox earns its reputation through deceit and simulation. He simulates inoffensiveness; he deviates from truth much like he deviates from straight lines. He also dissimulates his intelligence and breathing to ensure his survival. His fur, red because of its disguise, strengthens the association between himself and the devil.

Although the fox exemplifies the idea of deceit as a sin, this attribution is not the only judgment imposed onto (dis)simulation. The medieval bestiary treats deceit differently depending on who carries out the deception. In the tiger entry (figure 5.2), it is not the tiger but a human who deceives. The narrative tells of a tigress who chases after a hunter who has stolen her cub. The tigress, being the fastest of all animals, can outrun the thief on his horse, forcing him to devise a distraction. The thief thus throws a glass sphere behind him, and the tigress, thinking she sees her cub in her own reflection, gives up the chase.

In this instance, a man carries out the deception, not an animal. Though the term "thief" bears an obvious negative connotation, the bestiary chastises the fox for its cunning, not the man. The language that describes the thief's plan bears no remnant of moralizing. Many bestiaries, including the *Physiologus*, present a comparable situation with the unicorn: to trap the swift creature, the hunter must resort to luring it with a virgin woman, before which the unicorn is rendered docile. In this case, also, neither virtue nor sin enters the equation: the deceit is simply part of the folklore attributed to its respective animals. The fox, tigress, and unicorn reveal medieval religious and literary authorities' attitudes on simulation and dissimulation. The negative connotations associated with the fox's incarnation of the abstract idea suggests that the pure concept of deceit belongs in the realm of evil. Once deceit is assigned to a human purpose, however, it is treated neutrally.

The evolution of the bestiary allows for nuance regarding the idea of evil-deceit, which opens the discussion to venture beyond the prevalent "deceit–truth" and "evil–good" binaries. Borges complicates truth and fiction in *Manual de zoología fantástica* and *El libro de los seres imaginarios*. He deliberately misquotes and misattributes sources. He tweaks his fictions just so, making his book an unreliable source for cultural referents. Monterroso also deceives his readers with a little-known term for "cannibal," a detail that, when discovered, turns the epilogue to *La oveja negra* on its head. Playful tricks in avant-garde and Boom bestiaries are more obvious than those in their medieval counterparts, but they remain part of a greater tradition. Each representation is but a minor feature of the larger work, rather than one of its defining characteristics.

Borges's and Monterroso's deceitful play is refined beyond mere curiosity in contemporary bestiaries. Some, unfettered by the orthodoxy of a proper suspension of disbelief, choose to (dis) simulate in their bestiaries, misleading or at least confounding the reader by simulating another genre entirely. Pioneering this trend are *Animalia exstinta* and *Informe sobre ectoplasma animal. Animalia exstinta* disguises its bestiary as a pseudo-environmental manifesto. Officially, it advocates for the conservation of animal species by showcasing the extinction of fictional animals as the direct consequence of human destruction. *Informe sobre ectoplasma animal* offers a compiled report of the apparition of different animals' ectoplasms in the cities of Buenos Aires, Argentina, and Montevideo, Uruguay. The first half of the work contains the bestiary, a series of entries unrelated except for the repetition of names and institutions. These names are explained in the second portion of the work, which reads like an epistolary novel.

Bestiaries comprising the corpus examined in chapter 5 simulate other genres, consequently blurring the divisions between fiction and nonfiction. To boost credibility, both borrow from a pseudo-scientific discourse that is obscure enough to make readers second guess their understanding of the text. Here, it is worth recalling that although unintentional, the *Physiologus* and its derivatives are commonly classified as pseudo-scientific works. Despite the confusion spurred by the works' authors and illustrators, and the break in tradition brought about by a disregard for the genre, the form persists. Thus, a casual flip through these two works provides the best way of categorizing them, as anything longer than a glance would raise too many questions. The genre of the works will thus seem to fluctuate depending on what and how much attention one pays to their various aspects.

Animalia exstinta*, by Esteban Seimandi, illustrated by Hugo Horita, and designed by Juan Cruz Bazterrica (2010)*

Animalia exstinta simulates an ecological manifesto, a documentation on lost animal species. It employs ecological discourse to lend its claims an air of moral seriousness and superiority. Ecology, its prologue states, is an important topic. The disappearance of an animal or plant species every forty minutes deeply troubles the author, as does the fact that Pekinese dogs are still bred while species like the (fictional) *vitrolitas de Corrientes* or the samurai beetle are left to perish. According to Seimandi, the work is, above all, "in truth, a task of moral and aesthetic rescue because it is immoral to privilege particular and mercantilist interests above humanity's natural heritage, but, even more so, it is antiaesthetic" (2010, 7; my translation).[2] This message appeals to the hypersensitivity that characterizes current times, and to the human desire to hide one's ignorance. Lest the reader be accused of indifference and ignorance before mother nature, they must vigorously nod along with the author's claims. As stated, the *vitrolitas de Corrientes*' extinction is a serious matter – the reader *should* feel guilt over a plausible connection between ecological loss and their pet's lifestyle. The reader's ignorance of the *vitrolitas*' existence only furthers their sense of inadequacy before the prologue's indoctrination. Of course, the reader is not familiar with the creature because it never existed. The prologue's tone causes the reader to hesitate, however – a fear of further revealing their ignorance. The reader's unfamiliarity with various animals and their destruction are at the root of the ecological disasters presented in the work. For Seimandi's project to work, the prologue needs to instill doubt, guilt, and ignorance in the reader, because they might otherwise see the work as it is: a fake, a phony, a simulation. Here, hyper-morality dissimulates an absence of morality. Seimandi's quest must be nobler than the reader's: it must be placed on a pedestal or it must not be at all. He must keep up the charade because otherwise the reader might utter, "the emperor has no clothes."

A sliver of the work's intentions is revealed when it presents the problem of extinction as a problem of aesthetics. Perhaps, the reader's guilt should not lie with their inability to prevent the disappearance of certain species. Rather, the reader should take issue with the net beauty left in the world because of the protection of certain animals (such as the short-snouted, foreign Pekingese dog) and the destruction of others (the local *vitrolita de Corrientes*). As mentioned, this moral stance crumbles once the reader realizes, after minimal research, that the latter animal never existed. The author's moral superiority derives from the same fabrication of which he accuses the Pekingese breeder: Seimandi and Horita also design boutique animals. They, perhaps, long for the same recognition as the toy dog's breeders, but because they do not have time for centuries of experimentation, they must accelerate the process. Thus, Seimandi places the creatures in the past and emphasizes humanity's role in their disappearance. He constructs a moral platform from which to preach and gambles on minimal questioning from the reader so that he might uphold the illusion. With this, the bestiary dives into its creatures.

Animalia is divided into five sections, each introduced by a brief paragraph. The first section presents birds as metaphors for human freedom and vessels for spirituality. Seimandi insists that because humans could not fly like birds, they became envious, leading to their role in the disappearance of certain bird species. Fish are next, deemed by the fictional philologist, architect, and *bon vivant* Carlos Mendes da Mosqueira to be psychic creatures because they swim in the depths of the subconscious. Insects are the third group, distinguished by their ability for survival despite humans' creation of atomic bombs and insecticides. The author points out that these insects do not always survive human-made massacres, as was the case for the (again, fictional) *escarabajo serengeti*. The fourth category consists of reptiles and amphibians, condemned in the book of Genesis. Seimandi states that although crawling might suggest a submissive, humiliating existence, reptiles once dominated the Earth and are the closest link to Jurassic prehistory. Finally, the reader encounters mammals, the last class to emerge on the Earth. Seimandi laments that boasting the biggest brains and hearts has not deterred humans from causing destruction. In the book, scientific names accompany their respective beasts and, along with the prologue and subsection introductions, serve to feed the reader a curated reality. In most cases, the terminology forgoes Latin in favour of English, in recognition of the lingua franca of contemporary society. Examples include creatures like the "Patito feo" ("ugly duckling," listed in pseudo-Latin as *cairina uglys*) and the "Cocodrilo somnífero" ("Somniferous crocodile," *Crocodylus valiumae*). The shift from a classical language to a modern one winks at the overall playfulness at work.

Under the first category, the reader finally encounters the *vitrolita de Corrientes* (figure 5.3). The *vitrolita*, a type of toucan boasting brown and gold feathers, is native to Corrientes, a province in the north-east of Argentina. Its beak functioned much like a funnel, trapping flying insects, and its song was hoarse and choppy and could be heard kilometres away. Locals hunted them for use as speakers, which, along with the steady cutting down of trees in their habitat, led to their extinction in 1969 (Seimandi 2010, 11).

The entry invites different possible interpretations. The reader can either engage with the text's surface meaning, with its

Figure 5.3 | The *vitrolita de Corrientes*, a fictional extinct bird, boasts a gramophone for a beak (Hugo Horita, 2010).

intentions to exist as a reality constructed via simulacrum (a surface reading), or they can engage with its unexpressed truths (a symptomatic reading). A brief digression is necessary to discuss the surface/symptomatic dichotomy, as the former concept is often overlooked in literary criticism. With a symptomatic reading, meaning is understood to be hidden and repressed, and in need of analysis and disclosure by an interpreter (Best and Marcus 2009, 1). It speaks to the oppositions of present/absent, manifest/ latent, and surface/depth (4). As seen with the allegorical beasts of the medieval bestiary, a symptomatic reading boasts a long tradition. Fredric Jameson, an advocate of symptomatic reading, depicts the literary critic as an author, able to extract or provide meaning, and rewriting a text according to an interpretive master code (1981, 9–10). This method of reading and interpreting complicates the role of the critic – now a critic-as-author – making them responsible for infusing meaning where there is none and extracting significance when the text proves hermetic, always running the risk of altogether altering the work.

Surface reading, as the name suggests, does not seek to penetrate the depth of a text. In a 2009 special issue of the journal *Representations* dedicated to surface reading, editors Stephen Best and Sharon Marcus define the surface as what is evident in a text, not hiding – replacing thickness or depth with length and breadth (9). Because this "depthlessness" demands to be looked at, rather than looked through, inviting a "shallow" analysis, surface reading is often stigmatized or dismissed as a weak methodology. Furthering the challenge issued at those who employ the methodology, Anne Anlin Cheng proposes that both the "philosophic history that perceives the visual as deceptive [and] an epistemological history that thrives on a hermeneutics of suspicion," both of which characterize contemporary critical practices, must be overcome in order to read the surface as something beyond a mere covering (2009, 99). Because bestiaries are so replete with tradition and meaning, surface reading allows for appreciation without suffocation. An open, unassuming approach often reveals more than would trapping the animals in various frameworks.

This work cedes to different beasts' interpellations by alternating between symptomatic and surface reading. Though the methodologies can and have overlapped, the (dis)simulating qualities of these works require that the next few examples make explicit what has thus far been tacit. Whether (dis)simulation succeeds or fails – both in these readings and in general – is dependent on the reader's interaction with the material. While not passive, surface reading spreads itself over the surface of a text, as if across a flat plane. It does not wrestle meaning from a source, making it a more suitable candidate for the alternate reality created by (dis) simulation. A symptomatic reading, on the other hand, will break the spell of (dis)simulation and reveal the workings of its mechanism. The following examinations thus interpret the *vitrolita* with both approaches, inviting those approaching the text to play the role of both reader and critic.

Let us first cling to the *vitrolita*'s gold and brown feathers, and not ruffle them in hopes of Oedipal confessions. Let us take the text at (sur)face value – as simulation. Seimandi tells a tragic story in few words, conveying reckless human behaviour. Because of direct human action and indirect neglect, the *vitrolita* is now extinct, and Corrientes, a Mesopotamic paradise infused with pastoral subtext, is deprived of a characteristic creature. Seimandi's use of the word "*ostentar*" (flaunt, boast) raises the stakes of the *vitrolita*'s loss, as Seimandi presents flora and fauna as being central to what makes Corrientes valuable. Recalling the aesthetic mission as stated in the prologue, the reader is reminded of the significance of the beautiful *vitrolita*'s extinction. No part of the text suggests deceit, and aside from an unusual number of poetic flourishes, it reads as an encyclopedic entry. The text betrays no hint of being fictitious, nor misleading. Though surface reading certainly does not require that the reader take fiction as reality, the content and form of the *vitrolita*'s description demands a fidelity to the text – rather than a suspension of disbelief. There are no unbelievable occurrences, as animals being used for human purposes and the destruction of habitats are, unfortunately, all too common. Choosing to remain on the surface is therefore choosing to read *Animalia exstinta* as nothing more than a catalogue of exquisite, extinct beasts.

The use of conjugation in the entry reinforces the entry's various temporal aspects. All information regarding the province of Corrientes is written in the simple present, an ambiguous tense that in this case spans both present and past. Like in English, the present, when not inflected with the gerund (-ing), can refer to past, present, future, or habitual actions. Present tense is thus used to indicate that Corrientes was, is, and continues to be, despite the changes its landscape may suffer under human influence. The imperfect, undefined tense of past events is used to describe the *vitrolita* exclusively. A sole use of the preterit tense appears in the entry, reserved here to emphasize the *vitrolita*'s 1969 disappearance. The perfect tense signals finality, denying the reader any hope of ever encountering the beautiful, bizarre bird.

The presence of the diminutive morpheme (-ita) and its effect on the reader also demand reflection. The Argentine dialect is less prone to the use of the diminutive than Colombian, Mexican, or Puerto Rican dialects, making its use an interesting choice. The *vitrolita* is described as a variety of toucan, with a beak of an unusual size – likely meaning large – so the reader can infer that the use of the diminutive is not because of the bird's stature. Discarding linguistic idiosyncrasy and physical description, then, and once again acknowledging the verb "*ostentar*," the *vitrolita*'s diminutive suffix must be born out of a familiarity, a protective feeling, or even an affection for the birds by locals. The use of "-ita" is a form of manipulation that endears us to an unknown bird, promoting Seimandi and Horita's pseudo-environmental cause.

As warned in the prologue of the work, a surface reading plays along with a simulation of morality and a dissimulation of aesthetic interests. The symptomatic reading finds a departure point in the entry's epigraph: "Sing with me this chamamé / sing loudly my friend / the accordion sounds like piporé / and the *vitrolita* will accompany you" (Seimandi 2010, 11).[3] These four lines, quoted from a *chamamé* song "La vitrolita" by Isaco Fillol, deceive the naïve reader and wink at the informed one, as neither song nor singer ever existed. In fact, the only truth in the reference lies in its paratextual footnote, in which the author explains that *chamamé* is a musical genre belonging to the northern provinces of Argentina, similar to polka.

A surface reading requires a naïve reader, or at the very least a reader willing to play along. It requires a reader unfamiliar with birds, wildlife status, provincial regions of Argentina, *chamamé*, and, as will be seen in the following analysis, commercial gramophone brands. The work depends on both readers – "naïve" and "informed" here bare no negative connotations. An informed reader – in this instance one familiar with cultural referents from early to mid-twentieth century Argentina – will encounter a different book than a reader from another country or generation. To succeed in its multifaceted goal, *Animalia exstinta* must suspend its material between the reader who will believe the (dis)simulation and the reader who will understand the elements at play.

The "informed" and symptomatic interpretation departs from a nostalgic and humorous reimagining of an obsolete object, a common thread in the entries of this work. As foreshadowed by the *chamamé* lines, the name *vitrolita* is reminiscent of the Victrola brand of gramophones.[4] This connection is furthered by the *vitrolita*'s scientific name, "*Ramphastos victor*," which alludes to its kinship with both the toucan (also of the genus *Ramphastos*) and the gramophone company, and the fact that *vitrolita*'s beaks were supposedly used as hearing aids. Victrola gramophones came on the market in 1906, produced by the Victor Company, and were the first successful mass-marketed phonographs (Coleman 2003, xix–xx). The *vitrolita*'s brown and gold plumage matches the colours of the phonograph, as the company's premium models featured fine woods and gold trim. The allusion to the Victrola brand is consistent with Seimandi's quest for aesthetics: the Victrola was the first of its kind to hide its turntable and amplifying horn (its machinery) in favour of aesthetic beauty. The most expensive models, for instance, were designed to "harmonize with beautiful furniture," made by placing the horn in fine wood cabinets from the Pooley Furniture Company of Philadelphia (Barnum 1994, 40).

This first (dis)simulating bestiary thus opens with a creature inspired by one of the earliest simulation machines brought into the home. Musicians recorded on gramophone discs by playing into horns that would channel sound into a diaphragm. The diaphragm transferred sound vibrations into a needle that inscribed the sound into a record topped with a layer of wax. The record was treated to fix the recording, and the reverse process ensured playback (David, n.d.). Although simulation is, according to Baudrillard, a characteristic of postmodernity, the modern gramophone demonstrates an early process of the disappearance of reality, thus foreshadowing the second half of the twentieth century. The description from the machine's manual, "Reproduction, perfect in every detail, is made at will through the medium of the needle, the sound box and the amplifier," recalls Baudrillard's statement on simulacrum, which he deems "Not unreal ... but exchanged for itself, in an uninterrupted circuit without reference or circumference" (1994, 6). Victrola records offered copies of an original encased in permanent repetition, or, in the words of Walter Benjamin, a technical reproduction that "enables the original to meet the beholder halfway, be it in the form of a photograph or a phonograph record. The cathedral leaves its locale to be received in the studio of a lover of art; the choral production, performed in an auditorium or in the open air, resounds in the drawing room" (2019, 221). Although the sound of a phonograph recording pales in comparison with contemporary technology and destroys the authenticity of the piece (220), its advent represented an undeniable democratization of a privilege denied to many. The phonograph reproduced the voice of the opera singer or the orchestra and served as a warning that reality is merely that which can be simulated and copied. It could be reset, replayed, and rewound, its volume turned up or down; it was not the opera but better, as its referents were liquidated and Baudrillard's uninterrupted circuit was created.

A 1915 *Literary Digest* ad featuring Enrico Caruso, Italian operatic tenor and the first voice to be recorded for the commercial purposes of the Victor Company, underlined the impending blurring of reality (Barnum 1994, 79). The ad displays an image of the recorded disc next to an image of Caruso and reads: "Both are Caruso," and yet, neither of the images is Caruso himself. The ad's guarantee, "It actually *is* Caruso – his own magnificent voice, with all the wonderful power and beauty of tone that make him the greatest of all tenors," caters to the hyperreality that Baudrillard ascribes to postmodernity. Not only does the disc claim to be the real Caruso; it also claims that Caruso is the greatest of all tenors, multiplying the incredibleness of the reproduction, making the opera no match for a wax disc. Although the two different readings – *vitrolita* as reality and *vitrolita* as simulation – can remain parallel, indifferent to each other, their overlap is an intriguing possibility. The surreal image to the *vitrolita* entry functions as a weld, attaching fiction and reality, sustaining or prohibiting the reader's belief in Seimandi's words.

To better understand the role of images in a surface reading of the work, it is helpful to return to the concept of the simulacrum. Baudrillard presents Disneyland as the ultimate simulacrum, a place that exists with the purpose of making one believe that the surrounding display is a real America (1994, 12). Disneyland, with its miniature countries, promise of magic, and endless fun, is hyperreal in that it proposes to be better than any real place. It is neither a real nor a fake place, but a "deterrence machine that rejuvenates the fictions of the real in other camps" (13). Like Baudrillard's Disneyland, the images in *Animalia exstinta* disguise the simulacrum taking place in the text. The images – impossible when compared to the tone of the text and its introductory claims – are surely loose interpretations of the description of the animal. This simulation depends on the perceived relationship between text and image. The reader can consider the images to be deterrents to reality only if the reader assumes an *a priori*, traditional hierarchy of text over image in an illustrated text. *Animalia exstinta* relies on being perceived as an illustrated text, on the supporting qualities of image in relation to word, and not as a collection of annotated images. In other words, it needs the reader to assume that the illustrator took inspiration and ran with the words of the writer, not the other way around. The relationship of "Disneyland > America," in which Disneyland is more fantastic and thus lends credibility to America, finds a parallel in *Animalia exstinta* with the understanding of "Images > Text." In this case, a symptomatic reading of the disconnect between the text's tone and the image's surrealist depiction could encourage the reader to remain on the surface of the text.

Paradoxically, if the reader wishes to delve deeper into latent elements of the text, they must look to the surface of the image as well. Aside from the suggestive colouring of the *vitrolita*, the illustration of the bird shows a fusion between the biological and the mechanical. This aesthetic choice is that of steampunk, a subgenre of science fiction that serves as a main aesthetic and philosophical influence in *Animalia exstinta*, as both point to an intricate relationship between humans and technology. Steampunk artists tinker with contemporary objects to make them simulate Victorian machinery. Steampunks call for "cross pollination between historical times, materials and markers" (Forlini 2010, 77). Through these methods and practices, they look to challenge current design trends and to call into question the value of things (72–3). Rebecca Onion calls steampunk a "creative anachronism," further specifying: "Steampunk, in some sense, stands outside of chronological periodisations of modes of thought – such as 'modern,' 'anti-modern,' or 'postmodern' – and defies categorisation within the ideologies of previous technology-based social movements" (2008, 142). Seimandi echoed this sentiment in an interview, stating that what defines the current zeitgeist is a constant remixing and a preference for never working on a blank canvas (2017). This treatment of time and referents is evident in *Animalia exstinta*'s postmodern blend of modern elements: the gramophone, a modern object, becomes subject to postmodern criticism through the repurposing of its parts. Initially foreshadowing the simulations to come during the latter half of the twentieth century, the gramophone becomes a new entity altogether when remixed with a bird and placed in a medieval form in a contemporary context.

The creation of a mythology from the visual is also common to both steampunk art and *Animalia exstinta*. Steampunk art prioritizes aesthetics over function, as a piece need not function particularly well, but instead must be skilfully put together. The manifesto for a 2008 steampunk show held in Seattle claimed that its artists were uniting nostalgia with design and technology, imagining a past capable of overriding the future, creating "a dazzling future-perfect" (Doctorow 2008). In this creation exists the potential for a strange simulation that seeks not only to act as reality, but also to do so via incorporating a past that never occurred. The notion of a "future-perfect," a "would be" that is firmly rooted in a parallel past, also inspires *Animalia exstinta*'s entries, as evident in that which drives the works' aesthetic: a merging of past technologies with believable creatures. Although acquiescing to a vertical hierarchy of text over image has been entertained in previous bestiaries, this is not the case with Seimandi's project. Horita's images were the departure point for Seimandi's mythologies, making *Animalia exstinta* a collection of annotated images after all (Seimandi and Bazterrica 2016). Seimandi's texts, based on images, mean that his prioritizing of beauty is greater than that to reality or morality, recalling the steampunk aesthetic and philosophical influences that make for anachronistic, symptomatic readings.

Aside from reaffirming the aesthetic mission of the bestiary, Seimandi's confession that the prose is based on images also challenges the examination of the text thus far. The aforementioned simulation in *Animalia exstinta* relies on an inherent hierarchy of text above image. W.J.T. Mitchell proposes in *Picture Theory* that one must remove the slash to turn "image/text" into "imagetext" in order to rightfully describe the phenomena between the two arts: "Imagetext ... designates a composite, synthetic works (or concepts) that combine image and text" (1994, 89). And yet this analysis does not work when contemplating *Animalia exstinta*. Although there is no question that the entries are comprised of this composite, this unity is veiled, and the playful, simulating characteristics of the work thrive. Because Seimandi and Horita neglect to inform the reader of the process behind the bestiary, the reader understands their bestiary as a traditional, illustrated text.

While the *vitrolita de Corrientes* hints at a nostalgia better suited to a universal collective unconscious, the *trucha Mascardi* (Mascardi trout) (figure 5.4) hones the feeling of nostalgia for a specific audience,[5] invoking a particular audience and inversely amplifying the affective nature of its interpretation.

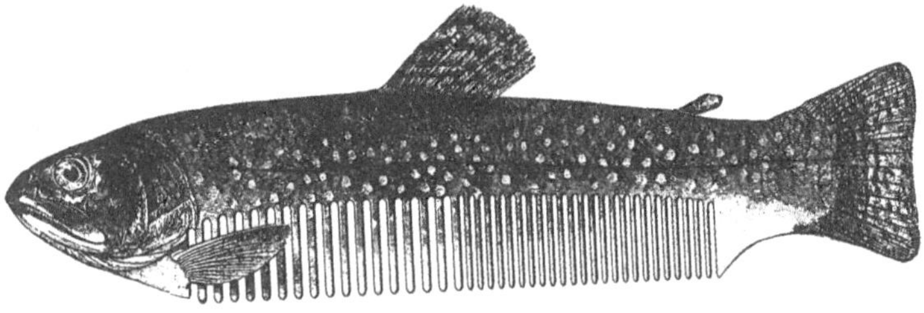

Figure 5.4 | The *trucha Mascardi*, a fictional extinct trout, had comb teeth for gills (Hugo Horita, 2010).

According to *Animalia exstinta*, the *trucha Mascardi*, autochtonous to the lakes of Patagonia, was discovered in 1945 by Alfredo Mascardi Combs. Mascardi Combs described the ventral fin of the fish as a comb, confusing it for a defence mechanism. In 1964, after being overfished by sport fishermen, the *trucha* was deemed a protected species. It was during the annual dinner of the Patagonian Foundation for Aquatic Fauna, however, after members ate the last specimens, that the species was declared extinct (Seimandi 2010, 29).

The *trucha* is a more likely creature to prompt the "informed" reader's nostalgia, as it is the namesake of three separate yet interrelated Argentine entities. Lake Mascardi, located in the Nahuel Huapi National Park in the Argentine province of Río Negro, is the first referent, as the author informs that the trout is autochthonous to the Patagonia region. The lake is a popular destination for sport fishing; it is easily navigated and contains a large variety of trout. Lake Mascardi is, in turn, named after the Italian Jesuit Nicolás Mascardi, who established his mission near Lake Nahuel Huapi in the second half of the seventeenth century. Like Alfredo Mascardi Combs, Nicolás Mascardi moved from Chile to Argentina, where he was martyred in 1673 by the Indigenous populations he sought to convert (Biedma 1986, 281). Finally, the Mascardi firm is among the largest plastic manufacturers in Argentina, specializing in household products, including hair combs. Founded in 1975 in the city of Ezeiza, Buenos Aires, the Mascardi brand is commonplace in Argentine life.

The nostalgia for a creature that never existed, and the cultural referents it evokes, owes its persuasiveness to the simulacrum at play in the entry. Baudrillard identifies the final phase of the simulating image as having no relation to any reality whatsoever and as being self-encompassing as its own pure simulacrum (1994, 6). The consequence of this final detachment gives way to a multiplicity of imagined past referents:

> When the real is no longer what it was, nostalgia assumes its full meaning. There is a plethora of myths of origin and of signs of reality – a plethora of truth, of secondary objectivity, and authenticity. Escalation of the true, of lived experience, resurrection of the figurative where the object and substance have disappeared. Panic-stricken production of the real and of the referential, parallel to and greater than the panic of material production: this is how simulation appears in the phase that concerns us – a strategy of the real, of the neoreal and the hyperreal that everywhere is the double of a strategy of deterrence. (6–7)

Considering this, a question emerges: In the case of the *trucha*, from what disenfranchised reality is this nostalgia feeding? As will be examined shortly, the referents of the Mascardi trout no longer hold warm connotations. Because this reality is not what it was, the *trucha Mascardi* provokes nostalgia by offering a parallel origin story to that held in the memories of many Argentines. Simulation need not have a genuine original from which to reproduce itself and can thus morph, amassing memories, offering more poignant ruminations than any one thought could ever have.

Animalia exstinta's presentation of fish foreshadowed their ability to swim in the subconscious; the *trucha* relishes in the deconstruction and reassignment of nostalgia. The undoing of reality may be the mere realization that the companies present during one's childhood are, after all, simply companies. Despite being one of three leading Argentine plastic manufacturers, the fall of the internal market and an increase in imports in 2016 caused Mascardi sales to drop by 60 per cent that year, significantly more than the sector's average. Consequently, Roberto Reid, founder and owner of the company, dismissed 43 of 130 workers. The decision led to a strike by the remaining workers. Reid claimed that his intention was to continue producing, and downsizing was a necessary step (Ensinck 2017). The articles that covered this story in 2016 were read by Argentine citizens who might have grown up in the 1970s, 1980s, or 1990s. The adult, confronted with this story, might then find that the same comb their mother used to ready them for school no longer holds the magic it once did. Now, it belongs to the same complex capitalist dynamics as the rest of their complicated, adult lives.

A similar process unfolds with the lake linked to the trout. Lake Mascardi is both a national and an international tourist destination. Like with the Mascardi comb, it holds positive connotations for those who have vacationed there: rest, relaxation, time spent with family, proximity to nature, and outdoor activities. The nostalgia attached to an uncomplicated time is heightened by the shattering of its idyllic reality: today, Lake Mascardi has become one of the stages on which Indigenous Mapuche resistance has been taking place in recent years. In November of 2017, the Mapuche of lof Lafken Winkul Mapu announced that they had reclaimed territory in Nahuel Huapi National Park. This prompted a negotiation between the national government and the Mapuche community, which resulted in the decision to peacefully displace the Mapuche community to another territory, outside the park (Dinatale 2017). Despite this agreement, the displacement was violently carried out by three hundred federal agents of the Agrupación Albatros, a unit of special security forces belonging to the Argentine Navy Prefecture. According to a Mapuche woman who described the operation, gunshots were heard around 4:30 a.m., and government forces shot indiscriminately and threw tear gas at children ("El testimonio" 2017). Rafael Nahuel, a twenty-two-year-old Mapuche man, was shot and killed by the armed soldiers. However, the official discourse has made both sides of the battle seem evenly matched, and served to discredit Mapuche witnesses ("El gobierno defendió" 2017). Ramón Chiocconi, doctor to the wounded protesters, came forward, claiming that only those on the Mapuche side had suffered wounds and a death ("Habló el médico" 2017). Despite the death of an unarmed man, Minister of Security Patricia Bullrich insisted that the government forces had taken legal, legitimate action ("El gobierno defendió" 2017).

The unjust murder of Rafael Nahuel sparked mass protests. Workers at the national park, who were among the enraged protestors, pointed to the relationship between environmental preservation, biodiversity, respect for all human life, and an acknowledgment of the dark history of Argentina's beautiful national parks: "'When these same territories turn into a stage on which the fundamental rights of people are violated, their purpose is delegitimized,' they stated, adding, 'There is no possible conservation of biodiversity on territories irrigated with blood'" ("Trabajadores de parques nacionales" 2016; my translation). The statement by the Nahuel Huapi workers recalls the paradoxical consumption in *Animalia exstinta* of the last samples of the *trucha* by the Patagonian Aquatic Fauna Foundation, while questioning the history of the parks themselves, reminding those who stand against the Mapuches that the qualifier "national" is only the result of usurpation and genocide. This connects to the final "original" referent, Nicolás Mascardi himself. Because enough time has passed between his attempt in the seventeenth century to annihilate the same Mapuches who today protest at Lake Mascardi – or at the very least, their customs, faith, culture, and way of life – this referent is the weakest, and not coincidentally, the least evident in the entry.

The events and reactions I have described, particularly the murder of Rafael Nahuel and Nicolás Mascardi's mission, exemplify the opposite realities that can occupy a physical or figurative space, complicating single-faceted imaginings of the Lake as something exclusively positive. All three referents of the *trucha Mascardi* are, either by the maturing of a person or of a society, complicated by the permeating of reality into nostalgia. The once paradisiac understanding or reality of Lake Mascardi is now implicated with the crimes and inhumanities that have recently taken place, simultaneously recalling the crimes and inhumanities of a less recent past. This poses the question: Why does the simulation of the *trucha Mascardi* become an attractive vessel for nostalgia? To think of Lake Mascardi as a purely nostalgic place would be an "[e]scalation of the true, of lived experience, resurrection of the figurative where the object and substance have disappeared" (Baudrillard 1994, 7), where true, lived experience can be understood as subjective truth, personal lived experience, or individual memories, all leading to a resurrection of the non-literal, the non-real. In other words, a fully nostalgic outlook on Lake Mascardi based on personal enjoyment and memories would mean disregarding the experience of Indigenous peoples and sanctioning the unjustifiable death of a young man. The appeal of the *trucha Mascardi* thus becomes clear: it is a target to which different origins and myths can be attributed, once the reality of Mascardi-related referents can no longer be what they once were, unless one makes a valiant effort in cognitive dissonance. It allows a reader who is familiar with all the referents to indulge in nostalgic ruminations, a non-existent hyperreality that is not complicated by historical tragedies.

To readily offer up the trout's nostalgic, deterrent charms, Seimandi and Horita once again depend on the reader's assumption that the image is a loose interpretation of the text. Seimandi's paratext in this entry also reveals an increasing comfort with deceit as the bestiary progresses. Whereas the *vitrolita*'s *chamamé* footnote had some footing in reality, here the sources serve only pseudo-academic purposes: "Alfredo Mascardi Combs, Notes on the Thorn-Bellied Patagonian Trout, Santiago de Chile, Científica Cogno-Cimientos Editorial, 1947, p. 23" (Seimandi 2010, 29; my translation).[6] The footnote is confidently deceitful, and as the entries progress, this phenomenon becomes common practice. Seimandi's footnote points to the strengthening of the simulation throughout *Animalia exstinta*, as the entries detach from reality altogether, as if certain that the reader will not verify its content.

As a final reflection on the bestiary's aesthetic mission, we must acknowledge the form of the entry. Seimandi's stunning description of the movement of the fish school mirrors that of a comb moving through hair. The *trucha*'s innately uniform swimming leaves satisfyingly straight trailings in its wake. Unlike the medieval fox that fails to hide its deceitful nature in its crooked walk, the *trucha*, pure simulacrum, glides effortlessly through the waters of a new era. The *trucha* schools swim in perfect formations, even through whirlpools. Although the literal Spanish–English translation of "*remolino*" is "whirlpool," the word is also used to describe unruly locks of hair, much like a cowlick. That these trout can comb through whirlpools tells of their ability to smooth knotty memories and reattribute them to themselves, where they will prove less problematic. Seimandi paints the fish in readers' minds, inviting them to imagine the crisp white line of a scalp revealed by a comb moving through wet hair: a beautiful promise of nostalgia protected.

Through a blend of object and animal, the simulation of environmental documentation, and a moralistic tone, *Animalia exstinta* dissimulates its place in the evolution of the bestiary. The work and its mix of fiction and reality rely on two different readers to come alive: a reader to believe its simulation and a reader to appreciate the simulacrum. The hyperreality that *Animalia exstinta* creates allows for a rewiring of the feelings of nostalgia, removing the problematic aspects of certain referents and allowing subjective personal experience to override objectivity. The disconnect of referent and nostalgia from reality adds to the work's appeal for those who have come to realize that a nostalgia based on reality can mean pain and injustice for another entity or group of beings. The innovation of the bestiary hinges on assumed hierarchies between text and image, an assumption that Seimandi and Horita exploit and put to work in service of the simulacrum.

Informe sobre ectoplasma animal, *by Roque Larraquy, illustrated by Diego Ontivero (2014)*

Informe sobre ectoplasma animal is a bestiary comprised of reports on the materiality of dead animals, followed and contextualized by a short narrative. It is relayed by documentation and letters from the father of ectography, Severo Solpe – a fictional character created by Larraquy. Through his writings and reflections, the reader learns that the birth of ectoplasm photography is as deceitful as the bestiary itself. Severo Solpe was an event photographer, hired to stage the first "ectoplasmic photograph," or "ectograph," by a senator wishing to use the image as a party trick. Solpe hung a sedated monkey from the ceiling to achieve the illusion of a creature in a state of religious ecstasy. The senator loved it. Because of the trick's success, Solpe continued taking similar pictures, until an accident caused his camera to fall and capture the image of a real spectral duck or goose in Buenos Aires' Parque Centenario. Inspired by this event, Solpe founded the Sociedad Ectográfica Argentina (SEA), which eventually hired Julio Heiss and Martín Rubens, two ectographists who weave in and out of the bestiary's text. Ectoplasmic remains of animals comprise the entries.

To avoid confusion due to unfamiliar terminology, I will here summarize three important definitions of the pseudoscience, as explained by *Informe*'s main investigator, Solpe. There is the *spectre*, a sort of material residue left behind by an animal: salivations, smells, differently sized prints of its body as it grows, etc. From this spectre, *ectoplasm* can be distilled with the electric aid of the ectographist's body. The result is an *ectograph*, an image that holds something of the dead animal and the live ectographist, who willingly gave up something of themselves to create the image (Larraquy and Ontivero 2014, 49). The ectographist must stand on a slab of cesium to provide the necessary electricity that renders the ectoplasm an ectograph (Larraquy 2014, 11).

Unlike *Animalia exstinta*, which describes extinct animals, *Informe* focuses on the apparitions of various animals' postmortem spectra as they surge into the cities of Montevideo and Buenos Aires. For instance, the entry titled "Federico, Buenos Aires, 1949" describes a family who finds the entry to their home obstructed. They believe it to be Federico, the beloved family dog who died at the threshold in 1948. The ectographists lure it with meat, and Federico appears, glowing at two to five watts. Several attempts to move the dog fail, and the obstruction is resolved by building a step over the apparition (9).

Even more so than in *Animalia exstinta*, *Informe* employs a rigorous tone and language for the sake of unadorned communication. On the surface, "Federico, Buenos Aires, 1949" borrows from scientific reports and reads like the product of a scientific investigation. The reader is presented with all necessary aspects of scientific literature: introduction (contextualization of the problem of a dog's death and its ectoplasm blocking the stoop), materials and methodology (baiting Federico with medium-rare bovine meat; measuring the glow of his ectoplasm in watts), discussion (commenting on the animal's love of meat), and conclusion (the acceptance that the ectoplasm will not leave of its own volition; the construction of steps to avoid the obstacle that Federico poses). The entry even offers a dismissal of spiritual and religious practice, noting the ineffectiveness of prayers and matches. The undermining of the spiritual and religious draws a line in murky territory: lighting matches and prayers are for old wives and the superstitious, the uneducated. Federico's ectoplasm, however, belongs to the serious field of science, with the investigation carried out by a White, male Argentine of German descent.

The above interpretation of "Federico, Buenos Aires, 1949" highlights one of many surfaces in *Informe*. Although it is counterintuitive to layer surfaces and claim that there is no depth, one can mentally place the following elements beside each other, expanding the text in surface area but not in volume. First, there is the already examined surface of the entry and its pseudo-scientific rhetoric, the simulation to be believed if one does not question the authoritative, succinct tone of the text. Then, there is the spectre of Federico, an entity that Solpe later describes as made up entirely of surface: "Ghosts are pure visible surface. The simultaneous transparency of all their secrets. What they dreamt of in their sleeping state, the proportions and weight of their gaze; all is there like a phosphoric weaving in their ether skin that can be recorded" (Larraquy 2014, 55; my translation).[7] This innocent surface contrasts starkly with Baudrillard's superficial hyperreality. Hyperreality, the element of simulation that confuses the real and imaginary, flattening any depth, comes to be significant the moment that a spectre becomes reproducible. While Baudrillard's simulation creates a flat hyperreality based on automatized deceit, and while Larraquy's spectra are transparent by and in nature, there is a juncture between the two surfaces. The moment that transparent, innocent spectra become reproducible, a surface starts to translate into superficiality. A precarious, potentially non-existent real (spectre) is copied, landing in the domain of (dis)simulation. The indifference of Federico before his own superficiality reinforces the process of simulation taking place, in the entry and in the work itself. In light of this, the spectre's transparency and passivity can be compared to one of the most recognizable, unidimensional elements of simulating postmodernity: pop art. Baudrillard presents Andy Warhol's art as the elevation of image to pure figuration, void of transcendence and signification, and completely artificial (Baudrillard 2008, 78). This art offers total transparency, it is a superficial, artificial object free from signification. This void of meaning, a fetish, simultaneously has no value and has absolute value, living off the ecstasy of value (77).

Indeed, the transparency of Federico and its kin is enigmatic. There exists the obvious enigma of a transparent animal in spiritual limbo. There is also the metaphorical transparency of an idle entity that refuses to be enticed, that is and is not, that obstructs with its passivity. Much like with Warhol's images, spectra are at once insignificant in their (lack of) materiality and substance, and, through this precise insignificance, made to be of absolute value, as their emptiness is cause for a fascination that culminates in the creation of an entire discipline. Both pop art and spectra no longer hold desires but rather are pure image, pure artificiality that must be taken at face value. This notion is furthered not only by the content of the images in *Informe*, but also by the fact that the images accompanying the report act independently from their text, as is the case with "Federico, Buenos Aires, 1949" (figure 5.5). The authors of *Informe* intended little correlation between text and image, something that was achieved with varying degrees of

Figure 5.5 | Image depicting Federico, a family dog, whose spectral remains block the entrance to its former home (Diego Ontivero, 2014).

success. In an interview, Larraquy and Ontivero revealed that the project was initially based on pictures of animals, and they decided to keep image and text as separate as possible. "Federico, Buenos Aires, 1949" involves one of the more explicit links, an exception in the overall work.

All the images in the book are characterized by a geometric abstraction influenced by Ontivero's background in graphic design. This contemporary vector art creates a separation between prose and illustration – a break as opposed to a relationship. Ontivero reveals that he sought to remove temporality from the aesthetic equation, since temporality would have contradicted the dates seen in the work (the first decades of the twentieth century and the 1950s). The only remnant of the temporal context of the text is what Ontivero defined as "library map colour" (Rodríguez Gimeno 2015): desaturated colours that hint at archived paper. This disjuncture between colour and form favours function above beauty. It reinforces the link between *Informe*'s spectra and pop art, in turn solidifying the superficiality common to the elements and the era of simulation. Although Ontivero's art is not strictly defined as pop art, its sense of superficial absolute value and use of colour can certainly be traced to the movement. In fact, if the work replaced the image in "Federico, Buenos Aires, 1949" with Warhol's *Portrait of Maurice* (the painting itself being a copy of a copy), the entry would not change much. Although Warhol's *Portrait of Maurice* would make a more explicit counterpart to "Federico, Buenos Aires, 1949," the complete entry would not lose its essence. *Portrait of Maurice* depicts a spectral dog, its colours similarly desaturated and its gaze, though more alert, just as impenetrable as Federico's meditative state. Neither image will reveal social or romantic truths if further examined; both further the simulacrum and remain superficial.

One way of approaching the text in order to further the dissection of simulating mechanisms involves the flat triangulation of discipline-observer-observed. Baudrillard chooses ethnology as a discipline through which a paradox that is applicable to the ongoings in "Federico, Buenos Aires, 1949" can be identified. The object of ethnology must die, according to Baudrillard, for the discipline to live. Through its death, the object avenges the act of being discovered, in turn defying the science that wishes to understand it (1994, 7). By leaving behind a mere copy of a former self for study, the animals' spectra take revenge on Solpe and his ectographists. On 9 April 1914, we read, Solpe ruminated on the physical origins of spectra: "A dead animal's inscription in the ether, which can be measured by its brightness in watts, is a result of the animal's recurring habits during its lifetime as well as of intense physical suffering. Habit and pain form the gramophone stylus that records

Figure 5.6 | Image showing a glimpse of the duck haunting the Richmond Café (Diego Ontivero, 2014).

the trace of sound for its later reproduction" (Larraquy 2014, 51; my translation).[8] The reader thus encounters a simulation comprising the study of a (literally) unreal object by a (literally) unreal discipline. All that the ectographists are left with are formulaic repetitions, repetitions incapable of change and bound to carry on in death as indiscriminately as they did in life.

Curiously, Solpe's theory for the origin of spectra makes reference to the function of the gramophone. Whereas in *Animalia exstinta* the device was presented as a triumph of modernity and a democratizer of the arts, here it stands as a metaphor for the reproduction of pain and the mundane. What now dents the wax disc is not the "real" Caruso's voice, but that which is worn, heavy, and tired. Simulation requires reproduction without a real or live original. Still, painful habits and the nostalgia brought on by poignant memories, death, and obsolete technology make the spectre an unlikely confidant, encouraging the reader to stay immersed in the (dis)simulation if only a little longer.

Informe dissimulates its ties to the bestiary by assuming a no-nonsense tone anchored in the (pseudo)scientific. This tone, which is an indispensable accomplice in the simulacrum that is the bestiary, can also be found in the entry "Confitería Richmond Buenos Aires, 1952" (Richmond Café, Buenos Aires, 1952), in which a voyeuristic, spectral duck (figure 5.6) plays panopticon, to the detriment of the Confitería Richmond's reputation and to a customer's vision (Larraquy 2014, 13).

The dry tone with which ridiculous occurrences are described does more than incite laughter. Ectographists exemplify a desensitization before reality, the stagnant feeling that draws people towards the hyperreal, a more real than real, that might conjure up certain desired feelings. Due to the lack of fear and mystery brought on by their daily contact with the dead, ectography professionals are prone to a condition called "cesium syndrome." In the *Nomenclador*, an eclectic encyclopedia mentioned in *Informe* that encompasses all ectographic knowledge, the condition is compared to that of a deaf person walking through crossfire, dependent on reading the fear in the eyes of others to keep themselves safe. The entry "Cuadro o síndrome del cesio, Buenos Aires, 1951" (Cesium Syndrome, Buenos Aires, 1951) recalls the example of D. Peller as a cautionary tale. Hired by the Ministry of Public Works, he is called in to investigate the phenomenon of a lead ball falling from a building, veering a full metre to one side, then correcting itself and returning to its original trajectory toward the ground. The deviation to the left is found to be caused by the ectoplasm of a Great Dane that fell from the nineteenth floor in 1944. To test the theory, Peller proceeds to throw ten lead balls, the first two of which are enough to prove the phenomenon. The third lead ball accidently crushes the skull of another Great Dane, walking past with his owner. Despite the dog's death and its owner's screams, Peller continues with his experiment until he has thrown the tenth ball. Peller's indifference can be understood as a symptom of being in constant contact with the simulations that are ectographs; his repetitive immersion in the world of the departed has irreparably affected his perception of the real.

Rendering ectoplasms real though a camera lens is partly, here, what composes the hyperreal. To further illustrate this theoretic parallel – and with the disclaimer that the following is in no way a comparison between literary mishap and war – let us turn to Baudrillard's most polemical essays: "The Gulf War Will Not Take Place," "The Gulf War: Is It Really Taking Place?," and "The Gulf War Did Not Take Place" (1995). The essays played with a sensitive topic, claiming that the massacre that took place during the Gulf War was merely a simulation of war and that the postmodern deterrence of war translated into a simulacrum with real consequences. The adversaries never truly confronted one another, one side won its virtual war in advance, and the other lost in advance (62). If the Vietnam War was lost through the media, the Gulf War was fought through it. The Gulf War was the first time that images of war were relayed live, and reports and images were controlled more than ever before by the military (Patton 1995, 3). The curating of images and video footage of advanced weaponry made for a seemingly clean war, a video game that made carnage and blood seem like a barbarity of the past. The information and images used for war-training simulators were indistinguishable from those of the real war (4). On-site reporters confessed to watching CNN to find out what was happening in the war; in other words, "television news coverage appeared to have finally caught up with the logic of simulation" (2). Noam Chomsky echoed this sentiment, stating that he understood "war" to mean combat – two sides shooting at one another – which did not occur in the Gulf (Chomsky 1992, 51). With both the Gulf War and Peller's experiment, hyperreal simulacra resulted in real consequences. Much like with most people's experience of the war, the world of ectoplasms becomes real only through cameras, subject to interaction only through technology.

The simulation of a compilation of scientific reports, and of a science by extension, is supported by the para-bestiary information offered by the latter portion of *Informe*. The work is rife with bureaucracy, with the mundane ongoings of the SEA, confusing the real and fantastic, creating a hyperreality.[9] Solpe's letters and journals, along with the descriptions, describe the process of refining the discipline. On 6 April 1914, for instance, he defines *espectro* and *ectoplasma* in his journal for the first time. In 1928, he describes the accidental discovery of the methodology with which to capture images on plaster.

The realistic details provided by the documents help to historically contextualize the entries of *Informe*. Each report archived by an ectographist reveals that the spectra are a nuisance to those who call the SEA in search of aid. Federico the dog blocked the door, the duck made customers uncomfortable, a spectral sea urchin dug itself into an office worker's calf, etc. The constant nuisance played by the ectoplasms of domestic animals and animals otherwise typically raised for consumption is significant when historically contextualized. The entries are scattered through the first half of the twentieth century. During this period, Argentina was a prosperous nation, the "granary of the world," decidedly moving towards modernity. In contrast to medieval animals, which were used to prescribe a good life, *Informe*'s departed animals merely obstruct progress – perhaps they even warn against it.

In the latter half of the work, Solpe writes to Eugenio Dubarry, a national senator of the city of Buenos Aires, in the hopes of gaining legal recognition for the science of ectography and securing grants and subsidies. In one of these letters, Solpe describes a sleepless night interrupted by a protest on the morning of 6 September 1930. He confessed to not knowing the cause of the commotion that woke him and how he moved with the protest as it approached the Avenida de Mayo due to fear of the protesting masses entering the SEA building. The events describe the military coup d'état of 1930, also known as the September Revolution, consisting of the overthrowing of President Hipólito Irigoyen by fascist leader José Félix Uriburu. *Informe* closes with the arrival of the dictatorship, also announcing that during Juan Domingo Perón's 1947 widening of the Avenida 9 de Julio, the block on which the SEA was located was demolished. The cluster of ectoplasms and the mundane annoyances they caused by appearing in the decades leading up to and following the dictatorship comprise a passive defiance to the changes that lead Argentina towards its present state. *Informe*'s scientific tone conveys "objective" phenomena that, when compiled, point at the refusal, by animals, of an alarming national trend. The book's anchoring of the ectoplasm sightings and the development of ectography during the coup also strengthens the credibility of the reports, furthering the (dis)simulation in the work.

CONCLUSION

This chapter identified and explored the (dis)simulating qualities in both the entries and the overall content of *Animalia exstinta* and *Informe sobre ectoplasma animal*. Although each work involves smaller (dis)simulations on an entry-to-entry basis, there are two defining characteristics in each stage of the texts: the simulation of other genres and the dissimulation of the bestiary tradition. While other chapters explore the many changes to content, with the most radical being the replacement of beasts with humans, the works explored in this chapter alone challenge the form. The authors' use of scientific reports and an exposé on extinct animals problematizes the categorization of their works as bestiaries. Their inclusion here as examples of an evolution of the genre is based on my redefinition of the genre (i.e., a collection of titled, independent short texts, largely descriptive but sometimes anecdotal, often accompanied by an image, about real, mythical, or implied beasts).

The push and pull implicit in these bestiaries – between surface and symptomatic reading, the naïve and informed reader, and simulation and dissimulation – is constant. Each of the former terms (surface, naïve, simulation) rely on a suspension of disbelief unlike in other bestiaries before them. They ask the reader to ignore the nonexistence not just of certain creatures, but of entire disciplines, cultural referents, and ultimately a literary genre. These elements form a specific approach to *Animalia exstinta* and *Informe sobre ectoplasma animal*, and depend on an agreement between author and reader for the entries unfold on a plane informed by, yet far from, the real. Certain preconditions – the ties to materiality and substance that Baudrillard links to hyperreality – need to disappear in order to allow the collective unconscious, objects, the real, obsolete objects, bodily remains, and fantasy, among other elements, to mix freely, allowing for a flourishing of referents and information carriers. Because, as the myth goes, all great criminals wish to be caught and thus recognized, dissimulation in the text exists. Symptomatic, informed, and dissimulating elements all pull towards an acknowledgment of the games present in the works, so that the artistic value of the words and images in both bestiaries may be recognized.

The simulation in these bestiaries is both pertinent and successful, a timely reimagining of a re-emerging genre. In a lecture on Baudrillard, Professor Rick Roderick identifies the fad of constant change as being capable of producing an ecstasy not of the sublime, but rather of a more visceral, direct quality that leads to the hyperreal feelings that society demands. The quick doses demanded of everything in contemporary Western society – news, interaction, love, etc. – must be succinct and effective if they wish to seduce. The combination of flash fiction and attractive images make the bestiary a compromise between what these attention-deficit–riddled times demand and literature with a strong aesthetic dimension.

The dissimulation of the bestiary tradition can also betray practical motivations. Originality is a valuable quality in literary works, and to push the somewhat obscure bestiary form to entirely simulate another creates buzz, as demonstrated by the attention *Informe sobre ectoplasma animal* has received.[10] This signifies a much stronger connection to the tradition than would be noticed at first glance and ties in the two bestiaries examined here as part of a wider evolution within the genre. If their lineage to the bestiary genre is deliberately hidden, the lie by omission would presuppose a familiarity with some of the works. The innovation on the genre thereby not only enriches it greatly, but also confirms the trajectory of the evolution of the bestiary genre that I have proposed here, originating in the medieval period, being rediscovered during the avant-garde and Boom periods, and finally proliferating in contemporary Hispanic literature. The purposeful dissimulation of the genre protests too much, and by its omission points to the trajectory of the genre, presenting *Informe sobre ectoplasma animal* as an instance interlinked to many other works and to a tradition, as opposed to representing an isolated event.

6

USURPING BEAST TERRITORY

While the title of the medieval bestiary announced the animals encased within its pages, the works often included beings beyond the kingdom Animalia. Save for the innovations of Nicolás Guillén, the previous chapters discuss how, despite moulding and experimenting with the genre, the authors of Hispanic bestiaries left the genre's animal/creature foundation untouched. This chapter explores the human/animal connection in two bestiaries that share the peculiarity of being exclusively populated by humans: *200 años de monstruos y maravillas argentinas* (2015) by Gabo Ferro, Christian Montenegro, and Laura Varsky; and *Bestiario médico* (2000) by Carlos Ferrándiz and Carlos Baonza. This chapter focuses on how these works invoke two opposing yet related instances of "human as animal," and the significance of placing humans in the literary space of animals.

The notion that the bestiary is a place exclusively reserved for animals denies an important aspect of the genre's history. However subtle, a human current exists in the *Physiologus* and medieval bestiaries. Humans were, of course, responsible for illustrating, editing, and writing the bestiaries. Their presence, however, was not solely production based. The human form appeared in many entries, depicting aspects of some mythical creatures, or in allegories in keeping with the bestiary's metaphoric characteristics. Firestones, for instance, first found in the *Physiologus* and later transferred to medieval bestiaries, were anthropomorphized. These stones warned of the dangers in unions between a man and a woman, particularly for those committed to a monastic life. While apart, the male and female firestones did not ignite. When the

Figure 6.1 | Shown as male and female, the firestones cautioned medieval audiences about the dangers of lust (*The Aberdeen Bestiary*, ca. 1200).

female drew near to the male, however, their fire kindled at once, burning everything in their vicinity. The reader is thus warned to steer clear of women, lest the contact between them ignite and burn the goodness that Christ has placed upon him.[1] Through making an explicit connection between moral teachings and the audience, the human embodiment of the firestones made the association between sexuality and eternal damnation more compelling (figure 6.1). These early bestiaries used the human form as a sensuous encasement for abstract teachings. Though unusual, the human-as-animal motif can be traced back to the origin of the genre. The authors and illustrators seen in this chapter simultaneously venture into untouched territory and dive back into the bestiary's tradition to rescue one of its most obscure branches.

The human presence is felt beyond the content of medieval manuscripts, as pointed out by Sarah Kay, who highlights the fascinating parallel between the effects of medieval bestiary teachings on people and the animal flesh used to convey them. She sees the animal-derived parchment as a juncture between incompatibles, "between bare life and intellectual life, livestock and literacy, the history of the book and the seemingly ahistorical existence of nonhuman animals" (2017, 7). Parchment also offers a space for ambiguity, for once the animal is stripped of its fur, its skin appears uncannily like human skin. Kay observes that with every touch, every transfer of oil from the reader's bodies onto the page, the material becomes more and more skin-like (7). The pages that tell of human virtues and vices acquire a different meaning, or perhaps they become more meaningful, when the human and allegorical planes are bridged. The carnal undertones of the firestones' warning against lust, for instance, could be emphasized by the experience of seeing and touching the dry, rough skin upon which that warning was written. The skin and its macabre undertones anchored the allegorical in the sensuous, making the bestiary's teachings tangible in the physical world. Though today's bestiaries are not printed on animal skin, this past practice foreshadows a "practical" turn in some interpretations of the genre. Language, images, and documents provide a tangible tie between the allegorical aspects of literature and the world in which they find relevance.

The aforementioned aspects of the human presence in content, form, and manufacturing are of particular interest for the works featured in this chapter, which suggest a compelling dialectic. These works not only embrace the human/animal dynamic, reviving an often-ignored branch of the genre, they also offer its most radical interpretation yet: a bestiary exclusively featuring humans. This rendition allows for constant play, in which the authors, through their choice of genre and title, announce the critical content of their work. Because of these choices, much of the allegorical aspect of the entries is lost. The message no longer requires an animal as a vessel, as humans now accomplish the mission themselves.

200 años de monstruos y maravillas argentinas, *compiled by Gabo Ferro, illustrated by Christian Montenegro and Laura Varsky (2015)*

200 años de monstruos y maravillas argentinas (2015) is the product of three artists, whose mission is to redeem and recover the subjects of history omitted by the Argentine elite and hegemony. The disregard of these figures was not done by neglect alone, but also by constructing them as Other, abnormal, or, more pertinently, monsters. With the traditional formatting of the bestiary – short texts, titled entries, illustrations, a beast theme – *200 años* studies the devalued figures whose negated and inconvenient presence has systematically been used to validate the practices and figures of official Argentine history (Ferro 2015, 10). The following are among the work's entries: "Las multitudes rurales del litoral" (The rural populations of the coastal region), "Los anfibios" (The amphibians), "El pederasta" (The pederast), "El sodomita" (The sodomite), "El onanista" (The onanist), "El anarquista" (The anarchist), "Los internados en los hospitales" (Those hospitalized), and "Las muchachas peronistas" (The Peronist girls). The allusion to animals, monsters, and creatures in the title of the work, as well as the context in which the subjects are represented, allows for an ontological debate and destabilizes Argentina's identity through a form traditionally reserved for the moulding of a uniform society.

All three collaborators belong to a larger cultural trend that seeks to understand the national identity beyond the classic Argentine *civilización/barbarie* (civilization/barbarism) dichotomy. Gabo Ferro, the compiler of this work, was an acclaimed musician, poet, and historian. The names of his other works, *Barbarie y civilización: Sangre, monstruos y vampiros durante el segundo gobierno de Rosas* (2009) and *Degenerados, anormales y delincuentes: Gestos entre ciencia, política y representaciones en el caso argentino* (2010), bear a resemblance to the text featured in this chapter. Ferro often worked to reclaim forgotten figures. In his 2018 show "Loca," for instance, he mounted an homage to female tango singers such as Libertad Lamarque, Ada Falcón, Tania, Rosita Quiroga, Azucena Maizani, and Sofía Bozán at the Torquato Tasso theatre in Buenos Aires. This project, like many of Ferro's, began with a historical axis. "Loca" initially sought to explore the gender fluidity that these women portrayed despite the society in which they lived. During the show, Ferro paid homage to this phenomenon, singing in the first person through a female perspective with his characteristic voice – often compared to that of a woman (Romero 2018).

While there is less press about Laura Varsky and Christian Montenegro, both boast impressive achievements. Varsky, a graphic designer, is also a navigator of traditionally subversive spaces, as her career began in the rock-and-roll scene. In 2006 she won a Latin Grammy for the art direction of "Café de los maestros" (A. López, n.d.), and she taught typography at the School of Design at the Universidad de Buenos Aires for a decade. Montenegro is a versatile illustrator who has lent his talent to numerous books, media articles, and television, commercial, and animation projects. In 2009 he was awarded the Swatch Special Prize Young Illustrator Award.

200 años emerges after a significant shift in Latin American literature that brought matters of biopolitics to the forefront. In this shift, occurring around the 1960s and identified by Gabriel Giorgi in works such as Guimarães Rosa's "Meu tio o Iauaretê" and Esteban Echeverría's "El matadero," humans are no longer held to be the absolute opposite of animals, and the traditional, modern dichotomy is replaced by "lines of continuity, contiguity, passage, and ambivalence between human and animal bodies" (Giorgi 2014, 29). In Giorgi's analysis, the animal condenses political intensities and functions as a privileged zone in which intersection, thematic knots, the cultural, and the biopolitical can be read (14). While Giorgi's analysis mainly focuses on the emblematic qualities of the animal body that blur the definition of what it means to be human, this chapter focuses on the mechanisms used to deny a person's humanity.

The representation of humans in contemporary Hispanic bestiaries can be divided into two distinct yet interrelated categories, broadly falling under what Greg Garrard labels "zoomorphism" (2023, 131). The first type of representation draws from the darkest qualities of humankind: greed, bigotry, racism, idiocy, and so on. It speaks to a long-standing conflict, one encapsulated by Giorgio Agamben in *The Open: Man and Animal*, in which he reduces Western politics to biopolitics, the crucial conflict being the internal one between the animality and humanity of humans (2004, 80). These undesired, repressed instincts work to challenge the idea that humans are superior to animals. They highlight the gap between the most pompous assumptions of human superiority and a less flattering reality, an idea that has accompanied bestiaries for centuries: "In medieval iconography, the ape holds a mirror in which the man who sins must recognize himself as *simia dei* (ape of God). In Linnaeus's optical machine, whoever refuses to recognize himself in the ape, becomes one: to paraphrase Pascal, *qui fait l'homme, fait le singe*" (Agamben 2004, 27). The second manifestation of the human/animal connection occurs when humans animalize other humans for selfish gain. The description of a fellow human as an animal, whether implicit or explicit, is a self-serving enterprise in which a person seeks to elevate their own status. While the goal of devaluing the Other is carried out successfully by comparing them to an animal, it invokes the first instance of human as animal. The utterance of the Other as animal backfires on they who utter, turning them into the first type of animal: the greedy, the bigot, the racist, the fool. Both sides of the human/animal dynamic bear negative connotations, as the comparison to the animal, traditionally perceived as being below humans, is not a positive one.

Much of *200 años*' impact relies on its status as bestiary, which in turn hinges on the relationship between text and image. The term "bestiary" mocks, demanding that humans meet certain moral standards or suffer the disgrace of being reduced to an animal. Disenfranchisement was not limited to people during the formulation of Argentine historical discourse. The art permitted to accompany official discourses was to be as "realist" and "naturalist" as possible (Ferro 2015, 8). Thus *200 años* showcases a type and use of art denied in official historical sources. During the twentieth century, illustrations of texts and comics accompanying historical accounts with subversive or sardonic tones came under fire as a result of Argentina's numerous dictatorships. Héctor Germán Oesterheld and Alberto Breccia's 1968 graphic novel on the life of Che Guevara, for example, was banned in the 1976 to 1983 dictatorship. Oesterheld, whose 1957 *El eternauta* already contained anti-establishment tones, was disappeared in 1977. Foreign illustrators also saw their images censored by the Argentine junta: in 1979, Jorge Rafael Videla sent soldiers to cover up nude male drawings by Richard Corben (Gociol and Rosemberg 2000, 48). Art was meant to be decorative; art was to faithfully and submissively illustrate a text. In keeping with the objective to tell an untold story through unused methods, *200 años* has estranged itself from this artistic tradition in such a way that the entries would be incomplete without Montenegro's and Varsky's design and images. Their images are intrinsic to the thesis of the work, as they interpret and engage in dialogue with each compiled document. The dynamic between text and image demands engagement; one retroactively informs the other, offering a continuum of increasingly telling interpretations, forcing the viewer-reader to confront their own understanding time and time again. Ferro (2016) identified himself as a "cultivator of the ephemeral," and this collaboration is no exception, as the space between text and image exists only while the reader holds the bestiary and oscillates between the two elements. The image now demands the same detailed attention as the text, and the elements can only be interpreted as a whole. Three colours carry out the historical correction: light blue and white, the colours of the Argentine flag, and an abundance of black, to remind the reader of history's dark underbelly that was denied: "The ones who deviated from the good path of history, the undisciplined ones, the failures of civilization, the ones who deviated from the path of order, the ones who subvert the canon" (Ferro 2015, 9; my translation).[2]

Ferro draws from a variety of historical sources, untethered by the prestige of one or the obscurity of another. The following verses in the entry "Los negros" are quoted from the Argentine epic *Martín Fierro* by José Hernández: "God made the white, and Saint Peter the brown, / At least so I've heard men tell; / But the devil himself made the black, / As coals for the fire of hell" (Ferro 2015, 34; quoting Hernández 1936, 52).[3] The lines are uttered by the gaucho Fierro, when, after returning defeated from a forced governmental defence against Indigenous peoples, he encounters a Black woman at a dance. Though *Martín Fierro* was not written in colonial Argentina, the gaucho's words betray centuries of colonialist ideology. Despite the character Fierro himself being impoverished, outlawed, and hunted by the same establishments that condemned Black and Indigenous peoples, he remains convinced of his superiority. Fierro's offensive comment is not dismissed by the woman's companion, the two men duel, and Fierro kills his opponent. The inclusion of the Black person as opposed to the Indigenous character in *200 años* may seem counterintuitive, particularly when *Martín Fierro* condemns the latter more consistently than the former. In light of this, it is important to note that official Argentine discourse has worked diligently to deny Black history in the country. During the settlement and colonial periods, the ratio of White people to Black people was equal, with any uneven distribution tipping in favour of the Black population (Tannenbaum 1946, 10; Scobie 1974, 31; Rosenblat 1954, 34). The population of Black people began to steadily decline around the nineteenth century, because Black slaves were volunteered by their owners to fight in independence wars. This in turn forced Black women to turn to White, mulatto, or Indigenous men for intimate partnerships (Castro 1988, 12), further dwindling the numbers of the Black population. These events, paired with Bartolomé Mitre's success in unifying Argentina as a porteño-oriented[4] society (15), manifest today in an almost complete eradication of Black history from the Argentine consciousness.

The line "as coal for the fires of hell" ("para tizón del infierno") reifies the Black population, reducing them to fuel for unholy fires. But because they are living and breathing people, the objectification settles somewhere between "human" and "object": it settles on "animal." In *The Wretched of the Earth*, Frantz Fanon articulates the colonizer's vision of colonized subjects as animals:

> In plain talk, he is reduced to the state of an animal. And consequently, when the colonist speaks of the colonized he uses zoological terms. Allusion is made to the slithery movements of the yellow race, the odors from the "native" quarters, to the hordes, the stink, the swarming, the seething, the gesticulations. In his endeavors at description and finding the right word, the colonist refers constantly to the bestiary. The European seldom has a problem with figures of speech. But the colonized, who immediately grasp the intention of the colonist and the exact case being made against them, know instantly what he is thinking. This explosive population growth, those hysterical masses, those blank faces, those shapeless, obese bodies, this headless, tailless cohort, these children who seem not to belong to anyone, this indolence sprawling under the sun, this vegetating experience, all this is part of the colonial vocabulary. (2004, 7)

The use of language and insults deriving from animals has also been explored by Jacques Derrida in *The Animal That Therefore I Am* (2002). In this work, Derrida looks at Western culture's treatment of the animal, and he grapples with their philosophical dismissal and reduction, particularly by Descartes, Kant, Lacan, and Levinas. He explores how, in a tradition that has built up

European man and crushed all Others, Othering becomes a tool to belittle humans, further adding that authentic idealism consists in insulting the animal within the human, or treating the latter as animal, contesting their dignity (103). Language is essential in the shaping of the animal–human and human–human discourses. The person who possesses animal qualities thus becomes a lesser being, a non-subject that is devoid of an identity, an "I." Crucially, to hold the "I" and to deny it to another is a form of power, as the "I" raises the human above all other earthly beings (92). In the human/animal dichotomy, the "I" belongs to the human; in the colonizer/colonized, it belongs to the colonizer, and so on. The "I"/Other dichotomy is fluid and unrestricted in the restrictions it imposes.

Since in the battle between Martín Fierro and the Black man there is no European, the figures of speech belong to Fierro, the man who is closer to the "ideal." The fight, in fact, is the result of the figures of speech Fanon attributes to the colonizer, and Derrida to the "I." The following quotes are not featured in *200 años*, but rather are from the scene in *Martín Fierro* discussed above. The Black man, angry at Fierro's insult, replies, "You're the only ass that's loose to-night, / You drunken beast" (Hernández 1936, 52), attacking the gaucho as a man.[5] Fierro does not return the courtesy; during the fight he states, "gentlemen ... leave this bull to me" (53),[6] marking the stark difference between gentleman and animal. This dynamic is further illustrated when, after having killed his opposition, Fierro describes the woman who accompanied the murdered man: "Like a she-wolf there she began to howl" (55).[7] Ferro's quote thus prompts us to reread the epic and recognize that in the epic, persecution and dehumanization were not limited to the gaucho.

To accompany the entry, Monterroso and Varsky draw inspiration from the colonial European imagining of its subjects as savage and promiscuous. The image has its roots in the colonists' obsession with the perceived sexuality and exoticism of the colonized subject. This perversion of the perverse forces the viewer-reader to engage with the true motivations behind European depictions of African descendants. The artists ridicule the idea that Hottentot Venus[8] was ever exhibited in the name of anthropological study, satirizing the attempts at justifying the clear exploitation, objectification, and exoticization at the hands of, ironically, repressed societies. By exaggerating the already grotesque traditional Black caricature, the colonists expose their own weak attempts to justify such depictions. In the book, defiance is represented as people who copulate before the Pirámide de Mayo, in Buenos Aires, and the selective freedom the act represents, as the power that is recognized and celebrated by the monument belonged exclusively to White, landowning males. The Pirámide de Mayo is located at the centre of the Plaza de Mayo, at the city centre, surrounded by the government house, the Metropolitan Cathedral, the Secretariat of Intelligence, and the Bank of the Argentine Nation, among other important institutions. The pyramid was erected in 1811 as a way of commemorating the May Revolution, which involved the removal of the Viceroy Baltasar Hidalgo de Cisneros, a key step towards independent nationhood. The monument's shape represents a proximity to the heavens and the symbolic concentration of power. In this case, the power being recognized and celebrated belonged to a privileged few, marking the "savage" display of defiance all the more irreverent. The interaction between the entry's text and image becomes a defiant gesture made toward a traditionally respected symbol of anti-colonial power and reminds the reader-viewer that the pyramid's celebration is a premature one, for many in Argentine society have yet to enjoy the agency and absolute freedom it boasts.

The medieval understanding of authorship as it pertains to the practices of writing, drawing, and painting offer an interesting layer of meaning to the mission of *200 años*. In *The Luminous Trace*, Thea Burns (2012) writes that in the early Middle Ages, the Old English verb *awritan* could mean to write, describe, transcribe, draw, or delineate. These activities, particularly drawing, painting, and writing, were not understood in exclusive terms (45). While the visual commentary examined in this chapter belong to a contemporary context, the notion of writing and drawing as extensions of a single expression aids the interpretation of the entries in *200 años*. Were it not for the entries, the compilation of documents would serve as a purely historical work featuring a corpus of objectionable documents. While the interaction between Montenegro's images and the text gathered by Ferro is undeniably different than that between a medieval text and image, the medieval notion that all aspects of a text need be considered together contains the key to understanding the critical nature of the work. The text and image of the bestiary along with its author/compiler's and illustrators' decisions to present humans as bestiary subjects weigh equally in *200 años*.

Figure 6.2 | Image of a child living on the street, whose human face has been covered with an abstract, monstruous one, thus othering the child (Christian Montenegro and Laura Varsky, 2015).

The view of the Other as animalistic is not limited to the colonized Other, as can be seen in the entry "Los niños de la calle" (Street children), taken from a thesis entitled "Razas humanas y su distribución" (Human races and their distributions). The thesis describes the population of children aged six to seven who live on the street, exposed to "all the contagions of miserable, immoral life" (Ferro 2015, 88) (figure 6.2). According to the author of the thesis, Salvador Elmi, three factors contribute to these children's unfortunate situation: their parents' negligence and passing down of poor habits; the environment, conducive to all manner of deviation; and finally, a lack of education (88).

By calling the street children "extraordinary" and mentioning their "diverse professions," the author creates a comfortable partition between the spectators (or readers) and reality. The first two sentences of the entry could be narrated by David Attenborough for a less-than-comely nature documentary, to reassure the reader that *that* reality, the one where children are equated with fauna, is far away. The animal–child connection is not explicitly made in the text. When the text is observed in play with the image, however, the first two sentences give the sense that urban pigeons, not children, are being described. The child's surroundings hint at a habitat that is not a comfortable, respectable home. Each explanation that is offered is almost correct, almost helpful, but ultimately overlooks the causes behind the complex problem of poverty, as attempts to untangle cause and effect fail. The author of the thesis begins to point to social factors but ultimately opts for the discourse that blames the child or their family, thus creating an image of little monsters who run around the streets of Buenos Aires, without faulting those with means. This creation of the Other is echoed in the image accompanying the entry.

The edges and styling of the image emulate a photograph that could have circulated during the time that the source was written, and the agreeable background could have well been used as a photography set. The child's mask thus creates a fascinating dynamic; she is rendered anonymous, lost in a multitude of other children left to fend for themselves. Simultaneously, the mask's fangs and exaggerated eyes ensure that this alienation is perpetuated by keeping the reader-viewer frightened, unwilling to come closer. The child's dress, shoes, and stockings point to someone who may be loved and cared for, yet her mask allows for her to be exoticized in a manner reminiscent of Picasso's *Les Demoiselles d'Avignon*, a different sort of outcast. Most importantly, the mask allows the reader to comfortably remain a spectator. Emmanuel Levinas (1998) sees the encounter with the face of the Other as crucial in a being's shift from the "in-itself" and "for-itself" into the "ethical self." One who can prioritize the Other, the ethical "I," chooses a responsibility for the Other – choosing to see their defenceless nakedness, misery, and mortality (202). To face the Other is to have one's ideatum, or reality, destroyed and overflowed at each moment, preventing a fake or plastic image from being formed (Levinas 1991, 51). A mask, then, places these children under primitivist, totemic, foreign, and esoteric categories, certainly not a part of the European educated construct as prescribed by the president of the time, Domingo Sarmiento, and far from being a problem of the elites, who hold and cultivate hegemony. Despite Fanon's French colonialist context, the leap necessary to apply his theory to impoverished children is not a big one. The refusal to see the face of the Other and the language that denies the humanity of a subjugated person are two sides of the same coin. Both tactics deny those who challenge hegemony through their existence alone.

The entry titled "Los médicos" (The doctors) presents a different animal exhumed by the playful dialogue between text and image. "Los médicos," fuelled by the positivist currents dominating Argentine society in the nineteenth and twentieth centuries, exemplifies the dangers of only attributing value to knowledge derived from the experimentation and observation of the scientific method. The excerpt, from Ricardo Berdier's 1900 *Introducción a las enfermedades del espíritu* (Introduction to the illnesses of the spirit), reads: "To us physicians the first position in intellectual combat ... to find solution to the evils of the present: the rags of humanity belong to us ... We are the beast with its appetites and needs, but the intellectual beast *par excellence*, the beast creator of worlds, dominant of the earth" (Ferro 2015, 61; my translation).[9] Their portrait tells otherwise (figure 6.3).

The text's use of the word *bestia*, intended to transmit elitist power, is corrupted by the artists' interpretation. Depicted as creatures best left unimagined, Montenegro and Varsky's medics are a far cry from the pedantic, elitist figures that Berdier invites the reader to imagine. The creatures are not the avant-garde of knowledge, rationality, or excellence. Rather, they embody the dialectic of Enlightenment, the renouncing of religion in favour of the dogma of science and capitalism, progress at the cost of

Figure 6.3 | Image depicting physicians as bloodthirsty crocodile-like creatures, and their patient as a victim (Christian Montenegro and Laura Varsky, 2015).

lives and human dignity, though progress nonetheless. Their eyes betray their ill desire for the patient, for a carcass with which to feed the physician's noble enterprise. The talons, obscene in colour and length, are a depiction of greed and lust. They function as an allusion to something deeply sinister as they ogle and grope the victim on the operating table. The darkness that surrounds them and the eagerness of their dynamism unearths something best left hidden in history, to be shelved with experiments in eugenics and lobotomies. If, as the text states, the humans charged to their care are "rags," leftovers, waste, and decaying matter, the physicians that excitedly flock to such misery must be vultures.

By inviting the image to throw around the same weight as its accompanying document, *200 años de monstruos y maravillas argentinas* creates a dialogue that takes place in the negative space between its entries. The images demand that their sources be accountable, highlighting the animalistic nature inherent in humans and satirizing the human/animal discourse used to dehumanize the Other of Argentine history.

Bestiario médico, *by Carlos Ferrándiz, illustrated by Carlos Baonza (2000)*

Bestiario médico assumes a reader who is familiar with the great sacrifices and consequent advances made in medicine by those who defied ignorance, religion, and politics. Author Carlos Ferrándiz states that the book seeks to offer medicine's "photographic negative" in order to demonstrate how incorrect data and unchecked prejudice in medicine has caused neglect of and outright violence against certain groups based on categories such as race, gender, and sexual orientation (Ferrándiz 2000, 15). Though animals such as the bubonic plague's rat make an appearance, the bestiary focuses on humans. In it, erroneous scientific and medical conclusions responsible for prejudice and suffering serve as reminders that there is no definitive worldview, and that believing otherwise leads to dogmatism and impedes human progress: "Scientific paradigms are like living organisms: they're born (with a lot of pain) causing a revolution in ideas, they develop, and, finally, they die" (Sainz 2000, 12; my translation). The work is a cautionary tale of the dangers of operating without an awareness of past mistakes – and a call to question what is circumstantially considered the pinnacle of progress.

Little is known about Ferrándiz, who tells of tortures, purgings, disease, and alchemy as medicine slowly became separated from philosophy and magic, and took its first independent – albeit wobbly – steps at the end of the seventeenth century. His history of medicine is condensed into short episodes, written as plays, poems, and flash fiction, and illustrated by Carlos Baonza's sardonic, sharp lines. Carlos Baonza is a Spanish engraver, sculptor, and painter. He studied engraving and stamping under Dimitri Papagueorguiu and had his first exposition at the Universidad de Pontificia Comillas in 1979 (Los sueños y miedos 2019). Baonza has illustrated poetry books as well as bestiaries (*Bestiario* 1999, *Bestiario* 1993). Although he usually illustrates works with engravings, Baonza likely used black ink on paper for his illustrations in *Bestiario médico*, as they lack the characteristic crisp lines of his engraving technique.

Ferrándiz opens his bestiary with "El enfermo mesopotámico" (The Mesopotamian patient), the poeticized tale of Arad-Nonoi, an ill man in Ur. The cause of his abdominal pain is uncertain, so Arad-Nonoi makes speculations based on what he knows. He wonders if his pain is cause by demons of the dead, the spirit of an aborted fetus, the demon Askakku, or an ekimmu ghost. After praying and imploring his protector, Ea, to gain him favour with the god Marduk, he finally gives up and tries calling a doctor. Guided by the doctor, the man commences an examination of his conscience, and he turns up empty handed. They investigate the sins of family members: "The sin lies with my parents or grandparents. / We recited all possible faults. / So that naming them would become an act of penance, / despite not remembering having committed any faults, / and I would gain the gods' favours once again" (Ferrándiz 2000, 17–18; my translation).[10] His initial resource was religious: he looked to otherworldly possibilities and divine motives for whatever had caused him harm; only once his mystical reasoning proved fruitless did he look to a doctor. And yet the doctor ultimately deflects responsibility back to religious authority, calling for the aid of a priest and an exorcist, costing Arad-Nonoi a total of thirty coins (18). The three healers then continue, by killing insects, examining the sick man's dreams, suggesting prayers to him, sacrificing the rest of his lambs, and urging him to drink pungent concoctions. In Baonza's illustration, Arad-Nonoi is depicted as exhausted, in the middle of sacrificing a sheep (figure 6.4).

Figure 6.4 | Arad-Nonoi is forced to sacrifice a sheep as a final attempt to cure himself (Carlos Baonza, 2000).

Man and sheep stare at each other; the sacrifice weighs on the man, and this shows on his face. A nebulous ectoplasm outlines his body, perhaps along with the spectre of inherited sins. The pain is personified as a dark, albeit playful, demon: the only character that seems to enjoy the mystery and the ridiculous attempts to unveil it. Much to Arad-Nonoi's distress, the cures amount to nothing. The man's fate is mirrored in the medicinal process depicted throughout the pages of *Bestiario médico*: assurance in the validity of an antidote based on a cosmovision, which gives way to letting life run its course when all possibilities and solutions are exhausted. The archetype slowly changes throughout the course of the book as physicians turn to their own solutions and begin to consciously – the unconscious aspect takes longer – divert away from religious teachings.

Bestiario médico lays bare the mechanics of large-scale mistakes brought about by a lack of skepticism and overconfidence in unchecked discourse. In another entry, reflective of a period influenced by the Greek physician Galen of Pergamon (129–216 CE), the entry "El sofoco de la madre" (The suffocation of the mother) demonstrates that little has changed since Arad-Nonoi's time, many centuries earlier. It explores the ideas that, rooted in medicine, fuelled sexism. Ferrándiz begins his text with Aristotle's and Galen's theories that presented women as imperfect due to their lack of male-like genitalia and their cold, humid humours. The account invites the reader to reflect on the power of popular ideas, as the dominant perception of menstruation and its physiological causes, together with the intrinsic misogyny in medieval European Judeo-Christian religion, proved devastating for women's societal power. This way of thinking peaked with the burning of women at the stake in the witch hunts of the sixteenth and seventeenth centuries and has yet to be fully corrected (Ferrándiz 2000, 107).

Ferrándiz quotes the sources that guided medieval authorities in order to reveal the bones of this pillar of sexist discourse. In referencing Pliny the Elder's view that a menstruating woman's touch can cause plants to dry up, fruit to fall from trees, seeds to become sterile, and blades of steel to blunt, Ferrándiz creates a juncture between the medieval and contemporary bestiaries, revealing the dance with form and content that is inherent to the genre. Pliny the Elder's depiction of women is reminiscent of the basilisk, a reptile-like beast that was also capable of destroying shrubbery, grass, and rocks with its breath – a comparison that brings to mind the tired snake/woman trope. Under Pliny and Galen – authorities to medics, scholars, and bestiary editors – a woman is subject to the same gaze as a mythical animal. Incorrect data and incorrect assumptions helped establish a powerful agenda – one that is still relevant today. Whether intentional or not, the ludic, critical tone and the use of antique and medieval authorities in this entry, and in *Bestiario médico* at large, allows for a subversion of previously uncontested sources in the genre that once venerated them.

Figure 6.5 | A woman contemplates the medical treatment of menstruation over the centuries (Carlos Baonza, 2000).

The bestiary's formula (header, short text, image) is here used to expose the roots of many contemporary conflicts, the various connections of which had previously been dispersed through the allegorical teachings of its medieval form.

The attempt to normalize the overly debated aspects of a woman's physiology is not limited to menstruation, as menopause does not offer any societal relief: "and it is because the retention of menstruation engenders bad humours and, already being of a certain age, they don't have the natural heat to consume and cook said matter; and poor women above all, that don't live off of anything but bad meats, are more poisonous than the others" (110; my translation).[11] The suffocation of the mother could be better described not as a physical illness but as a suffocating existence, a consequence of an opportunistic, historical understanding of female anatomy. Of course, suffocation hardly begins at the moment of menopause: "When the woman is young, she is a passive victim of a demonic possession by an incubus; when she becomes old, especially if she is 'thin and cold of complexion,' she becomes an active subject of evil: she becomes a witch" (110; my translation).[12] Thus, all stages of the woman's life provide reason for control or fear. The conclusion of the woman as witch – or goddess, for that matter – encourages the use of a dehumanizing discourse. Removing women from a practical, human plane became a pervasive practice whose correction we have only begun to see over the past couple of centuries. Simone de Beauvoir wrote that women such as Rosa Luxemburg or Marie Curie only began to appear once women's position in society began to feel natural (1968, 151), alluding to the fact that any supernatural manner of speaking about women, be it worship or damnation, is a symptom of the agency that has been denied them as human beings (162). Witch, snake, infant, goddess: all these are rhetorical tools for removing women from a human sphere, moving them away from their own bodies and from the decisions and autonomy that living in them requires. Despite the obvious possibility of denying autonomy by way of force, Beauvoir points to a systematic suffocation of women, spanning as long as the course of the bestiary's history. There is, for instance, no good way to oblige a woman to procreate. One can, however, ensure that motherhood is her only option through laws that impose marriage, through banning contraceptives and abortion, and through forbidding divorce (67). Progress has been made in some aspects to relieve the suffocation of women in society, but laws on abortion, support for basic rights such as birth control, and the expectation that women bear the brunt of reproductive responsibility point to the entrenchment of the medieval mentality in contemporary society.

As Beauvoir claimed, the woman is demoted as a result of being categorized as "lower than" (329, 360, 718). This has linguistic repercussions, as Eva Feder Kittay points out in "Woman as Metaphor" when she states, "the woman is always available as the metaphoric vehicle for his self-conception" (Feder 1988, 66). In other words, the abundance of metaphors regarding femaleness and the lack of metaphors about maleness reveals an internalization of maleness as "I." Both Ferrándiz and Ferro draw attention to the historical use of metaphors and linguistic symbolism to deny the humanity of the Other. This ambiguity, this need of an Other in order to represent the self – to then deny and oppress the Other – is representative of the human/animal dynamic fuelling these bestiaries.

The weight of this societal inheritance is captured by Baonza, who depicts the castrated impulse of a woman, her contradictory existence, replete with metaphors and a denied autonomy (figure 6.5). The image embodies the Scylla and Charybdis of the woman's condition as seen by medieval authorities – their simultaneous damning and dismissal.[13] The woman, physically an adult, sits like an infant. Helpless, in a puddle of her own blood, she is unable to participate in life as a result of her pre-existing condition. Her expression contrasts with her posture; the anger in her look does not correspond to her position on the floor. Whether the anger is the manifestation of her evil, supernatural powers or her disdain for her forced encasement in society is unclear. Her frustration is contagious, and Baonza's lines capture her flustered attempts to move in any one direction, her isolation, and the physiological cause tethering her to her condition.

Ferrándiz continues to exploit the aggressive/defenceless dynamic held within an individual person throughout his work, pushing it to its most extreme form in his final entry, titled "Adivina quién soy …" (Guess who …), in which he simultaneously depicts the present and the past with a modern conundrum that parallels the issues seen in the entry on the sick man, Arad-Nonoi. As the culmination of the book, it represents the biggest challenge yet to the readers' ego: having enjoyed laughing at past follies, the time has now come for the reader to laugh at themselves. In the poem, microscopic matter returns humans' gaze and slings taunts from beyond the sphere of the known. Unlike with the first poem, however, here the poetic voice transforms into a purposeful disease, rather than a distraught person. Its monologue calls into question assumptions, processes, and advancements assumed to be correct by scientific authorities:

> You are very big.
> So huge
> that I don't see you,
> nor do you me
> (if a stream of electrons
> don't help you).
> In my case
> given that I lack eyes
> I have a better excuse. (Ferrándiz 2000, 225; my translation)[14]

The first lines allude to a sensorial problem: neither party can see the other, resulting in an initial shared ignorance. Yet, somehow, the creature reveals knowledge of what surrounds it, despite its lack of basic senses. The lack of vision, as well as of touch, hearing, and smell, highlights the debate that sits at the crossroads between a sensorial and a total approach to observation. Further questioning the methodology behind scientific observation, the poem's entity speaks to the observer directly, ignoring the possibility of observational and scientific objectivity in a subject. It plays with the Western notions of the objective observer, and with the idea in that tradition that the observer must be removed in order to formulate an objective narrative of experience. This crossroads between "objective" and "total" observation is the subject of Dieter Schulz and Michael Sauter's (2012) article "Thoreau's Excursions, Science, and Hermeneutics," in which they contrast two figures who are representative of each philosophy. The first is Francis Bacon's ideal observer, distilled from his writings on the scientific method: an empirical scientist who seeks to understand within a sterile vacuum. The second is Henry David Thoreau's walker, who exemplifies a holistic observer, simultaneously watching and watched, changing alongside his environment and subject.

Bacon's observer employs the induction method, slowly working from the specific to the general, from ignorance to power. This knowledge translates into total control, a kingdom of men, and absolute rational power supported by the deductive reasoning of Bacon's contemporary, Descartes. Recognized as the father of empiricism, Bacon sought to eliminate prejudice, anticipation, and subjectivity (his *idola tribus, idola specus, idola fori, idola theatri* – idols of the tribe, den, market, and theatre) from observation to create as objective a plane of knowledge as possible (206). Aside from the argument that there is no experience without anticipation and prejudice (Hans-Georg Gadamer, *Wahrheit und Methode*, 356–62; *Truth*, 345–51; as quoted in Schulz and Sauter 2012, 206), the most pertinent critique of Bacon's methodology in light of the message in *Bestiario médico* is in keeping with the outcome of the Enlightenment – that is, in the quest to eliminate religious dogma and to think rationally, a new dogma is created. Regardless of the objectivity demanded of the experience, the observer is necessarily, irreparably subjective, as is the nature of experience (Schulz and Sauter 2012, 206). Believing the subjective to be objective and infallible simply ends up limiting the observable. This reduction of the observable in turn gives way to the accounts that fill the pages of *Bestiario médico*.

Thoreau's walker, much like with the hermeneutics of the medieval bestiary, seeks to find hints of truth and greater truth in what is inscribed in nature, asking: "is not Nature, rightly read, that of which she is commonly taken to be the symbol merely?" (Thoreau, quoted in Schulz and Sauter 2012, 203). The walker is a part of the world, simultaneously the observer and the observed, each aspect changing the other in a manner that foreshadows the observational mysteries of quantum mechanics. Thoreau stresses the importance of a familiarization with the subject of observation as a way of being close to it, demanding more than empirical observation: "We do not learn by inference and deduction, and the application of mathematics to philosophy, but by direct intercourse and sympathy. It is with science as with ethics, we cannot know truth by contrivance and method; the Baconian is as false as any other" (Thoreau, quoted in Schulz and Sauter 2012, 209). The walker is a scientist-philosopher who seeks to bridge the now accepted and normalized gap between the sciences and humanities. The lack of a bridging figure is highlighted by the poetic voice in this entry, who frustrates the existing categories for classification and understanding:

Am I alive?
Says the physiologist:
"No, it does not produce
any excrement
and it is true
that he who lives shits
and he who does not shit
obviously doesn't live."

And the geneticist:
"Yes, the sonofabitch
reproduces well, breaking
the mother or the matrix
that feeds him,
and killing upon its exit,
the damned fetus."

Discuss!
You can't even manage that. (Ferrándiz 2000, 226; my translation)[15]

The poetic voice in *Bestiario médico* confounds the physiologist and the geneticist by existing beyond binaries and heckling from afar. It questions what it means to be alive, calling upon a discourse explored by Agamben in *The Open*: to ask why a certain being is called living means to seek out the foundation by which living belongs to this being. Among the various criteria attributed to the term "to live," one criterion must be raised above the others, and be used to attribute life to a certain being. In other words, what has been separated and divided is precisely what – in a sort of *divide et impera* – allows for the construction of the unity of life, as the hierarchical articulation of a series of functional faculties and oppositions (2004, 14).

The creature thus manages to live outside of the foundation that is attributed to living things. What must then necessarily take place is a questioning of this foundation, and a reconsideration of what comprises a living being. The creature speaks directly to the reader, demonstrating its aliveness, without regard for its problematic classification. It presents itself as an end, not a means. It exploits the constant unknown seen in *Bestiario médico*, the unknown against which the only viable option is to humbly accept before attempting to decipher. It is also one of the few entries in the work that remains unillustrated, mimicking the reader's inability to conceive the creature in the poem.

CONCLUSION

The bestiaries in this chapter highlight ethical debates by placing humans and animals at the same level. The authors bring scholars, medics, schizophrenics, women, and colonial subjects, among other groups, down to this same level, in literary exhibits traditionally reserved for animals. The bestiary presents a textual space for this to happen: the tradition has evolved alongside society, and it has diverged in order to criticize rather than to unify. The blend of traditionally advantaged and disadvantaged groups keeps the definition and dynamic of human/animal constantly oscillating, avoiding it settling on any one interpretation. It allows humans to be compared to the nature that mainstream Western society has denied and oppressed, simultaneously seizing those who have gained the most advantage, and returning them to the whole. Having accompanied ever-shifting currents of thought from the Western world, the bestiary offers a space for a long-opposed connection between human and animal, a space for the two to meet and draw new conclusions.

In the bestiaries featured here, the two possibilities for the human/animal contrast – that is, the likening of humans to animals as a mode of marginalization, and the baring of the visceral savageness within the person who demeans the Other by calling them an animal – operate under an *a priori* human/animal binary. In both instances, the human aspect of *200 años de monstruos y maravillas argentinas* and *Bestiario médico* leads to a critical depiction of humans. Here, the animal aspect, the *bestia*, is used to convey darkness, barbarity. This darkness often manifests when a person is faced with someone or something unrelatable, allowing the concept of the Other to surface time and time again. This aspect of human nature has been subject to much writing, as seen with Fanon, and in Levinas's more general version, of encountering the face of the Other. Fanon's and Levinas's ideas, however, still function under the assumptions implied in Ferro's and Ferrándiz's decisions to pit human against animal. While the reader might be prompted to scrutinize the treatment of women by men, of Black people by White people, or of orphaned children by governmental authorities, an underlying hierarchy persists: that of animals beneath humans.

This presumed hierarchy stems from the position that Western society's most influential thinkers (Descartes, Kant, and, more recently, Levinas) held regarding animals, in that "all that is anomalous, that is, alive and non-predictable, is erased or subdued in the Newtonian/Cartesian epistemological paradigm" (Donovan 2016, 356). The hierarchy also consists of, consciously or unconsciously, a neglect of thinking about the animal altogether, as Derrida well points out, along with Levinas (Derrida 2002, 107). Together, these philosophical traditions leave the animal, along with Othered human subcategories, neglected. Advocacy for an ecocentric understanding of human/non-human relations is not novel, but one need not look further than factory farming and mass habitat destruction to understand the incompatibility between ecocentrism and capitalist gain.

The two bestiaries also demonstrate the importance of language, and the true meaning in animal-based insults or comparisons. Like Beauvoir's woman, the animal is a vessel for the metaphors that allows for the conceptualization of the self. Thus, the use of the name "bestiary" to describe a work that features the worst aspects of human nature, though provocative and certainly tongue in cheek, assumes that the animal and its qualities, physiognomy, and nature, are undesirable and alien. It deepens the division between the Other and the self, and the notion that any resemblance between the two entities represents a failure in humankind's journey. Reduction and negligence go hand in hand, as the denial of animals becomes simpler when creatures as different as the blue whale, the crow, the bee, and the ant are assimilated together into one homogenous group. This discounting of animals allows humans to outweigh other beings, in a continuation of a philosophical tradition that provided little space for non-human creatures.

The abovementioned assumptions and the currents of thought from which they evolve in no way to subtract from the works' novelty, beauty, and value. They do, however, highlight common ground between the authors' just critiques of society and their use of the animal kingdom to depict them. Racism, sexism, and speciesism are all rooted in unfounded, interconnected, arbitrary decisions and ideas of one group's sense of superiority over another. It is the inheritance of thinking in terms of means and ends that, when driven to an extreme, manifests in tragedies such as witch hunts, environmental racism, and fascism. The otherness of the animal, once identified, can become a means towards understanding and solving such problems as those explored in the two bestiaries. To break down the barriers simultaneously pointed out by and reinforced in the works explored here, the reader must begin to conceptualize a crossroads whereby factory farming and massacres are closely related, where a mass famine and habitat destruction are two sides of the same coin, or where Beauvoir's constricted women and hormone-filled cows are derivatives of the same ideology.

CONCLUSION

The experimental works of Jorge Luis Borges, Juan José Arreola, Augusto Monterroso, Pablo Neruda, Nicolás Guillén, and José Emilio Pacheco inspired the revival of the bestiary genre in contemporary Hispanic literature. Basing themselves on the medieval form, these five authors infused the bestiary with their flair and interests, demonstrating that new creatures and concepts could reside in an old framework. As a result of these authors' examples, contemporary writers, illustrators, and designers from all corners of the Spanish-speaking world have published original interpretations of the medieval genre, demonstrating the form's plasticity and adaptability across hundreds of centuries and thousands of miles.

The bestiary is thus emblematic of the ethos of Hispanic literature. Themes of political and civil unrest, a preoccupation with existential matters, a simultaneous knowledge of and irreverence for tradition, and the gleam of magic are woven through the entries of the contemporary interpretations of the genre. Perched on a rather obscure branch of the Hispanic literary tradition, the bestiary serves as a case study on the persistence of a literary genre across continents and centuries, traversing cultural and religious transformations and shifts. Each work serves as a glimpse into the preoccupations of the society into which it is published, and the phenomenon as a whole showcases the flair of authors and artists alike, broadcasting the talent and varying styles of an entire generation.

In order to better understand the genre's resurgence, its origin, and its consequences in Hispanic literature, the first section established a foundation that tied the medieval to the contemporary. Through this groundwork I traced the trajectory of the genre, from its origins as the prototype *Physiologus* to the wildest of interpretations in newer works. Elastic in nature, the bestiary genre has managed to fit itself into contexts across centuries and continents, most recently adapting itself to the virtual territories of video and digital applications. In order to stretch the limits of what could be encompassed under the term "bestiary," we first had to modify the traditional understanding of the genre, and this book offered the following definition: "A collection of titled, independent short texts, largely descriptive but sometimes anecdotal, often accompanied by an image, about real, mythical, or implied beasts." Aside from the addition of "implied" beasts, as best illustrated in chapter 5, this definition omits the adjective "medieval" that was used in previous definitions, both in English (Oxford English Dictionary: "A descriptive or anecdotal treatise on various kinds of animal, especially a medieval work with a moralizing tone"), and in Spanish (Real Academia Española: "In medieval literature, a collection of narratives, descriptions, and images of real or fantastical animals"). Like any other, this definition remains fluid and subject to later discoveries on and interpretations of the topic. Certainly, because of the exciting, contemporary nature of the field, we can anticipate that new bestiaries are being written as this book is published, and that a revisiting of the topography of the genre will soon be in order.

Outlining the confines of the genre during the writing of this book proved challenging, and the investigation was filled with red herrings. The omission of Julio Cortázar's celebrated *Bestiario*, for instance, caused me a lot of uncertainty. While the title of Cortázar's work cannot be ignored, nor the fact that his work is animal-centric, his *Bestiario* is ultimately a collection of short stories, rather than independent, descriptive entries. In the case of Augusto Monterroso's *La oveja negra y demás fábulas*, the opposite is true, as the title announces a collection of fables, not a bestiary. Yet the length, verb tense aspect, and descriptive qualities of the entries, as well as the impact on later bestiaries, makes *La oveja negra* an undisputed member of the Hispanic bestiary canon. Both *200 años de monstruos y maravillas argentinas* and *Bestiario médico* offered another challenge: the inclusion and consequential implications of a bestiary inhabited by humans. Here, the recognition that humans also occupied medieval bestiaries, the works' short, titled entries and subheadings, and the allusions to animal themes all suggested that both works belonged in the corpus of bestiaries examined here. The bestiary is defined by form, independent of content. This is especially evident in chapter 5, with examples that attempt to pass themselves off as pseudo-scientific reports, obscuring any links to the literary tradition. While these bestiaries have proven to be as difficult to pin down as the animals they house, their form is what ultimately earned them a place in this book.

The pressure these works exerted on the traditional understanding of the term "bestiary" correlates with the new societal purposes they now fulfill. Beginning with the canonical works, and continuing through to the contemporary Hispanic bestiaries, the mission of the bestiary has changed. In most instances, the Christian moral teachings intrinsic to the medieval works is now either explicitly challenged or ignored. A strong anti-establishment current flows through these contemporary works, be it by showcasing beasts often neglected by contemporary mainstream culture, disputing biopolitical assumptions, or shifting the reader's gaze from the anthropocentric to the ecocentric. Although its purpose is no longer to teach within the Christian faith, the contemporary bestiary remains a fundamentally didactic enterprise. From this perspective, the contemporary bestiary has maintained one of the missions of its medieval ancestor.

This book has identified and explored some of the trends found in the most recently published examples of the genre. True to its trajectory thus far, however, the genre continues to evolve. The nature of the bestiaries published most recently, like *Animalia exstinta*, *Informe sobre ectoplasma animal*, *200 años de monstruos y maravillas argentinas*, and a bestiary not highlighted in this study titled *Animalario universal del profesor Revillod*, illustrated by Javier Sáez Castán and written by Miguel Murugarren (2003), demonstrate that bestiaries are moving towards abstraction and hybridity. These types of bestiaries are also the ones that receive the most press, reaffirming their relevancy in addressing contemporary preoccupations and concerns. In an entry titled "Monsters of the future" in *Bestiario mágico*, Jesús Callejo and Amelia Piñas predict that the monsters of the future will be the product of genetic testing. They predict a creature genetically modified to be five times the size of a "natural" salmon, aptly nicknamed *el salmonazo* (the giant salmon). Such is the terror inspired by the overgrown fish that in their closing lines, Callejo and Piñas write: "This is but an example of what awaits us. May God, Allah, and all gods on Olympus find us having confessed" (2000, 274; my translation).[1]

The consequences of experimenting with life, be it vegetal or animal, haunt not only literature, but society at large. This dystopian thread, which echoes the anxieties of works like Mary Shelley's *Frankenstein*, raises questions on the bioethical and biopolitical limits of human power over other beings, as pursued in the anthropocentric hierarchy by which Western society functions. In medieval bestiaries and in the medieval understanding of life, humans were the caretakers of God's creation. Along with the more structured aspects of medieval existence, this sense of responsibility has largely disappeared, and been replaced by the illusion of power. The abstract, hybrid, and modified bestiaries that are reflective of contemporary Western life, then, grapple with the disastrous consequences that this power, poorly wielded, wrecks – on beings, the environment, and the psyche.

While bestiaries reflect ongoing social, biopolitical, and environmental realities, their entries also have the effect of rendering the unknown familiar, of ushering creatures previously ignored into the cultural fold. In *Imagining Extinction: The Cultural Meaning of Endangered Species*, Ursula Heise states: "biodiversity, endangered species, and extinction are primarily cultural issues, questions of what we value and what stories we tell, and only secondarily issues of science" (2016, 5). She argues that species matter when they become part of the stories a culture tells about their origins, history, modernization, and future, and when they become a part of that culture's understanding of their humanity (237). In other words, bestiaries are one of the genres through which animals become relevant and familiar to audiences. As animals become part of the culture, they take on new meanings and become more important for audiences, leading to genuine interest and a connection between species. In *Ecocriticism*, Greg Garrard points out that "concern for endangered species is not lacking, but nor can it be conjured merely by placing a species on a scientifically determined list" (2023, 152). An organic, natural interest in other species stems from contact with them, not from an abstract directive to care. Not unlike the medieval bestiaries that told stories of fascinating, far away beasts, contemporary works can also serve to spark an interest in nature, its unique qualities and essence, and its preservation.

Despite more abstract and technologically altered creatures beginning to take centre stage, bestiaries have yet to permeate the virtual world in a significant manner. This is in part because of the book-object aura that exists around the genre. In many cases, bestiaries are obscure findings, produced by small publishers in limited quantities. Most bestiaries are printed in colour, beautifully designed, and with elaborate illustrations, making it almost impossible to imagine their existence in other media. Some crossover into the virtual world, however, has taken place. The most exciting example can be found in José Luis Trueba Lara's *Bestiario culinario de México* (Mexican culinary bestiary) (2018), a bestiary that uses augmented reality to make two of its pages come alive when viewed through a smartphone. Videos of Luisa Valenzuela's alliterative *ABC de las microfábulas*, for instance, have been created and can be found online. A version of *Animalario universal del profesor Revillod* was created for use on a tablet. This virtual version was not available for long, however, likely because the popularity of the work, unmatched by any other contemporary Hispanic bestiary, proved the digital version superfluous. The bestiary, if tweaked, would lend itself well to game-like applications. The creatures would fit into a model like that of Pokémon Go, an augmented reality game that allows players to find, battle, and capture Pokémon creatures in real-life locations. If the Pokémon were replaced with mythological creatures, the game could double as an educational tool, allowing players to populate their own digital bestiaries. Based on the trend thus far, further attempts to upload the beast seem imminent.

Guillén's and Tomeo's works also hint at other possible uses for the bestiary. The idea that these works (or in the case of Guillén, aspects of his work) avoided censorship because of their seemingly inoffensive nature, unlike more realist texts, offers a fascinating research opportunity. A study of censorship and the bestiary during past dictatorships in Latin America and Spain might reveal that the animal's literary disguise made it an optimal vessel for provocative or subversive material. Increasingly common tampering with public opinion by social media giants and companies during political elections, as well as the introduction of generative artificial intelligence, with its hallucinations and outwardly friendly demeanour, demonstrate that society remains as vulnerable as ever to censorship and language curation. Bestiaries, especially when populated by animals alone, could prove an interesting subject of study as seemingly innocuous vessels of complex, subversive material.

Collecting examples for this book meant begrudgingly passing up countless non-Hispanic bestiaries. Airline weight restrictions and the Hispanic-literature scope of the investigation demanded significant self-restraint. While this Hispanic-only delineation carved out a clear and necessary scope for the project, it also excluded exciting possibilities. A cross-linguistic, cross-canonical bestiary would be a fascinating perspective on the genre. Likely, bestiaries belonging to other canons were impacted very differently by their own renowned authors, or perhaps they emerged independently of each other, inspired directly by the medieval tradition. It would be intriguing to see whether contemporary, original bestiaries in other languages manage to equal or outnumber their once-prolific medieval counterparts.

As briefly outlined by the preceding paragraphs, the novel nature of the bestiary genre as a contemporary enterprise meant that for every question answered and each conclusion drawn, two equally significant ones emerged in its place. I offer this hydra to others interested in the trajectory and uses of the contemporary Hispanic bestiary and to encourage readers to draw their own conclusions and to challenge my own. While this book proposed one potential route that the genre might have taken to arrive on the American continent – the experimentation and renown of six canonical authors, and Borges in particular – not much more scholarship exists on the topic. There is also limited information regarding the existence of Spanish medieval bestiaries, which further complicates this matter. Perhaps the closest instance is that of Brunetto Latini's *The Medieval Castilian Bestiary*, originally written in French, and belonging to his encyclopedic work, *Livres dou tresor*. Due to the popularity of Latini's work in medieval Spain, a number of Castilian manuscripts survive, with the defining characteristic of being largely devoid of Christian moralization. Another example is that of the medieval author Ramon Llull, who wrote a Catalan bestiary titled *Llibre de les bèsties*, and bestiary-like works like José Durand's *Ocaso de sirenas: Manatíes en el siglo XVI* surface well before 1957, the date that Borges's *Manual de zoología fantástica* was published. They were not featured in this investigation because their form does not offer as clear a story as that of the proposed jump of the medieval bestiary, as is, straight into avant-garde literature, as a result of experimentation. Whether a clearer trajectory and evolution can be traced would be the undertaking of a different project.

In the hopes of facilitating further inquiry and inciting interest in the genre, the entire corpus can be found in the appendix of this book. My first hope for this corpus is that educators might incorporate it into their curricula. I invite teachers and parents to expose children to a wealth of readily available, beautifully illustrated autochthonous creatures, as well as Hispanic authors and artists through the bestiary. University instructors might also wish to consider the bestiary as a tool with which to build lectures from the specific to the general, and to study the bestiary from historical, literary, artistic, political, and design perspectives, among countless others. Finally, I hope other admirers of Hispanic literature might peruse these works, and perhaps incorporate the modern bestiary into their conception of this most superb literary tradition.

APPENDIX

BESTIARY CORPUS

Aceves, Raul. 1995. *Diccionario de bestias mágicas y seres sobrenaturales de América*. Universidad de Guadalajara.

Arístides, César. 2000. *Bestiario inmediato: Muestra de poesía mexicana contemporánea*. Ediciones Coyoacán.

Arreola, Juan J. 1972. *Bestiario*. J. Mortiz.

Arreola, Juan J., with Héctor Xavier. 2018. *Punta de plata: Bestiario*. J. Mortiz.

Avilés Fabila, René. 2001. *Bestiario de seres prodigiosos*. Illustrated by José Luis Cuevas. Ediciones Eneida.

Bajarlía, Juan-Jacobo. 1969. *Historia de monstruos*. Ediciones de la Flor.

Baltic, Leo. 1999. *Bestiario mitológico: Seres fantásticos de la Argentina*. Albatros.

Baonza, Carlos. 1999. *Bestiario*. Ediciones Eneida.

Bellido, Mercedes. 2019. *El libro oculto de los animales*. Lunwerg Editores.

Blanco Laserna, David, and María Espejo. 2018. *El bestiario de los números*. Tuhle.

Borges, Jorge L., and Margarita Guerrero. 1957. *Manual de zoología fantástica*. Fondo de Cultura Económica.

– 1967. *El libro de los seres imaginarios*. Illustrated by Silvio Baldessari. Editorial Kier.

Brizuela, Leopoldo. 2012. *La locura de Onelli*. Bajo la Luna.

Callejo, Cabo J., and Amelia Piñas. 2000. *Bestiario mágico*. EDAF.

Carner, Josep, and Pere Vivas. 2013. *Barcelona bestiario*. Triangle Postals.

Colombres, Adolfo. 2002. *Nuestros seres imaginarios*. Ediciones del instituto movilizador de fondos cooperativos.

Colombres, Adolfo, and Luis Scafati. 2000. *Seres mitológicos argentinos*. Emecé.

Costa, Geògia, and Claudio Sánchez Viveros. 2017. *Monstruos del mundo.* Montena.

Doce, Jordi, and Rafael Gómez. 2001. *Bestiario del nómada.* Eneida.

Domínguez Luis, Cecilia. 2008. *Bestiario y otros desconciertos.* Ediciones Baile del Sol.

Feria, Luis, Ricardo Zamorano, and José Hierro. 1999. *Bestiario.* Ediciones Eneida.

Ferrándiz, Carlos. 2000. *Bestiario médico.* Illustrated by Carlos Baonza. Ediciones Eneida.

Ferrer, Lerín F. 2007. *El bestiario.* Galaxia Gutenberg.

Ferro, Gabo. 2015. *200 años de monstruos y maravillas argentinas.* Illustrated by Christian Montenegro and Laura Varsky. Beatriz Viterbo Editora.

Fitz James Stuart, Brianda. 2019. *Mi universo re-creativo: Curiosidades y otras bestias.* Editorial Planeta.

García López, Ángel. 2000. *Bestiario: Animalias.* Ediciones Eneida.

García-Orea, Almudena. 2004. *Animalario peregrino: Un bestiario del camino de Santiago.* Eneida.

González, Lanuza E. 1971. *Bestiario del Martín Fierro.* Cuadernos del Fondo Nacional de las Artes.

Guillén, Nicolás. 1967. *El gran zoo.* Illustrated by Jamís Fayad. Instituto del libro.

Hierro, Margarita. 1999. *Gatos gatos gatos.* Eneida.

Larraquy, Roque. 2014. *Informe sobre ectoplasma animal.* Illustrated by Diego Ontivero. Eterna Cadencia.

Lizalde, Eduardo. 1997. *Manual de flora fantástica.* Cal y Arena.

Llull, Ramon. 2017. *Libro de las bestias.* Edited and translated by Laureano Robles Carcedo. Tecnos.

López Lacomba, Guillermo. 2019. *Bestiario.* Espuela de Plata.

Machado, Wilfredo. 1994. *Libro de animales.* Monte Ávila Editores Latinoamericana.

Malaxecheverría, Ignacio. 1991. *Fauna fantástica de la península ibérica.* Kriselu.

Meza, Julián. 2010. *Bestiario de historia mexicana.* Equilibrista.

Montero Galán, Daniel. 2015. *El gran zooilógico: Bestiario de seres mitoilógicos.* Ediciones Jaguar.

Monterroso, Augusto. 1969. *La oveja negra y demás fábulas.* J. Mortiz.

Moreno, Alberto, and Catriel Tallarico. 2014. *Bestiario de seres míticos de la Patagonia.* Artemisia.

Morón, Enrique. 1979. *Bestiario.* V. Pozanco.

Muñoz, Isabel, and Carlos Baonza. 2000. *Bestiarios del libro ultramarino*. Ediciones Eneida.
Muñoz Ledo, Norma. 2016. *Bestiario de seres fantásticos mexicanos*. Illustrated by Israel Barrón. Fondo de Cultura Económica.
Muñoz Ledo, Norma, and Helguera y Hernández. 2012. *Supernaturalia*. Altea.
Muñoz Rengel, Juan Jacinto. 2003. *El libro de los pequeños milagros*. Páginas de espuma.
Navalón, Virginia. 2018. *Bestiario*. Editorial Pre-textos.
Neruda, Pablo. 1965. *Bestiary/Bestiario*. Illustrated by Antonio Frasconi and translated by Elsa Neuberger, Harcourt, Brace and World.
– 2019. *Bestiario*. Libros del Zorro Rojo.
Nesquens, Daniel, and Elisa Arguilé. 2001. *Hasta (casi) 100 bichos*. Anaya.
Pacheco, José Emilio. 1985. *Álbum de zoología*. Illustrated by Alberto Blanco. Cuarto Menguante.
Perucho, Juan. 1977. *Bestiario fantástico*. Cupsa.
Posada, José L., and Félix Guerra. 2000. *Criaturas insólitas o desaparecidas*. Editorial letras cubanas.
Pujol, Carlos. 2012. *Bestiario*. Ediciones Cálcamo.
Ramón Alonso, José, and Riki Blanco. 2017. *Seres asombrosos: De los avispones asesinos a los delfines soñadores*. A Buen Paso.
Retana, Salvador, and Alberto Manguel. 2005. *Bestiario*. Editorial Casariego.
Roldán, Gustavo, and Gabriel Berstein. 2005. *Bestiario*. Guadal.
Roldán, Gustavo, and Eugenia Nobati. 2008. *Bestiario de seres mágicos mitológicos e imaginarios*. Guadal.
Roldán, Gustavo, and Luis Scafati. 2013. *Dragón*. Sudamericana.
Roldán, Peniche. 1097. *Bestiario mexicano*. Panorama.
Romo, Claudio. 2018. *Bestiario mexicano*. Tipografia Negri.
Sáez Castán, Javier, and Miguel Murugarren. 2003. *Animalario universal del profesor Revillod*. Fondo de Cultura Económica.
– 2016. *El animalario vertical*. Fondo de Cultura Económica de España.
Sánchez Ferlosio, Rafael. 2019. *De algunos animales: Bestiario ilustrado*. Edited by Ignacio Echevarría and illustrated by Alfred Brehm. Penguin Random House.
Santamans, Joana, and Ernest Santamans. 2016. *Vida*. Casa Catedral.
Seimandi, Esteban. 2010. *Animalia exstinta*. Illustrated by Hugo Horita and designed by Juan Cruz Bazterrica. Tres en Línea.
Tomeo, Javier. 1988. *Bestiario*. Montena.
– 2000. *Bestiario*. Las Tres Sorores.

Tomeo, Javier, and Natalio Bayo. 2007. *Bestiario*. Prames.

Toriz, Rafael, and Edgar Cano. 2015. *Animalia*. Vanilla Planifolia.

Toro, Montalvo C. 1999. *Reyes, astros y enanos*. Palabras del Oráculo.

Trueba Lara, José Luis, and Margarita de Orellana, eds. 2018. *Bestiario culinario de México*. Artes de México.

Uhart, Hebe. 2017. *Animales*. Adriana Hidalgo.

Urdapilleta Muñoz, Marco. 1995. *Bestiario de Indias*. Universidad Autónoma del Estado de México.

Valenzuela, Luisa. 2009. *ABC de las microfábulas*. Illustrated by Rufino de Mingo. Del Centro Editores.

– 2013. *Zoorpresas zoológicas*. Illustrated by Lorenzo Amengual. Editorial Macedonia.

– 2018. *ABC de las microfábulas*. Illustrated by Lorenzo Amengual. Fondo de Cultura Económica.

Vázquez Gloria, Andrés. 2013. *Bestiario para Mateo*. UAM.

Vela, David, and Ramón Gómez de la Serna. 2007. *Bestiario de greguerías*. ACVF Editorial.

Vilchis, Abraham. 2006. *Animalario: Manual de zoología imaginaria para uso diario*. Ediciones y Gráficos Eón.

Wamba, Carlos. 2011. *Bestiario personal*. Editorial Baile del Sol.

NOTES

INTRODUCTION

1 There are a number of researchers doing excellent work in both the more general field of bestiaries and the stricter field of Hispanic bestiaries. In his thorough 2016 article "Nuevos bestiarios en la literatura española contemporánea," Francisco González García also notes the need for a more inclusive definition of the term "bestiary," one that does away with the temporal tethering to the medieval period, as well as including those works that do not have a moralizing tone. Esperanza López Parada dedicated an entire doctoral dissertation to the topic, entitled *Bestiarios americanos: La tradición animalística en el cuento hispanoamericano contemporáneo* (2002), in which she highlights some of the innovative features of the bestiaries I classify as "canonical" in a comparative type of analysis. Claire Mercier traces a history of monstrosity and uses a post-humanist lens to examine Alexis Figueroa and Claudio Romo's bestiary, *Fragmentos de una biblioteca transparente*.

2 The term "beast" is a loaded one in both English and Spanish, ranging in its meaning and used as insult and emphatic compliment depending on context. An analysis on the implications and consequences of labelling humans as such will be explored with more nuance in chapter 6. Unless otherwise indicated, however, this analysis will use the term interchangeably with "animal," insinuating no connotation, in keeping with the tradition of texts such as *Physiologus* and medieval bestiaries.

CHAPTER ONE

1 The date of the *Physiologus* is greatly debated, and the theories that support the various date claims prove too extensive to cite here. Though some outliers claim that the book could have been written before the second century, most scholars argue for a date between the second and fourth century, as by the fourth century, the *Physiologus* was being cited in other works. For more information on dating the *Physiologus*, please see Alan Scott's "The Date of the *Physiologus*" (1998).

2 Transcriptions and translations of all citations of *The Aberdeen Bestiary* were done by Morton Gauld and Colin McLaren, as cited in the Aberdeen University's digital archive of the work.

3 *The Aberdeen Bestiary*, fol. 11r, MS 24, University of Aberdeen Library, Aberdeen.

4 *The Aberdeen Bestiary*, fol. 11r, MS 24, University of Aberdeen Library, Aberdeen.

5 During the classical period, Cicero and Quintilian were concerned with the use of the allegory as a rhetorical tool, with the latter emphasizing it as "a figure of inversion, where it is one in words and another in sentence of meaning," focusing on the gap between lexical and semantic function. It was also during this period that the device became a tool through which to achieve the syncretism of Judaism and Greek and Roman polytheistic religions in the Roman world (Tambling 2010, 21). Isidore of Seville, among the noted bestiary contributors, stated: "Allegory is 'other speech,' for it literally says one thing, and another thing is understood" (2006, 63).

6 For more information on whether people in the medieval period believed that the fantastic creatures in bestiaries existed, please see Pamela Gravestock's "Did Imaginary Animals Exist?" (1999).

7 Another instance of the modification of visual evidence of religious practices for emerging Christian doctrine can be found in J. Holli Wheatcroft's essay on Classical influences in iconography, "Classical Ideology in the Medieval Bestiary" (1999).

8 The phoenix's ties to the Egyptian city of Heliopolis is not explicitly stated in the *Physiologus* entry. Heliopolis is mentioned, but Curley makes his assumption based on one version of the beast's mythology.

9 Genesis 1:26 (New Revised Standard Version)

10 Matthew 6:26–27 (New King James Version)

CHAPTER TWO

1 When relevant, the English translation of the title of a work will be provided. Once introduced, the original name will be used in the analysis.

2 "Platón (si terciara en esta investigación) nos diría que el niño ya ha visto al tigre, en el mundo anterior de los arquetipos, y que ahora al verlo lo reconoce" (Borges and Guerrero 1957, 7).

3 Borges once stated: "I consider Scholem a friend of mine and I think he considers me his friend, although we must have seen each other no more than eight hours in our lifetime ... But since I have read him and reread him so much ..." (Alazraki 1988, 6). And on a separate occasion, "When I was asked in Israel what I wanted to see, I said: Don't ask me what I want to see because I am blind, but if you ask me whom I want to see I'll answer, right away, Scholem" (6).

4 "El nombre de este libro justificaría la inclusión del Príncipe Hamlet, del punto, de la línea, de la superficie, del hipercubo, de todas las palabras genéricas y, tal vez, de cada uno de nosotros y de la divinidad. En suma, casi del universo" (Borges and Guerrero 1967, 7).

5 "Un libro de esta índole es necesariamente incompleto; cada nueva edición es el núcleo de ediciones futuras, que pueden multiplicarse hasta el infinito. Invitamos al eventual lector de Colombia o del Paraguay a que nos remita los nombres, la fidedigna descripción y los hábitos más conspicuos de los monstruos locales" (Borges and Guerrero 1967, 7).

6 The 1967 Editorial Kier and 1979 Emecé editions, for example, contain the same animals in a different order.

7 "En cada escalón se intensifica su color, su forma se perfecciona y la luz que irradia es cada vez más brillante. Testimonio de su sensibilidad es el hecho de que sólo logra su forma perfecta en el último escalón, cuando el que sube es un ser evolucionado espiritualmente" (Borges and Guerrero 1967, 12).

8 "El capitán Burton registra la leyenda del A Bao A Qu en una de las notas de su versión de las *Mil y una noches.*"

9 "Según mitología de los egipcios, Abtu y Anet son dos peces idénticos y sagrados que van nadando ante la nave de Ra, dios del sol, para advertirlo contra cualquier peligro. Durante el día, la nave viaja por el cielo, del naciente al poniente; durante la noche, bajo tierra, en dirección inversa" (Borges and Guerrero 1967, 23).

10 "Por lo demás, no pretendemos que este libro, acaso el primero en su género, abarque el número total de los animales fantásticos. Hemos investigado las literaturas clásicas y orientales, pero nos consta que el tema que abordamos es infinito" (Borges and Guerrero 1967, 9).

11 Unfortunately, very few first editions of *Bestiario* were printed, and they are sold at astronomical costs. As a timely and happy coincidence to this book, in 2018 the publisher Joaquín Moritz published a commemorative edition of Arreola's *Punta de plata*. This edition fell on the centennial of Arreola's birth and joined together the Jaliscan writer's texts and Xavier's images, which until that point could only be appreciated together in elusive first editions.

12 "Hubo que resolver para ellas algunos problemas biológicos que más parecen ingeniería y de mecánica: un circuito nervioso de doce metros de largo; una sangre que se eleva contra la ley de la gravedad mediante un corazón que funciona como bomba de pozo profundo; y todavía, a estas alturas, una lengua eyéctil que va más arriba."

13 "Veloces lanzaderas, las focas tejen y destejen la tela interminable de sus juegos eróticos. Se abrazan sin brazos y resbalan de una en otra improvisando sus rondas *ad libitum*. Baten el agua con duras palmadas; se aplauden ellas mismas en ovaciones viscosas. La alberca parece de gelatina. El agua está llena de labios y de lenguas y las focas entran y salen relamiéndose."

14 "Como en la gota microscópica, las focas se deslizan por las frescas entrañas del agua virgen con movimiento flagelo de zoospermos, y las mujeres y los niños miran inocentes la pantomima genética."

15 "En un lejano país existió hace muchos años una Oveja negra. Fue fusilada. Un siglo después, el rebaño arrepentido le levantó una estatua ecuestre que quedó muy bien en el parque. Así, cada vez que aparecían ovejas negras eran rápidamente pasadas por las armas para que las futuras generaciones de ovejas comunes y corrientes pudieran ejercitarse también en la escultura" (Monterroso 1969, 23).

16 "Los animales se parecen tanto al / hombre que a veces es imposible / distinguirlos de éste."

17 "y no me iré de este planeta / sin saber qué vine a buscar, / sin averiguar este asunto, / y no me bastan las personas." The pages in this work are not numbered, so no exact reference can be given.

18 "Yo tengo que ir mucho más lejos / Y tengo que ir mucho más cerca"

19 "Sin duda me preguntaréis por el marfil maldito del / narwhal, para que yo os conteste / de qué modo el unicornio marino agoniza arponeado" (Neruda 1990, 577).

20 “marítimo y enigmático / tiene una cresta de cristal / el lomo azul, la cola verde, / vientre de compacto coral”
21 “Para la red / para el arpón / naciste / Para anzuelos / asfixias / y sartenes / Inficionamos por usura tu mar / Ahora te haces justicia / envenenándonos”
22 “Grandes tribus flotantes / migraciones / áisbergs de carne y hueso / islas dolientes / Suena en la noche triste / de las profundidades / su elegía y despedida / porque el mar / fue despoblado de ballenas / Sobrevivientes de otro fin de mundo / adoptaron la forma de los peces / sin llegar a ser peces / Necesitan salir a respirar / cubiertas de algas milenarias / y entonces / se encarniza con ellas la crueldad / del arpón explosivo / Y todo el mar se vuelve / un mar de sangre / mientras las llevan al destazadero / para hacerlas lipstic / jabón aceite / alimento de perros / *Sus ojos son los párpados del alba / De sus narices sale humo / como de olla o caldero que hierve / En su cerviz está la fuerza / y delante se esparce el desaliento** / *Job, 41:18–22”

CHAPTER THREE

1 *The Aberdeen Bestiary*, fol. 7r, MS 24, University of Aberdeen Library, Aberdeen.
2 “Yo también hubiera podido ser reina, quede eso muy claro. Para ello hubiera sido suficiente que, durante mi vida larval, hubiera sido alimentada jalea real.”
3 “nada importan las costumbres y las tradiciones cuando se nace con los sentidos revolucionados.”
4 “Vigilo no sé qué, el aire invisible / acaricio nocturnos desvaríos, / y en la memoria guardo soledades / extraviadas de perro vagabundo”
5 “con miedo a hacer preguntas / interrogo al silencio y no hay respuesta. No sé si soy un perro imaginado, pero si puedo recordar existo”
6 “Algunos dicen que soy ave de mal agüero y que mis chillidos anuncian la muerte. En otros tiempos, sin embargo, hubo poetas que me entronizaron como rey de todas las aves nocturnas y me consagraron a Juno, esposa de Júpiter. No faltaron incluso quienes me vieron a los pies de Minerva, la diosa de la ardiente mirada, protectora de los artistas. Vivo pues en la duda.”
7 “Hoy en día la ciencia nos prohíbe / Creer cosas así, / Imposibles y bellas”
8 “se limita a ser un urodelo / Bestezuela digamos del montón, / Sin ningún privilegio”

9 "Todavía no tengo muy claro, sin embargo, a qué fuerzas represento."
10 "Parece que pregunto: ¿Y tú quién eres? / Nadie responde, la sabiduría / ¿consiste solamente en preguntar? / Me interrogan y yo guardo silencio"
11 "Más de una vez, contemplándome en el espejo del estanque, me pregunto: ¿Y si yo no fuese ese insecto cruel que pienso ser? ¿Y si yo fuese, en realidad, una flor?"
12 "a) aniquilarnos, a pesar de la suprema belleza de nuestros ojos. b) conservarnos vivos, gozar de esa belleza, pero a despecho de soportar nuestras dolorosas picaduras y recordar que, a pesar de todo, continúan vivos."

CHAPTER FOUR

1 *Bestiario de seres prodigiosos* is an extended version of *Los animales prodigiosos* (1989), by the same author. Because of the latter edition's collaboration with famed artist José Luis Cuevas, and the change in title to include the word *bestiario*, this chapter examines the latter edition, which in any case contains all the original entries.
2 The pages belonging to this bestiary are not numbered, and thus not referenced here.
3 "Terrible y poderoso / Duende espantoso / Para él la carne humana / Es lo más apetitoso"
4 "Ante sus blancos dientes de jaguar / El miedo deberás dominar / Sólo ríe a carcajadas / Y caer muerto lo verás."
5 "Todo cabe en su lamento / Tristeza, angustia y sufrimiento / ¡ay mujer que su dolor derrama!"
6 "Horario de los funerales y del nacimiento: Cada cien años, aproximadamente a las 12:30 del día, se le prende fuego a la canela, el nardo y la mierra que conforman el nido del ave («que es –según palabras de Ovidio – su propia cuna y sepulcro de su padre»). A las 13:30, luego de que las llamas aromáticas han cesado, el Fénix resurge triunfal, con su hermosísimo plumaje dorado y carmesí de sus propias cenizas. Sea usted puntual."
7 This is not the only instance of this phenomenon. The entry "Zoofilia" inserts Rubén Darío into the same tradition as Dante and Virgil, much like how Dante inserted himself into the Classical tradition.
8 "Ésta es la jaula destinada / a la resurrección del Ave-Fénix. / (En diciembre llegarán sus cenizas)"
9 "En la Frick Collection de Nueva York hay un pasmoso bronce que representa a una mujer sátiro cargando a su hijo. Mitad cabra, mitad

fémina sugiere la posibilidad de una raza que desapareció de manera misteriosa. Por ello es preferible no pensar en sátiros poseyendo brutalmente mujeres, sino en sátiros cotejando con elegancia a seres de su misma especie."

10 "Primero: ya no hay por qué recurrir a anticonceptivos, abortos, y cosas sacrílegas. Segundo: se cumple con un antiquísimo precepto cristiano: comed que éste es mi cuerpo, bebed que ésta es mi sangre."

11 "Las nuevas quimeras, los seres fantásticos que pueden ser adquiridos en tiendas de rarezas, a lo sumo provocan curiosidad o el deseo irrefrenable de tenerlos en calidad de mascotas. El miedo a lo desconocido, a lo sobrenatural, por desgracia ha sido desterrado en este siglo en que todo es posible merced a la ciencia."

12 Two previous editions exist of this bestiary. The first is the 2009 edition of *ABC de las microfábulas*, illustrated by Rufino de Mingo. The work's cover is handmade, and the pages of the bestiary, which also look handmade, are loose, allowing for a rearrangement of the various entries. The second is *Zoorpresas zoológicas* (2013), which includes all the *microtextos* featured in *ABC de las microfábulas*. Because the 2009 edition was limited and is difficult to find, and the 2013 edition is not illustrated, I am featuring here the 2018 edition, which was published for mass distribution.

13 "Las moralejas suelen ser muy breves y al grano, sin embargo la que están leyendo nada contra la corriente y es una Macromoraleja de pretensiones abarcativas, concebida en torno a la idea de complicidad."

14 "La dulzura es el camino más directo a la felicidad" (54); "La fatua autoconfianza muchas veces te impide ver las trampas" (41); "Ni vale la pena hacerse el macho cuando la genética no te favorece" (62); "La comida macrobiótica no es para todos, mejor no insistir" (64).

15 The translation of this literary game is best read out loud, as I did my best to preserve the sound as opposed to the letter. The letter *f*, for instance, makes the same sound as the English letters *ph*.

16 "Focas fastidiosas no faltan. Fantasean fábulas ficticias, falsifican frases famosas y filosofías frenéticas. Fraudulentas, las focas, felices, feroces, fingen fragilidad para fabricarse favores. La fiebre las favorece, fulgen como faros al fagocitar faunas flotantes. Frígidas, se fijan en las fachas de los flamencos y farfullan falsas finezas fingiendo fervor. Fluctuantes, en el flujo fabrican frunces para frustrar la fruición de los flamencos y finalmente fumárselos a la fuerza. Los flamencos con fémures fracturados forcejean fenomenalmente formulando fulfurantes flatulencias de fuego. Farra para las focas, fascinadas, que fanáticas filman la farándula hasta el final de la fiesta. Moraleja: A los pedos nunca te vas a salvar."

17 "Lugar donde florecen los ñuños, por supuesto. Barrio periférico de Santiago de Chile."

18 "La ele, por ejemplo, es una letra líquida, basta con escuchar su sonido. Atención con derramarlas."

19 "Parque nacional argentino con importante catarata que no afecta la vista, todo lo contrario."

20 Gorilas y gusanos gustan de la globalización. La gente gime, golpeada por garrotes de generales gorilas, guapos guarangos que galopan al grito de "¡Genial!" Grandes gimnastas, los generales gorilas y gusanos se gratifican en grado gozoso, con el gaznate gárrulo. ¡Guai del gurí gay que los gaste! Son guapos, gelatinosos, gigantescos. Grandiosos gritones como guacamayos glorifican la guerra, los gladiadores, los gendarmes glaucos, los guardiacárceles, y gozan del graznido de los gansos. En grupo, los muy gandules le granizan las guindas a la gente. Gobiernan con guardias y guaruras. Los gerentes les garpan grandes guarismos, pero golosos no gastan en guisos gremiales, no son gregarios, son grasientos granujas guardianes de la guillotina. Moraleja: Un pasito a la izquierda suele mejorar la vida propia y la ajena.

21 Lluisa Llorent, la llama de Port Lligat, no halla la llave. Llena de lluvia, una llaga, llama llorando a su llamo que no llega. Lluwellyn Llorent, su amo, no le lleva la llave. En la llanura del Llobregat, las llantas llenas, una llamarada su llavero, leyendo a Vargas Llosa, a Llinás y "El llano en llamas," Lluwellyn llora sólo por llorar. Todo le llueve. Moraleja: Nunca dependas de los intelectuales, por más parientes cercanos que sean.

CHAPTER FIVE

1 *The Aberdeen Bestiary*, fol. 16r, MS 24, University of Aberdeen Library, Aberdeen.

2 "Una tarea de rescate moral y estético porque es inmoral privilegiar intereses particulares y mercantilistas por sobre el patrimonio natural de la humanidad pero, antes que eso, es antiestético."

3 "Cantá conmigo este chamamé / Cantá fuerte, chamigo pará. La acordeona suena a piporé / y la vitrolita te vua acompañá."

4 From here on, the terms "phonograph" and "gramophone" will be used interchangeably, as for the purposes of this chapter, the difference of disc versus cylinder for music storage is irrelevant.

5 The specificity of the audience and the ludic nature of the entry are both linked to the term *trucha*. In colloquial Argentine vocabulary, *trucha* means fake or of poor quality. If, for instance, an article of clothing or a

piece of jewelry is *trucho*, it means to pass itself off as a brand name that it is not.

6 "Alfredo Mascardi Combs, Notas sobre la trucha patagónica de vientre espinado, Santiago de Chile, Editorial Científica Cogno-Cimientos, 1947, p. 23."

7 "Los espectros son pura superficie visible. La transparencia simultánea de todos sus secretos. Lo que soñaron estando dormidos, las proporciones y el peso de su mirada, todo está presente como un tramado fosfórico en su piel de éter y puede registrarse."

8 "La inscripción en éter de un animal muerto como espectro, mesurable por su claridad en watts, resulta de los hábitos que el animal supo reiterar en vida y del sufrimiento físico intenso. Hábito y dolor son la púa del gramófono que graba en pasta la huella del sonido para su reproducción."

9 The reader is partly warned of this false reality by the allusion to the subjunctive tense for the verb "to be" (ser) in the acronym of the organization itself (SEA).

10 The authors have given several interviews in Argentine newspapers; further, a free translation of their work in English, German, French, Italian, and Portuguese can be found online, along with countless reviews and recommendations from other Argentine authors, including Esteban Seimandi.

CHAPTER SIX

1 *The Aberdeen Bestiary*, fol. 93v, MS 24, University of Aberdeen Library, Aberdeen.

2 "Los desviados del buen curso de la historia, los no disciplinados, los fallos de civilidad, los desviados del camino del orden, los subversivos del canon."

3 "A los blancos los hizo Dios / a los mulatos San Pedro / a los negros hizo el diablo / para tizón del infierno."

4 "Porteño" is the designation for someone from Buenos Aires.

5 Although Walter Owen's translation has the Black man calling the gaucho an ass and a beast, in the original Spanish he does not. He instead says, "más porrudo serás vos / gaucho rotoso," calling the gaucho stubborn and pitiable.

6 "caballeros / dejen venir a ese toro"

7 "Y empezó la pobre allí / a bramar como una loba."

8 Hottentot Venus was the name given to a Khoekhoe woman from south-western African who was exhibited as a freak show attraction in Europe.

9 “A nosotros los médicos el primer puesto en el combate intelectual … para buscar solución á los males del presente: el andrajo humano nos pertenece … Somos la bestia con sus apetitos y necesidades, pero la bestia intelectual por excelencia, la bestia creadora de mundos, dominadora de la tierra.”

10 “En mis padres o abuelos estaba el pecado. / Recitamos todas las culpas posibles. / Para que al nombrarlas, fueran un acto de arrepentimiento, / aunque no recordaba haberlas cometido.”

11 “la retención de la menstruación engendra malos humores y siendo ya de bastantes años, no tienen calor natural para consumir y cocer dicha materia; y sobre todo las pobres, que no viven más que de carnes malas, son más venenosas que las otras.”

12 “Cuando la mujer es joven, es víctima pasiva de posesión diabólica por incubo; cuando se hace vieja, sobre todo si es ‘magra y fría de complexión,’ se convierte en sujeto activo del mal: en bruja.”

13 Scylla and Charybdis were sea creatures in Greek mythology, who came to be associated with the idea of being stuck between two evils.

14 “Vosotros sois muy grandes. / Tan enormes / que ni yo os veo, / ni a mí me veis tampoco / (si no os ayuda / un chorro de electrones). / En mi caso / como carezco de ojos / tengo mejor disculpa.”

15 “¿Estoy vivo? / Dice el fisiólogo / «No, que no produce / excremento ninguno / y es bien cierto / que caga quien vive, / y quien no caga, / seguro que no vive». / Y el genético: / «Sí, qué bien se reproduce / El hideputa, rompiendo / la madre o la matriz / que lo alimenta, / y matando al salir, / feto maldito». / ¡Discutid! / Ni eso sabéis.”

CONCLUSION

1 “Este es tan solo un ejemplo de lo que nos espera. Que Dios, Alá y todos los dioses del Olimpo nos pillen confesados.”

REFERENCES

Aberdeen Bestiary. ca. 1200. University Library MS 24. University of Aberdeen, Aberdeen.

Agamben, Giorgio. 2004. *The Open: Man and Animal*. Stanford University Press.

Alazraki, Jaime. 1988. *Borges and the Kabbalah*. Cambridge University Press.

Antón, Jacinto. 2018. "El gran zoo de papel." *El país* (Madrid), 7 December. www.elpais.com/cultura/2018/12/06/babelia/1544121365_630932.html.

Armstrong, John B., and George M. Malacinski. 1989. *Developmental Biology of the Axolotl*. Oxford University Press.

Arreola, Juan J. 1972. *Bestiario*. J. Mortiz.

Arreola, Juan J., with Héctor Xavier. 2018. *Punta de plata: Bestiario*. J. Mortiz.

Arreola, Juan J., and Saúl Yurkiévich. 1995. *Obras*. Fondo de Cultura Económica.

Ashmole Bestiary. ca. 1400. Bodleian Library MS, Ashmole 1511. Bodleian Libraries, University of Oxford.

Avilés Fabila, René. 2001. *Bestiario de seres prodigiosos*. Illustrated by José Luis Cuevas. Eneida.

Baonza, Carlos. 1993. *Bestiario*. Universidad Popular.

– 1999. *Bestiario*. Eneida, Ediciones.

Barber, Richard W. 1993. *Bestiary: Being an English Version of the Bodleian Library, Oxford M.S. Bodley 764; With All the Original Miniatures Reproduced in Facsimile*. Boydell Press.

Barnum, Frederick O. 1994. *His Master's Voice in America: Ninety Years of Communications Pioneering and Progress; Victor Talking Machine Company, Radio Corporation of America, General Electric Company*. General Electric.

Bartra, Roger. 1987. *La jaula de la melancolía: Identidad y metamorfosis del mexicano*. Grijalbo.

Baudrillard, Jean. 1994. *Simulacra and Simulation*. University of Michigan Press.

– 1995. *The Gulf War Did Not Take Place*. Indiana University Press.

– 2008. *The Perfect Crime*. Verso.

Beauvoir, Simone de. 1968. *The Second Sex*. Knopf.

Beneyto, María. 1996. "Del humor a la ironía en la obra de Juan José Arreola." PhD diss., Universitat de Barcelona.

Benjamin, Walter. 2019. "The Work of Art in the Age of Mechanical Reproduction." In *Illuminations*, edited by Hannah Arendt and translated by Harry Zohn. Mariner Books.

Benton, Janetta Rebold. 1992. *The Medieval Menagerie: Animals in the Art of the Middle Ages*. Abbeville Press.

Berger, John. 1991. *About Looking*. Vintage International.

Best, Stephen, and Sharon Marcus. 2009. "Surface Reading: An Introduction." *Representations* 108, no. 1: 1–21. https://doi.org/10.1525/rep.2009.108.1.1.

Bewick, Thomas. 1962. *1800 Woodcuts by Thomas Bewick and His School*. Dover.

Biedma, Juan M. 1986. *Crónica histórica del lago Nahuel Huapí*. Emecé.

Blanco, Alberto. 2008. "José Luis Cuevas: Un animal impuro." *Artes de México* 9: 12–7. https://www.jstor.org/stable/24316464.

– 2011. *Visual Poetry/Poesía Visual*. Athenaeum.

Borges, Jorge L. 1960. *Otras inquisiciones*. Emecé.

– 1975. *El libro de arena*. Ultramar.

– 1988. "The Kabbalah." In *Borges and the Kabbalah*, by Jaime Alazraki, 54–76. Cambridge University Press.

– 1999. "A Defense of the Kabbalah." In *Selected Non-Fictions*, edited by Eliot Weinberger. Viking.

Borges, Jorge L., and Willis Barnstone. 1982. *Borges at Eighty: Conversations*. Indiana University Press.

Borges, Jorge L., and Margarita Guerrero. 1957. *Manual de zoología fantástica*. Fondo de Cultura Económica.

– 1967. *El libro de los seres imaginarios*. Illustrated by Silvio Baldessari. Editorial Kier.

– 1974. *The Book of Imaginary Beings*. Translated by Norman Thomas di Giovanni. Penguin.

Burns, Thea. 2012. *The Luminous Trace: Drawing and Writing in Metalpoint*. Archetype Publications.

Callejo, Jesús, and Amelia Piñas. 2000. *Bestiario mágico*. EDAF.

Carothers, J.C. 1959: "Culture, Psychiatry, and the Written Word." *Psychiatry* 22, no. 4: 307–20.
Castro, Donald S. 1988. "El negro del acordeón: The Image of the Black in Argentina." *Afro-Hispanic Review* 7, nos. 1–3: 11–18. https://www.jstor.org/stable/23054118.
Cheng, Anne Anlin. 2009. "Skins, Tattoos and Susceptibility." *Representations* 108, no. 1: 98–119. https://doi.org/10.1525/rep.2009.108.1.98.
Chomsky, Noam. 1992. "The Media and the War: What War?" In *Triumph of the Image: The Media's War in the Persian Gulf: A Global Perspective*, edited by Hamid Molwana, George Gerbner, and Herbert I. Schiller. Westview Press.
Coleman, Mark. 2003. *Playback: From the Victrola to Mp3, 100 Years of Music, Machines, and Money*. Da Capo Press.
Cortázar, Julio. 1965. *Final Del Juego*. Editorial Sudamericana.
Curley, Michael J. 1979. *Physiologus*. University of Texas Press.
David, Isaiah. n.d. "How Do Gramophones Work?" *Techwalla*, www.techwalla.com/articles/how-do-gramophones-work.
Davis-Lett, Stephanie. 1981. "Revisando a Nicolás Guillén." *Explicación de Textos Literarios* 10, no. 1: 87–94.
De Costa, René. 1979. *The Poetry of Pablo Neruda*. Harvard University Press.
Del Popolo, Luis. 2012. "El silencioso humor de Silvio Baldessari." *Sonrisas argentinas*, 9 December.
Derrida, Jacques. 2002. *The Animal That Therefore I Am*. Fordham University Press.
Dinatale, Martín. 2017. "La historia secreta de la negociación entre el gobierno y los mapuches que terminó en tragedia." *Infobae*, 29 November. www.infobae.com/politica/2017/11/29/la-historia-secreta-de-la-negociacion-entre-el-gobierno-y-los-mapuches-que-termino-en-tragedia.
Dines, Ilya. 2012. "The Problem of the Transitional Family of Bestiaries." *Reinardus: Yearbook of the International Reynard Society* 24, no. 1: 29–52. https://doi.org/10.1075/rein.24.03din.
Doctorow, Cory. 2008. "Steampunk Gallery Show in Seattle: Anachrotechnofetishism." *Boing*, 11 September. https://boingboing.net/2008/09/11/steampunk-gallery-sh-1.html.
Donoso Aceituno, Arnaldo, and Juan Gabriel Araya Grandón. 2016. "Representaciones del animal en la poesía de Pablo Neruda." *Literatura: Teoría, historia y crítica* 18, no. 1: 29–51. https://doi.org/10.15446/lthc.v18n1.54678.

Donovan, Josephine. 2016. "Animal Rights and Feminist Theory." In *Animal Rights*, edited by Clare Palmer. Routledge.

Doudoroff, Michael J. 1989. "José Emilio Pacheco: An Overview of the Poetry, 1963–86." *Hispania* 72, no. 2: 264–76. https://doi.org/10.2307/343116.

Douglass Leyburn, Ellen. 1956. *Satiric Allegory: Mirror of Man*. Yale University Press.

Ellis, Keith. 1973. "Nicolás Guillén at Seventy." *Caribbean Quarterly* 19, no. 1: 87–94. www.jstor.org/stable/23050359.

Ensinck, María Gabriela. 2017. "Conflicto en una de las mayores fábricas de plásticos del país." *El cronista*, 9 February. www.cronista.com/negocios/Conflicto-en-una-de-las-mayores-fabricas-de-plasticos-del-pais-20170209-0027.html.

Fanon, Frantz. 2004. *The Wretched of the Earth*. Translated by Richard Philcox. Grove.

Feder Kittay, Eva. 1988. "Woman as Metaphor." *Hypatia* 3, no. 2: 63–86.

Feria, Fernanda, and Rosa Lince Campillo. 2010. "Arte y grupos de poder: El Muralismo y La Ruptura." *Estudios Políticos* 9, no. 21: 83–100. https://doi.org/10.22201/fcpys.24484903e.2010.21.

Ferrándiz, Carlos. 2000. *Bestiario médico*. Illustrated by Carlos Baonza. Ediciones Eneida.

Ferro, Gabo. 2015. *200 años de monstruos y maravillas argentinas*. Illustrated by Christian Montenegro and Laura Varsky. Beatriz Viterbo Editora.

– 2016. "Soy un cultor de lo efímero." Interview by Pedro Irigoyen. *Clarín*, 9 September. https://www.clarin.com/espectaculos/musica/Gabo-Ferro-cultor-efimero_0_H19t2vkn.html.

Figueroa, Quique. 2009. "Don Silvio, la Adriana Baldessari y su impronta en los irracionales." *Los parrafistas*, 31 March. http://losparrafistas.blogspot.com/2009/03/don-silvio-la-adriana-baldessari-y-su.html.

Fischer, María Luisa. 1996. "Zoológicos en libertad: La tradición del bestiario en el nuevo mundo." *Revista Canadiense de Estudios Hispánicos* 20, no. 3: 463–76. www.jstor.org/stable/27763310.

Forlini, Stefania. 2010. "Technology and Morality: The Stuff of Steampunk." *Neo-Victorian Studies* 3, no. 1: 72–98.

García Meza, Norma Esther. 2012. *La garza morena y la Venus de Zapotlán*. Universidad Veracruzana.

Garrard, Greg. 2023. *Ecocriticism*. Routledge.

Garrido, Felipe. 1997. "Prologue." In *Narrativa completa*, by Juan José Arreola. Alfaguara.

Gazdaru, Demetrio. 2010. "Vestigios de bestiarios medievales en las literaturas hispánicas e iberoamericanas." *Romanistisches Jahrbuch* 22, no. 1: 259–74. https://doi.org/10.1515/9783110244793.259.

George, Wilma, and Brundson Yapp. 1991. *The Naming of the Beasts: Natural History in the Medieval Bestiary*. Duckworth.

Giorgi, Gabriel. 2014. *Formas comunes: Animalidad, cultura, biopolítica*. Eterna Cadencia Editora.

"El gobierno defendió el accionar en el sur y criticó al juez: 'En el lugar todavía están los violentos.'" 2017. *Clarín*, 21 November. www.clarin.com/politica/patricia-bullrich-german-garavano-muerte-joven-mapuche-frente-grupos-violentos-respetan-ley-reconocen-argentina_0_HJCW7cFxM.html.

Gociol, Judith, and Diego Rosemberg. 2000. *La historieta argentina: Una historia*. Ediciones de la Flor.

Goldman, Judy. 2017. "Israel Barrón, ilustrador." Society of Children's Book Writers and Illustrators. https://www.scbwi.org/2019/03/10/israel-barron-ilustrador.

González, Omar. 2014. "El bestiario y la flor evanescente." *Las mil y una nota* (blog), 14 June. http://notasomargonzalez.blogspot.com/2012/09/manual-de-zoologia-fantastica.html.

Gossen, Gary H. 1996. "Animal Souls, Co-essences, and Human Destiny in Mesoamerica." In *Monsters, Tricksters, and Sacred Cows: Animal Tales and American Identities*, edited by A.J. Arnold. University of Virginia Press.

Gravestock, Pamela. 1999. "Did Imaginary Animals Exist?" In *The Mark of the Beast: The Medieval Bestiary in Art, Life, and Literature*, edited by Debra Hassig, 119–39. Garland Publishing.

Grout, James. n.d. "The Medieval Bestiary" *Encyclopædia Romana*. https://penelope.uchicago.edu/~grout/encyclopaedia_romana/britannia/anglo-saxon/flowers/bestiary.html.

Grusin, Richard A., ed. 2015. *The Nonhuman Turn*. University of Minnesota Press.

Guillén, Nicolás. 1967. *El gran zoo*. Illustrated by Jamís Fayad. Instituto del Libro.

Guillén, Nicolás, and J.A. George Irish. 1975. "Notes on a Historic Visit: Nicolás Guillén in Jamaica." *Caribbean Quarterly* 21, nos. 1/2: 74–84. www.jstor.org/stable/23050261.

"Habló el médico que atendió a los manifestantes heridos: 'Hubo balas de un sólo lugar.'" 2017. *El destape*, 27 November. www.eldestapeweb.com/hablo-el-medico-que-atendio-los-manifestantes-heridos-hubo-balas-un-solo-lugar-n36387.

Hassig, Debra. 1995. *Medieval Bestiaries: Text, Image, Ideology*. Cambridge University Press.

Heise, Ursula K. 2016. *Imagining Extinction: The Cultural Meanings of Endangered Species*. University of Chicago Press.

Hernández, José. 1936. *Martín Fierro*. Translated by Walter Owen. Farrar and Rinehart.

Hollander, Robert. 2001. *Dante: A Life in Works*. Yale University Press.

Honig, Edwin. 1959. *Dark Conceit: The Making of Allegory*. Northwestern University Press.

Huizinga, Johan. 1924. *The Waning of the Middle Ages: A Study of the Forms of Life, Thought and Art in France and the Netherlands in the XIVth and XVth Centuries*. Translated by Frederik J. Hopman. E. Arnold and Co.

Hutcheon, Linda. 1989. *The Politics of Postmodernism*. Routledge.

Hutchinson, Robert. 1962. "Introduction." In *1800 Woodcuts by Thomas Bewick and His School*, by Thomas Bewick, Dover Publications.

Isidore of Seville, Saint. 2006. *The Etymologies of Isidore of Seville*. Translated by Stephen A. Barney et al. Cambridge University Press.

Jackson, Richard. 1988. "Nicolás Guillén in the 1980s: A Guide to Recent Scholarship." *Latin American Research Review* 23, no. 1: 110–22. www.jstor.org/stable/2503322.

Jameson, Fredric. 1981. *The Political Unconscious: Narrative as a Socially Symbolic Act*. Cornell University Press.

– 2003. "Prologue." In *Todo Calibán*, by Retamar R. Ediciones Callejón.

Jensen, Lloyd B. 1963. "Royal Purple of Tyre." *Journal of Near Eastern Studies* 22, no. 2: 104–118. www.jstor.org/stable/543305.

Jidejian, Nina. 1975. *Baalbek: Heliopolis, City of the Sun*. Dar el-Machreq Publishers.

Jijon, Isabel. 2011. "'El eclipse' de Augusto Monterroso y las implicaciones éticas de la brevedad." *Latin American Literary Review* 39, no. 78: 61–72. www.jstor.org/stable/41478093.

Johnson, Gary. 2012. *The Vitality of Allegory: Figural Narrative in Modern and Contemporary Fiction*. Ohio State University Press.

Kadner, Maríen. 2017. "Mitología para entender la violencia en México." *Fondo De Cultura Económica*.

Kay, Sarah. 2017. *Animal Skins and the Reading Self in Medieval Latin and French Bestiaries*. University of Chicago Press.

Kearin, Chris. 2012. "Who Was Silvio?" Dreamers Rise (blog), 24 May. http://dreamersrise.blogspot.com/2012/05/who-was-silvio.html.

Kiely, Robert. 1993. *Reverse Tradition: Postmodern Fictions and the Nineteenth Century Novel*. Harvard University Press.

Koch, Dolores M. 1981. "El micro-relato en México: Torri, Arreola, Monterroso y Avilés Fabila." *Hispamérica* 10, no. 30: 123–30. www.jstor.org/stable/20541934.

Larraquy, Roque. 2014. *Informe sobre ectoplasma animal*. Illustrated by Diego Ontivero. Eterna Cadencia.

Latini, Brunetto. 1982. *The Medieval Castilian Bestiary: From Brunetto Latini's Tesoro; Study and Edition*. Edited by Spurgeon W. Baldwin. University of Exeter.

Leonard, Irving A. 1992. *Books of the Brave: Being an Account of Books and of Men in the Spanish Conquest and Settlement of the Sixteenth-Century New World*. University of California Press.

Levinas, Emmanuel. 1991. *Totality and Infinity*. Translated by Alphonso Lingis. Duquesne University Press.

– 1998. *Entre Nous: On Thinking-of-the-Other*. Columbia University Press.

López, Alejandra. n.d. "About Laura Varsky." Laura Varsky, https://lauravarsky.com.ar/about.

López, Carlos. 2003. *Tito: Biografía mínima*. Magna Terra Editores.

López, Enrique H., and José Luis Cuevas. 1966. "Entrevista con José Luis Cuevas." *Diálogos: Artes, letras, ciencias humanas* 2, no. 4: 20–8.

López Baca, Marilú. 2018. "Bestiario de seres fantásticos mexicanos." *Diario el mundo*, 6 February. www.diarioelmundo.com.mx/index.php/2018/02/16/bestiario-de-seres-fantasticos-mexicanos.

Malamud, Randy. 2000. "The Culture of Using Animals in Literature and the Case of José Emilio Pacheco." *CLCWeb: Comparative Literature and Culture* 2, no. 2:1–13. https://doi.org/10.7771/1481-4374.1072.

McCulloch, Florence. 1962. *Mediaeval Latin and French Bestiaries*. University of North Carolina Press.

McLuhan, Marshall. 1962. *The Gutenberg Galaxy: The Making of Typographic Man*. University of Toronto Press.

Mendoza Hernández, Enrique. 2016. "Presentan asombroso *Bestiario de seres fantásticos mexicanos*." *Zeta Tijuana*, 19 November.

Mercier, Claire. 2021. "El bestiario monstruoso de Alexis Figueroa y Claudio Romo en Fragmentos de una biblioteca transparente: Hacia una comunidad post-humana." *Confluenze: Rivista di Studi Iberoamericani* 13, no. 1: 478–99.

Mezzalira, Francesco, Guglielmo Cavallo, and Danilo Mainardi. 2001. *Beasts and Bestiaries: The Representation of Animals from Prehistory to the Renaissance*. Umberto Allemandi.

Mitchell, W.J.T. 1994. *Picture Theory: Essays on Verbal and Visual Representation*. University of Chicago Press.

Molinaro, Nina. 2002. "Los humores de Javier Tomeo." *Anales de la literatura española contemporánea* 27, no. 2: 597–606. www.jstor.org/stable/27742163.
Montagu, Ashley. 1969. *Man: His First Two Million Years; A Brief Introduction to Anthropology*. Columbia University Press.
Monterroso, Augusto. 1969. *La oveja negra y demás fábulas*. J. Mortiz.
– 1971. *The Black Sheep and Other Fables: Tales Wry, Sly, and Truly Fabulous*. Translated by Walter I. Bradbury. Doubleday.
– 1981a. *Movimiento perpetuo*. Seix Barral.
– 1981b. *Viaje al centro de la fábula*. Muchnik Editores.
Muñoz Ledo, Norma. 2016. *Bestiario de seres fantásticos mexicanos*. Illustrated by Israel Barrón. Fondo de Cultura Económica.
Muñoz Ledo, Norma, and Helguera y Hernández. 2012. *Supernaturalia*. Altea.
Murray, Les A. 1992. *Translations From the Natural World*. Carcanet.
Neruda, Pablo. 1965. *Bestiary/Bestiario*. Illustrated by Antonio Frasconi and translated by Elsa Neuberger. Harcourt, Brace and World.
– 1972. *Obras escogidas. Selección de Francisco Coloane*. A. Bello.
– 1977. *Estravagario*. Seix Barral.
– 1990. *Canto general*. Cátedra.
– 2007. *Bestiario*. Edited by Giuseppe Bellini. Visor Libros.
Neuman, Andrés. 2001. "Callar a tiempo: El microcuento y sus problemas." *Revista de crítica literaria latinoamericana* 27, no. 53: 143–52. www.jstor.org/stable/4531154.
Onion, Rebecca. 2008. "Reclaiming the Machine: An Introductory Look at Steampunk in Everyday Practice." *Neo-Victorian Studies* 1: 138–63.
Ovid. 2008. *Metamorphoses*. Translated by A.D. Melville. Oxford University Press.
Owens, Craig. 1980. "The Allegorical Impulse: Toward a Theory of Postmodernism." *October* 12: 67–8. https://doi.org/10.2307/778575.
Pacheco, José Emilio. 1993. *An Ark for the next Millennium: Poems*. Illustrated by Francisco Toledo and translated by Margaret Sayers Peden. University of Texas Press.
Pacheco, José Emilio. 1985. *Álbum de zoología*. Illustrated by Alberto Blanco. Cuarto Menguante.
Paley de Francescato, Martha. 1977. *Bestiarios y otras jaulas*. Editorial Sudamericana.
Patton, Paul. 1995. "Introduction." In *The Gulf War Did Not Take Place*, by Jean Baudrillard. Indiana University Press.
Paz, Octavio. 1961. *The Labyrinth of Solitude: Life and Thought in Mexico*. Grove Press.

Pliny the Elder. 1991. *Natural History: A Selection*. Edited and translated by John. F. Healy. Penguin Books.

Ponzoni, Federico. 2015. "*The Gutenberg Galaxy*: How McLuhan Opened a New Path in the Digital Age to the Socratic Ideal of the Examined Life." *Humanum: Issues in Family, Culture and Science* 4.

Pujol, Carlos. 2012. *Bestiario*. Ediciones Cálcamo.

Ragette, Friedrich. 1980. *Baalbek*. Chatto and Windus.

Richard, Nelly. 1992. "Postmodern Disalignments and Realignments of the Center/Periphery." *Art Journal* 51, no. 4: 57–9. http://dx.doi.org/10.1080/00043249.1992.10791598.

– 2004. *Masculine/Feminine: Practices of Difference(s)*. Duke University Press.

Roderick, Rick. 2012. "Rick Roderick on Baudrillard: Fatal Strategies" (lecture). The Partially Examined Life, 25 January. https://www.youtube.com/watch?v=2U9WMftV4oc.

Rodríguez Gimeno, Rafael. 2015. "Una conversación fantasma entre Roque Larraquy y Diego Ontivero." *Verlanga*, 19 September. https://verlanga.com/letras/libros/una-conversacion-fantasma-entre-roque-larraquy-y-diego-ontivero.

Romero, Ivana. 2018. "Recital en el Torquato Tasso: Gabo Ferro homenajea a las mujeres del tango." *Clarín*, 14 December. https://www.clarin.com/revista-enie/escenarios/gabo-ferro-homenajea-mujeres-tango_0_2Ayuuycaz.html.

Rosenblat, Angel. 1954. *El mestizaje y las castas coloniales*. Editorial Nova.

Rowland, Beryl. 1989. "The Art of Memory and the Bestiary." In *Beasts and Birds of the Middle Ages: The Bestiary and Its Legacy*, edited by Willene B. Clark and Meradith T. McMunn. University of Pennsylvania.

Sadurní, Teresa. 2005. "Rulfo, Arreola y Monterroso: Tradición y modernidad en el cuento mexicano." *Revista de Crítica Literaria Latinoamericana* 31, no. 61: 91–109.

Sáez Castán, Javier, and Miguel Murugarren. 2014. *Animalario universal del profesor Revillod*. Fondo de Cultura Económica.

Sainz, María. 2000. "La lectura de los espejos: a modo de prólogo." In *Bestiario médico*, by Carlos Ferrándiz, illustrated by Carlos Baonza. Ediciones Eneida.

Scholem, Gershom. 1941. *Major Trends in Jewish Mysticism*. Schocken Book.

Schulz, Dieter, and Michael Sauter. 2012. "Thoreau's Excursions, Science, and Hermeneutics." In *Literature, Ecology, Ethics: Recent Trends in Ecocriticism*, edited by Timo Muller. Universitatsverlag Winter Heidelberg.

Schulz-Cruz, Bernard. 1991. "Cuatro bestiarios, cuatro visiones: Borges, Arreola, Neruda y Guillén." *Chiricú* 6, no. 2: 20–9. www.jstor.org/stable/43506119.

Scobie, James. 1974. *Argentina: A City and a Nation*. Oxford University Press.

Scott, Alan. 1998. "The Date of the Physiologus." *Vigiliae Christianae* 52, no. 4: 430–41. https://doi.org/10.2307/1584835.

Seimandi, Esteban. 2010. *Animalia exstinta*. Illustrated by Hugo Horita and designed by Juan Cruz Bazterrica. Tres en Línea.

– 2017. "Selfinterview Con Esteban Seimandi." *Selfinterview Minutes*, 23 October. https://selfinterview.com/people.php?id=43.

Seimandi, Esteban, and Agustina Bazterrica. 2016. "Entrevista a Esteban Seimandi por Agustina Bazterrica." *Siga al conejo blanco*, 4 November. www.sigaalconejoblanco.com/single-post/2016/04/11/Entrevista-a-Esteban-Seimandi-por-Agustina-Bazterrica.

Sell, Stacey, and Hugo Chapman. 2015. *Drawing in Silver and Gold: Leonardo to Jasper Johns*. Princeton University Press.

Shklovsky, Viktor. 1965. "Art as Technique." In *Russian Formalist Criticism*. Translated by Lee T. Lemon and Marion J. Reis. University of Nebraska Press.

Steele, Cynthia. 1995. "'An Ark for the Next Millenium.' Review of An Ark for the Next Millenium, by José Emilio Pacheco." *Review: Literature and Arts of the Americas* 28, no. 51: 81–101. https://doi.org/10.1080/08905769508594461.

"Los sueños y miedos de Carlos Baonza." 2019. *Hoy es Arte*, 10 July. www.hoyesarte.com/evento/los-suenos-y-miedos-de-carlos-baonza.

Tambling, Jeremy. 2010. *Allegory*. Routledge.

Tannenbaum, Frank. 1946. *Slave and Citizen: The Negro in the Americas*. Alfred A. Knopf.

"El testimonio de una de las mapuches detenidas en el desalojo de Villa Mascardi." 2017. *Río Negro*, 24 November. www.rionegro.com.ar/bariloche/el-testimonio-de-una-de-las-mapuches-detenidas-en-el-desalojo-de-villa-mascardi-KI3974048.

Tomeo, Javier. 1988. *Bestiario*. Montena.

– 2000. *Bestiario*. Illustrated by Natalio Bayo. Las Tres Sorores.

– 2007. *Bestiario*. Illustrated by Natalio Bayo. Prames.

"Trabajadores de parques nacionales repudiaron la represión en Mascardi." 2017. *Tiempoar*, 28 November. https://www.tiempoar.com.ar/ta_article/trabajadores-de-parques-nacionales-repudiaron-la-represion-en-mascardi.

Trueba Lara, José Luis, editor. 2018. *Bestiario culinario de México*. Artes de México.

Urdapilleta Muñoz, Marco. 2014. "El bestiario medieval en las crónicas de Indias (siglos XV y XVI)." *Latinoamérica* 58: 237–70. http://www.scielo.org.mx/scielo.php?script=sci_arttext&pid=S1665-85742014000100010&lng=essnrm=iso.

Valenzuela, Luisa. 2009. *ABC de las microfábulas*. Illustrated by Rufino de Mingo. Del Centro Editores.

– 2013. *Zoorpresas zoológicas*. Illustrated by Lorenzo Amengual. Editorial Macedonia.

– 2018. *ABC de las microfábulas*. Illustrated by Lorenzo Amengual. Fondo de Cultura Económica.

Wagschal, Steven. 2018. *Minding Animals in the Old and New Worlds: A Cognitive Historical Analysis*. University of Toronto Press.

Warhol, Andy. 1976. *Portrait of Maurice*. National Galleries of Scotland, Edinburgh.

Washburn, Yulan M. 1973. "An Ancient Mold for Contemporary Casting: The Beast Book of Juan." *Hispania* 56: 295–300. www.jstor.org/stable/339020.

– 1983. *Juan José Arreola*. Twayne.

Wheatcroft, Holli J. 1999. "Classical Ideology in the Medieval Bestiary." In *The Mark of the Beast: The Medieval Bestiary in Art, Life, and Literature*, edited by Debra Hassig. Garland Publishing.

White, T.H., and Robertson Davies. 1955. *The Book of Beasts: Being a Translation from a Latin Bestiary of the Twelfth Century*. Cape.

Worksop Bestiary. ca. 1185. Vellum MS M.81. Morgan Library and Museum, New York.

Yúdice, George. 1991. "El conflicto de posmodernidades." *Nuevo Texto Crítico* 4, no. 1: 19–33. https://dx.doi.org/10.1353/ntc.1991.0000.

INDEX

Page numbers in italics refer to figures.

MCGILL-QUEEN'S IBERIAN AND LATIN AMERICAN CULTURES SERIES

Series editor: Nicolás Fernández-Medina

1 Populism and Ethnicity
Peronism and the Jews of Argentina
Raanan Rein
Translated by Isis Sadek

2 What Would Cervantes Do?
Navigating Post-Truth with Spanish Baroque Literature
David Castillo and William Egginton

3 The Pen, the Sword, and the Law
Dueling and Democracy in Uruguay
David S. Parker

4 From the Theater to the Plaza
Spectacle, Protest, and Urban Space in Twenty-First-Century Madrid
Matthew I. Feinberg

5 Death in the Snow
Pedro de Alvarado and the Illusive Conquest of Peru
W. George Lovell

6 Configurations of a Cultural Scene
Young Writers and Artists in Madrid, 1918–1930
Andrew A. Anderson

7 Beyond Intimacy
Radical Proximity and Justice in Three Mexican Poets
Christina Karageorgou-Bastea

8 Patriarchy's Remains
An Autopsy of Iberian Cinematic Dark Humour
Erin K. Hogan

9 Pasting Up Protest
The Art of Memorializing Violence in Mexican Printmaking
Annik Bilodeau

10 From Griffin to Axolotl
Reimagining the Bestiary in Contemporary Hispanic Literature
Ailén Cruz